FOUNDATIONS OF
EXPERIMENTAL
RESEARCH

FOUNDATIONS OF EXPERIMENTAL RESEARCH

THIRD EDITION

ROBERT PLUTCHIK
ALBERT EINSTEIN COLLEGE OF MEDICINE

HARPER & ROW, PUBLISHERS, New York
Cambridge, Philadelphia, San Francisco,
London, Mexico City, São Paulo, Sydney

1817

Sponsoring Editor: George Middendorf
Project Editor: Beena Kamlani
Designer: Robert Sugar
Production Manager: Willie Lane
Cover Designer: Miriam Recio
Compositor: Com Com Division of Haddon Craftsmen, Inc.
Printer and Binder: R.R. Donnelley & Sons Company
Art Studio: J & R Art Services, Inc.

Foundations of Experimental Research, Third Edition.

Library of Congress Cataloging in Publication Data

Plutchik, Robert.
Foundations of experimental research.
(Harper's experimental psychology series)
Bibliography: p.
Includes indexes.
1. Psychology, Experimental.   2. Psychological
research.   I. Title.   II. Series.
BF181.P56   1983   150'.724   82-11777
ISBN 0-06-045265-X

To My Children: Lisa, Lori, and Roy

Contents

Appendixes

Indexes

Preface

Experimentation in any science is a complex decision-making process. The decisions concern such issues as: definitions of key concepts; sampling of subjects as well as conditions; measurement; scaling; instrumentation; design; and statistics. The present book is an attempt to analyze the many decision-making problems faced by the experimenter, and to suggest, wherever possible, rational considerations for solving them. In order to accomplish this goal, I have drawn liberally upon research reports in various fields to illustrate different problems, and I have proposed some solutions. Because of the emphasis on issues of methodology and decision making, this book should be useful to students in all areas of psychology as well as those in related fields such as psychiatry and sociology.

This book is not intended to be a summary of research in different areas; it seems to me that a student can develop an appreciation for research only by going to original experimental reports published in contemporary journals. The book is not intended to be a statistics text, although four chapters have been included which deal with basic statistical procedures in the light of certain decisions the experimenter makes. Finally, although the book does not propose a philosophy of science, several important philosophical issues are critically explored; for example, the problem of operationism and the nature of measurement and scaling.

A number of recent writings have been critical of the concept of significance level when considered independently of the actual magnitude of the differences between groups. Because of the importance of these views, there is a section dealing with the problem of evaluating the magnitude of an experimental effect, or "effect size." A rationale and practical reference tables have been provided so that the student can make direct use of these ideas.

In recent years, experimental psychologists have become increasingly involved in applied research in settings such as hospitals, clinics, and businesses. When research is carried out in such settings, precise control of all relevant variables is seldom possible, but the desire to interpret findings in reasonable ways or to draw plausible (if limited) conclusions still exists. As a result, a methodology that is referred to as quasi-experimental design has evolved during the past two decades, enabling an investigator to draw meaningful conclusions from experimental data even when subject samples are not randomly selected. A chapter has therefore been added in the current edition of the book that describes three major quasi-experimental designs.

Another recent important development that has taken place is the tremendous expansion in the use of computers. Not very long ago computers were largely considered by psychologists as high speed calculators that enabled complex statistical problems to be solved rapidly. The revolution in microminiaturization technology that has taken place during the past ten years now permits not only rapid analysis of complex statistical problems, but also the control of stimulus conditions in laboratories and the provision of models of complex theoretical processes such as memory, concept formation, language learning, and personality. A new chapter has therefore been added that describes some basic ideas related to the use of computers.

I am indebted to the Literary Executor of the late Sir Ronald A. Fisher, F.R.S., Cambridge, to Dr. Frank Yates, F.R.S., Rothamsted, and to Messrs. Oliver & Boyd Ltd., Edinburgh, for permission to reprint Table No. III from *Statistical Tables for Biological, Agricultural, and Medical Research.*

My indebtedness to other people is great. Richard Trumbull, Gilbert Tollhurst, and James Prescott of the Office of Naval Research provided me with some support for the preparation of the book through an ONR contract. Philip Ziegler and Joseph Lyons were very helpful with their suggestions. Fred Lit provided generous counsel on my chapter on psychophysics.

In addition, various others contributed comments on one or another aspect of the book. I should like particularly to thank my wife Anita, Bernard Aaronson, Hope Conte, Joseph Fleiss, Sherwin Klein, Solomon Kugelmass, Philip Reese, Sherman Ross, John Paul Scott, Jack Werboff, and Joseph Zubin. Needless to say, the responsibility for the final form of the book rests entirely with me.

Robert Plutchik

FOUNDATIONS OF
EXPERIMENTAL
RESEARCH

The Role of
Observation and
Description

Many of us are harassed by relentless and importunate cravings for scientific maturity, which incline us to leap over all the tedious stages of observation, description, and classification through which chemistry and all the biological and medical sciences have passed.

—Henry A. Murray

The word *research* has its origin in a term which means "to go around" or "to explore" and was derived from an even earlier word meaning "circle." *Experiment* means to "try" or "test" and refers to some of the procedures used in trying to discover unknown facts. As the definitions of these terms suggest, research and experimentation refer to the process of exploration and testing used to achieve a fuller understanding of the nature of the world.

Such definitions emphasize two important aspects of research: First, it involves actively trying to find new facts; and second, it implies an attempt by scientists to order the facts they discover into meaningful patterns.

The purpose of this book is to describe the basic experimental methods used by psychologists to gather information about living organisms. These methods are applicable to almost all kinds of problems, from those associated with aesthetic preferences to those concerned with the analysis of international conflicts.

The integrating theme of the book is the idea that each experiment requires a series of decisions, from the initial definition of a problem to the final analysis and presentation of results. The chapters that follow are organized around this idea with each chapter devoted to a major class of decisions that must be made. In Chapter 2 the concept of experimentation as a decision-making process will be described in detail and will be followed by chapters on definitions, sampling, statistics, design methods, etc.

Before any laboratory research is undertaken, however, a great deal of information has usually been informally acquired either by careful observation or by "pilot" studies. In fact, all science starts from observation. Before formal experimentation is begun, we must have some idea, even if not very precise, about what to search for, what to observe, and what to measure.

The process of searching, observing, and describing has sometimes been called "naturalistic observation" and has been thought of as a rather primitive kind of research procedure. Although this is often the case, there have been some important improvements in recent years in the techniques concerned with accurate observation. Because of the fundamental role of observation in experimentation, this first chapter will illustrate, through a series of examples, the nature and significance of observational techniques.

Some Examples

Darwin on the Earthworm

Most of biology until about 1900 was concerned primarily with description. Animals and plants were observed and grouped into species, families, orders, genera, and phyla on the basis of structural or morphological characteristics. Animals or plants having many similar characteristics were considered closely related; those having few similarities were considered only remotely related. Careful description provided a basis for classification or taxonomy.

Based on previous observations by other biologists as well as many of his own, Darwin proposed his theory of evolution in the middle of the last century. To this day, his theory has had a profound influence on most sciences—both the descriptive and experimental aspects. It stimulated the extensive work in comparative anatomy, neurology, and physiology, and excited an interest in the comparative psychology of animals.

Recent issues of ethological journals contain articles dealing with the feeding habits, sexual behavior, care of the young, and aggressive behavior of such animals as the fly, the ant, the bee, the fish, the chicken, the sea lion, and the elephant. These studies usually involve systematic observations of these animals in their more-or-less natural surroundings. Such detailed descriptive information provides a background for interpreting in a meaningful way the results of laboratory experiments.

To take one interesting example, there has been a good deal of research dealing with "hoarding" tendencies in rats. In most cases, these interpretations are based on rats studied in isolation and under food-deprived conditions. However, a study made of the Norway rat under naturalistic conditions revealed that they are highly social animals who live in groups with well-established dominance hierarchies. Such naturalistic studies may throw new light on laboratory investigations. This point may be illustrated by the fact that the widespread use of food-deprived animals led to the assumption that physiological deficit was essential to the development of a drive state. However, Collier, Hirsch, and Hamlin (1972) have pointed out that under normal conditions in the wild, animals carry out a variety of functions—including learning, play, and socialization—without being hungry. These authors demonstrated that complex behaviors can be learned in a free-feeding continuous-session experiment, and they believe that such settings are closer analogues to the natural situations that an animal faces than are the severe deprivations that are typical of the laboratory. Knowledge of an animal's normal species-specific behavior patterns helps interpret the patterns of behavior seen in severely deprived animals. For example, it was found that response rate *increased* as pellet size decreased. This result would not be expected on the basis of the assumption that the larger the reward the more frequent the response. Another hypothesis, based on observations of animals in natural settings, is that the animal is trying to obtain a certain necessary level of total food intake.

There is nothing, of course, to prevent the combination of a naturalistic study with an experiment in which some of the conditions affecting the animal are varied systematically. A simple but interesting example of this is provided in the work of Darwin dealing with the sensitivity of worms to light, an excerpt of which is presented here.

Worms are destitute of eyes, and at first I thought that they were quite insensible to light; for those kept in confinement were repeatedly observed by the aid of a candle, and others out of doors by the aid of a lantern, yet they were rarely alarmed, although extremely timid animals. . . .

When the light from a candle was concentrated by means of a large lens on the anterior extremity, they generally withdrew instantly; but this concentrated light failed to act perhaps once out of half a dozen trials. The light was on one occasion concentrated on a worm lying beneath water in a saucer, and it instantly withdrew into its burrow. In all cases the duration of the light, unless extremely feeble, made a great difference in the result. . . .

From the foregoing facts it is evident that light affects worms by its intensity and by its duration. It is only the anterior extremity of the body, where the cerebral ganglia lie, which is affected by light. . . . If this part is shaded, other parts of the body may be fully illuminated, and no effect will be produced. As these animals have no eyes, we must suppose that the light passes through their skins, and in some manner excites their cerebral ganglia. . . . One thing was manifest, namely, that when worms were employed in dragging leaves into their burrows or in eating them, and even during the short intervals whilst they rested from their work, they either did not perceive the light or were regardless of it; and this occurred even when the light was concentrated on them through a large lens. . . .

. . . The different effect which a light produced on different occasions, and especially the fact that a worm when in any way employed . . . is often regardless of light, are opposed to the view of the sudden withdrawal being a simple reflex action. With the higher animals, when close attention to some object leads to the disregard of the impressions which other objects must be producing on them, we attribute this to their attention being then absorbed; and attention implies the presence of a mind. Every sportsman knows that he can approach animals whilst they are grazing, fighting, or courting, much more easily than at other times. . . . The comparison here implied between the actions of one of the higher animals and of one so low in the scale as an earthworm, may appear far-fetched; for we thus attribute to the worm attention and some mental power, nevertheless I can see no reason to doubt the justice of the comparison.

On the basis of the careful observation of a relatively small number of worms under conditions which were partly naturalistic and partly experimental, Darwin noted, first of all, the variability of response of the animals under given conditions. He then saw that sometimes when no reactions were observed, the worms were doing something else, like eating. Darwin drew a parallel between this observation and the fact that higher animals will act in a similar way; that is, they ignore certain stimuli if their attention is directed elsewhere. Reasoning by analogy, Darwin concluded that these observations therefore indicate the existence of a "mental power" in the earthworms.

Whether or not a contemporary psychologist would agree with each step of this chain of reasoning, it is interesting to see the interaction of observation and inference in Darwin's thinking. The main point of this illustration is that his observations combined with simple experiments led to conclusions which can provide the basis for future research.

Kraepelin and Freud on Diagnosis

At the beginning of the nineteenth century, several physicians noticed that there were certain patients in the mental hospitals who had fairly similar symptoms. These patients often had poor memory, defective speech, and difficulty in walking or doing skilled movements and yet, at the same time, maintained that they were capable of the greatest deeds. Invariably, these patients got worse and eventually died in the hospital.

During the course of the next 60 years it was gradually learned that more men than women were affected, that onset of symptoms was usually during middle age, and that certain reflexes were abnormal. It became increasingly evident that this complex of symptoms had a typical *onset,* a typical *course,* and a typical *outcome.* By the end of the nineteenth century it had been fairly well established that this disease, later called paresis, was caused by damage to the spinal cord and brain due to syphilitic infection. Once this was known, various methods of prevention and treatment were instituted.

During the latter part of the nineteenth century, a German psychiatrist named Emil Kraepelin began to study large numbers of case histories in the mental hospitals. His aim was to establish various groupings of symptoms that were associated by virtue of a common onset, common course, and common outcome, just as had been done previously for general paresis. Kraepelin eventually classified mental diseases into two major groupings which he called the manic-depressive psychosis and dementia praecox (or schizophrenia). Within each major grouping he proposed several subgroups.

This system, with relatively few changes, has been in use by psychiatrists up to the present time. It is used as a basis for the legal determination of insanity, the establishment of wards for custody, the screening of military personnel, the preparation of census data, the estimation of prognosis, and the treatment of patients. Experimental research with patient populations usually uses these categories as the descriptive basis for selection of subjects and evaluation of results. Here again, description and classification precede experimentation.

While Kraepelin was achieving renown as the great classifier of mental hospital patients, Sigmund Freud was beginning his studies of hysteria. Hysteria seemed to be a strange malady, recognized many centuries before, and characterized by a large assortment of symptoms which could include blindness, deafness, paralysis, anesthesia of parts of the body, and convulsions. For a long time it had been believed that hysteria was due to a disorder of the nervous system, but then some surprising observations came to light.

It was discovered that most of the symptoms of hysteria could be produced by hypnotic suggestions and then eliminated by further suggestions. It was then possible to show that in some actual cases of hysteria the symptoms could be removed by hypnosis. Other peculiar facts were the existence of anatomically meaningless symptoms and a lack of occurrence of certain symptoms while the patient was asleep.

In an effort to clarify these issues, Freud published an essay in 1893 which described the differences between paralyses due to organic lesions and those due to hysteria.

After giving a detailed description of these differences between organic and hysterical paralyses, Freud noted that the particular symptoms that develop seem to depend on common, popular ideas about the organs and parts of the body. He then predicted that no one would find hysterical symptoms in patients that mimic certain well-known effects of brain or nerve injury (e.g., certain visual field defects, or certain kinds of partial facial paralyses) because the symptoms seem strange to the unscientific mind. Finally, Freud concluded that in all cases of hysterical paralysis there is a strong subconscious emotional feeling associated with the organ whose function is lost, and that cure requires the elimination of the connection between the emotion and the organ.

It is interesting to see how Freud moved from acute observation, to generalization, to prediction, and finally to speculation. What is also interesting is that it is just these kinds of speculations which have stimulated a good deal of subsequent research.

Piaget on Language Development in the Child

A number of years ago, the Swiss psychologist-philosopher Jean Piaget set himself the task of trying to learn about the development of language and thought in the child. He approached the problem from the point of view of a naturalist. His method, in his own words, is as follows:

Two of us followed each a child (a boy) for about a month at the morning class at (a private school), taking down in minute detail and in its context everything that was said by the child. . . . The children work individually or in groups, as they choose; the groups are formed and then break up again without any interference on the part of the adult; the children go from one room to another (modelling room, drawing room, etc.) just as they please without being asked to do any continuous work so long as they do not themselves feel any desire for it. In short, these schoolrooms supply a first-class field of observation for everything connected with the study of the social life and of the language of childhood. . . .

Once the material was collected, we utilized it as follows. We began by numbering all the subject's sentences. As a rule the child speaks in short sentences interspersed with long silences or with the talk of other children. Each sentence is numbered separately. Where the talk is a little prolonged, the reader must not be afraid of reckoning several consecutive sentences to one number, so long as to each sentence containing a definite idea only one number is affixed. In such cases which are rare enough, the division is necessarily arbitrary, but this is of no importance for statistics dealing with hundreds of sentences.

Once the talk has been portioned out into numbered sentences, we endeavour to classify these into elementary functional categories (Piaget, 1955).

On the basis of these sentences Piaget proposed that the language of these children, who are both 6½ years old, may be classified as: monologue, repetition, commands, requests, questions, answers, etc. He noted that these categories are reliable since four different judges agree within 3% on the scoring. He then pointed out that all these categories can be subsumed under two broad classes which he called *egocentric* and *socialized* language. In the former case the child does not address himself to anyone in particular nor does he know whether he is being listened to, while in the latter case, the child exchanges his thoughts with others.

The results of about 1,500 remarks for the two children, Pie and Lev, are summarized in Table 1–1. The figures represent the percent of the total number of sentences used in each category.

On the basis of data such as these, Piaget proposed a number of hypotheses and interpretations that have had considerable influence on subsequent research using methods other than the ones he described.

Agonistic Behavior in Woodchucks

The branch of biology which is called ethology has tended to rely largely on naturalistic observation as a method for gathering information. One example of such an ethological study is given by Bronson (1964) in his attempt to study agonistic (i.e., fight and flight) behavior in woodchucks.

Observations were made on a 10,000-acre area where woodchucks were living in natural populations. Seven small subareas were chosen for detailed observation, and, on each, five neighboring woodchucks were trapped, marked with dye, and released. Then, for a period of three to four weeks each subarea

TABLE 1–1   TOTAL SENTENCES USED PER CATEGORY

Categories	Percentage of Subjects' Responses	
	Pie	Lev
Egocentric		
1. Repetition	2	1
2. Monologue	5	15
3. Collective monologue	30	23
Socialized		
1. Adapted information	14	13
2. Criticisms	7	3
3. Commands	15	10
4. Requests	13	17
5. Answers	14	18
Egocentric language	37	39
Spontaneous socialized language	49	43
Sum of socialized language	63	61
Coefficient of egocentrism	0.43 ± 0.06	0.47 ± 0.04

SOURCE: J. Piaget, *The language and thought of the child.* New York: Meridian, 1955.

was observed by the experimenter during the morning and afternoon activity periods of the woodchucks. At the end of each minute of observation a notation was made of the location and type of behavior exhibited by each woodchuck observed. The observations were made from May to September, producing a total of 11,648 "minutes" of data.

After the observation periods were over, the woodchucks were retrapped and subjected to a paired competitive situation for water, in order to compare the dominance-subordination relationships determined in the laboratory with those seen in the field. In other words, each animal was paired with every other animal.

In this study, the categories of analysis were established before the field observations were made and were based upon the prior decision to study only those behaviors which related to fighting or avoidance. Therefore such things as nuzzling, visual threat, vocalization, fighting, and social avoidance were all observed and recorded. In addition, signs of alerting with the head up or with the head down were also noted.

One of Bronson's observations was that there was only about one aggressive interaction per day for each animal, and that agonistic behavior accounted for only about 4% of the behavior of the woodchuck in the period after reproductive behavior had occurred. In contrast to this, in the laboratory tests using water competition, fights occurred in 50% of the encounters. This difference, it appeared, was largely related to the fact that subordinate animals simply avoided their dominant neighbors in the field. It is thus evident that laboratory studies alone do not permit generalizations to the natural setting unless there is an established relationship between the variables present in the laboratory and in the field. It is also worth noting that this study used a time-sampling plan; that is, recordings were made once every minute during each of the observation periods. A final point of interest in this study is the use of *both* field and laboratory techniques with the same population. This highlights the fact that these two methods of approach are supplementary and interrelated, and may often contribute valuable insights when used together. Another example of the interaction of theory, field description, and laboratory research may be found in Plutchik's discussion of the nature of emotion (1962; 1970; 1980).

Brain Stimulation in Monkey Colonies

The overlap and interaction of laboratory and naturalistic studies are illustrated very nicely in a study by Delgado (1965). It has been known for some years that electrical stimulation of certain subcortical areas in the brain will evoke behaviors of various kinds, for example, flight, biting, attack, erection of the penis, eating of food, and vocalizations. When large animals such as monkeys are used in these studies they are usually kept fairly restricted to prevent them from pulling on the wires to their heads. In order to minimize limitations on an animal's freedom, Delgado developed a technique for stimulating the brain of an animal by the use of implanted intracerebral electrodes and small radio receivers mounted on the head or back of the animal. This allows stimulation of the brains of free-ranging animals in natural settings without the experimenter being present.

From an established colony of 8 rhesus monkeys, Delgado selected 4 animals and implanted 12 electrodes in each animal in various subcortical areas. One of the selected animals was "boss" of the colony; that is, he was at the top of the dominance hierarchy. The selected animals were placed back into the colony 1 or 2 at a time for periods of 4 to 10 weeks. Stimulation was carried out for 5 seconds every minute for an hour, but in some cases for as long as 14 days.

In order to measure and evaluate the complex social behavior of the colony, time-lapse motion pictures were taken; that is, one frame was exposed every 10 or 15 seconds. When the film was later run at normal speed, a condensed but reasonably accurate record of the activities of the colony, both before and during stimulation, was obtained.

By the use of this technique of radio-controlled brain stimulation and time-lapse photography it was found possible to change the dominance hierarchy in the colony, to induce hostility between previously friendly animals, and to enable subordinate monkeys to modify the aggression of the "boss" by allowing them access to a lever controlling the radio stimulator.

The technique of radio telemetry undoubtedly holds great promise as a way of combining experimental manipulations and naturalistic observations.

Modification of Behavior in Natural Settings by Operant Conditioning

A further illustration of the interaction of naturalistic observation and laboratory technology may be seen in the recent attempts to modify the behavior of children and adults by the use of operant conditioning procedures. These attempts may be thought of as forms of behavior therapy; what is noteworthy about the treatments is that they are often applied in the usual social environment of the individual. The basic observations may be made in a home or in a hospital, institution, or school.

The methods that are used have been mostly derived from Skinner's operant conditioning paradigms. In the typical field-experimental study, data are collected in a systematic way to try to establish relations between antecedent conditions, reinforcement contingencies, and responses. A baseline status is first established to provide an index of the strength of a response under "normal" conditions. Several different measures can be used for this purpose: for example, the frequency, latency, intensity, or duration of the response. The second phase of the study requires the introduction of a change in the behavior of the parent, teacher, or therapist, such that reinforcements are provided only for desired behaviors and not for any others. To discount the possibility that a change in behavior is fortuitous, or unrelated to the reinforcement scheme, the third phase of the study requires the withdrawal of reinforcement. If the frequency or duration of the behavior returns to that of the baseline condition, then this is strong support for the idea that the altered reinforcement schedule was responsible for the desired changes. As a final step, the new reinforcement program is reintroduced.

It is important to note that decisions about the introduction of each new phase of the field study depend upon the kind of data obtained in each preceding phase. For example, if the initial baseline behavior shows great variability or an increasing or decreasing trend, then the data collection is stopped and the target behavior and/or the methodology of the study are reassessed. Similarly, if the introduction of a new reinforcement procedure does not change the behavior, a reassessment is made.

If the new reinforcement procedure is effective, the return to baseline conditions can be made in one of two ways: (a) by simply omitting the reinforcement being given or (b) by distributing the reinforcements on a random schedule. The second approach is used if one wishes to avoid the "frustration" effects of a sudden decrease in reinforcements. The same total number of reinforcements are given in the "extinction" phase, but some are contingent on desired behaviors and others are not (Hart et al., 1964). Finally if the differences found between the different phases of the field study are small, the investigator will usually modify his procedures and begin anew.

The following study illustrates the method as used to deal with the disruptive classroom behavior of a first-grade boy (Kubany, Weiss, and Sloggett, 1971). The child, Henry, was an intelligent 6-year-old who was hyperactive, demanding, and disruptive. His loud outbursts made it difficult for the teacher to carry on her normal routine. Among Henry's unacceptable behaviors were painting on the desk and floor, destroying toys with a hammer, and throwing temper tantrums. At the time the study was begun, the school principal was considering sending Henry to a special class for emotionally disturbed children.

In order to obtain a baseline index of the frequency of occurrence of unacceptable behaviors, Henry was observed every afternoon for 11 days, using a 20-minute observation period. Every 15 seconds during each period, the observer would look at Henry and record his behavior at that instant as "A" (attending), "P" (passive, i.e., not doing his task, but in his seat), or "D" (disruptive). For the next two seconds, the observer recorded any peer or teacher reactions to Henry's behavior. Reliability of behavior observations was obtained by having two independent observers on a number of occasions and tabulating the frequency of their agreements and disagreements. The reliability index was defined as the number of agreements divided by the number of agreements plus disagreements, and was found to average 0.88.

During the 11 days of baseline observation, Henry was found to be disruptive in 88% of all observations. During this same baseline period, the teacher tried to ignore Henry's behavior (she reacted to him on only 12% of the observations), but Henry's classmates paid him a good deal of attention during his outbursts (39% of the time). It was therefore tentatively assumed that peer attention was maintaining much of Henry's misbehavior.

The experimental procedure that was then introduced was as follows: A large 15-minute electric timer was fitted with a new face containing the numbers 1 through 6 at 2-minute intervals. The clock was labeled HENRY'S CLOCK; it was placed in front of the classroom, and as long as Henry remained quietly in his seat, the clock would run. For every two minutes of running time, he would earn a treat that was either a piece of candy or a penny trinket. These treats were placed in a "Sharing Jar" until the end of the day, when Henry would take one and distribute the rest to the class. If Henry was disruptive, the clock was turned off by the teacher; as long as the clock was not running, Henry would not earn any treats. If Henry became quiet and returned to his seat, the teacher would praise him for his appropriate behavior and turn the clock back on. At first, Henry received the first treat every day and passed the rest out to the class; but later, although he continued to distribute the treats, he was placed in the regular rotation like everyone else. Since there were not always enough treats to go to every child, this meant that Henry did not necessarily earn a treat every day.

The intervention period lasted for 31 days. During this time the frequency of disruptive behavior emitted by Henry dropped from 88% to 17% of the time.

In order to demonstrate that the improvement in Henry's behavior was due to the interventions used, the experimenter reestablished baseline conditions. The teacher told the class that "Henry's Clock" would no longer be used. During 3 days of observation under baseline conditions, Henry's disruptive behavior was noted in about 96% of the observations.

Finally, the "Henry's Clock" program was reintroduced. Henry's misbehavior decreased to 13% of the observations during a 6-day period. It was found that several behaviors with which the program had not been explicitly concerned also changed. For example, Henry became more punctual in returning to class from recess. Follow-up near the end of the school year showed that Henry continued to maintain reasonably high levels of acceptable behavior, even after the program was finally eliminated.

There is an important qualification that should be noted in regard to the design method used in this study. Sometimes the reinstatement of baseline conditions does not produce the same level of behavioral functioning found in the original baseline conditions. This does not necessarily mean that the reinforcement procedure was really irrelevant; it probably means that new reinforcers were acquired during the intervention. To unequivocally demonstrate a reinforcement effect requires more sophisticated experimental designs of the type described in Chapter 11.

This study illustrates the use of naturalistic observation in normal settings as a prelude to experimental manipulations. It emphasizes the fact that there need be no sharp dichotomy between naturalistic and laboratory methods.

The Problem of Sampling Behavior

Since behavior is a more or less continuous stream of actions and interactions, only through some kinds of analytic, abstractive processes can it be grasped, recorded, and understood. As shown in the previous examples, one aspect of this abstractive process is the use of categories of analysis; another is the use of sampling procedures.

Many different kinds of observational methods have been developed for obtaining data on complex social events; a number of the more common ones are summarized by Wright (1960) in the context of the study of child behavior and these are also relevant here. He describes several types of sampling plans which he calls *diary description, specimen description, time sampling,* and *event sampling.* These are outlined below on the basis of Wright's description.

Diary descriptions are designed to trace in sequence the procession of behavioral events including all that the observer can manage to record. In essence, the use of motion pictures and tape recordings are diaries which can be broken down later in any of a number of ways. Such records have been used mainly to study longitudinal day-to-day development and to provide the basis for extensive data collection in an area where the investigator does not have any strong presuppositions about what to look for.

Specimen descriptions are generally based upon a shorter time span than diary descriptions and refer to a particular context. It could be used, for example, to describe the free cage behavior of monkeys, or the process of interaction of pairs of animals. The records, however, must still be examined and categorized in some ways before they are useful.

Time sampling utilizes short time intervals (ranging from a few seconds to as much as 20 minutes) which are sampled at regular intervals. This has been illustrated earlier in the use of operant conditioning to modify a child's behavior. Descriptive categories are generally established in advance and judged during the sample period. One limitation of the method that has been suggested is that it can be meaningfully used only for events that happen fairly often, at least every 15 minutes on the average. A second limitation relates to the fact that certain sequences of behavior may last longer than the sample time period, thus producing judgments on "fragmented" sequences of behavior. A third criticism that is sometimes raised about the method is that it does not usually record changes in situational factors as well as individual behavior. Despite these criticisms this general method has probably been used more frequently than any of the others.

Event sampling requires that a particular type of event such as aggressive acts, or fear reactions, be defined and that each such event that occurs within a given time period be recorded and described as fully as possible. This method is limited in that it is applied only to one or two types of behavior while all other types are ignored, but its advantages include the fact that natural units of behavior are examined and that it can be applied to events that occur quite infrequently.

Wright notes that the various sampling plans do not differ generally in terms of reliability of observer agreement, and that it has been found that broader, vaguer categories are not necessarily judged with less reliability than more specific, smaller items of behavior. From the descriptions given above it can be seen that any one or more of these sampling strategies may be used in studies of behavior in natural environments.

Why Categorize?

The various examples that have been cited above emphasize the fact that scientists continually seek to establish meaningful categories for the description of events. What function do these categories perform?

In a general sense, the categories scientists use are designed to group large numbers of observations into a smaller number of classes. The more the members of the class have in common, the more satisfactory is the classification. People can be grouped by the color of their eyes, but this is related to very few other properties of a person. Whales, seals, and dolphins could be considered fish because they live in the ocean, but they have far more properties in common with mammals (e.g., warm blood and suckling of their young).

Sometimes categories are made too broad and many important differences are ignored. This is illustrated by the attempts to classify all people as introverted or extraverted, and the attempt to classify them by body types such as ectomorph, mesomorph, and endomorph.

Classifications are arbitrary to some extent but depend on the purposes of the scientist. For the fisherman, whales may be considered as fish, but this is not satisfactory for the marine biologist. The psychiatrist in a mental hospital may consider his patients in terms of such categories as schizophrenia and manic-depression, but such a system has little value for a psychologist who is director of personnel in a large business. A music teacher in a public school may be content simply with distinguishing the "listeners" from the "singers"; the same teacher in a music school might want to make much finer distinctions in musical talent.

However, it must not be assumed that categories are completely arbitrary. In many cases, they do reflect consistent natural groupings of properties and may thus be thought of as "laws." Metals tend to have different properties from nonmetals (although there is some overlap); the symptoms of tuberculosis tend to be different from those for malaria; and the expressive behavior in anger is different from that in depression.

Bruner et al. (1956) sum up the value of categorizing in the following ideas:

1. Categories make the environment seem less complex.
2. Categories enable us to label parts of our environment so that they seem more familiar.
3. Categories reduce the need to learn new things each time we encounter a new situation since there are usually some relations between the new event and our older experiences.
4. Categories help us to determine appropriate and inappropriate action in new situations.
5. Categories enable us to relate different classes of events.

In general, category systems will be of maximum value if (1) they use a relatively small number of categories, (2) they are based upon theoretical (rather than practical) considerations, (3) they have a wide range of possible applications (throughout the mammalian kingdom, for example), (4) they are exhaustive, that is, are able to incorporate all existing data into the system, (5) they are reliable, and (6) they are sensitive to certain experimental operations, such as reinforcement, deprivation, or stress.

Summary

Naturalistic studies, sometimes called field studies or clinical studies, are usually concerned with an accurate description of an individual's behavior as it is found to occur outside of the laboratory. They are concerned with relations between the individual and the physical environment as well as with relations between individuals. The ideal of such studies requires the observer to interfere as little as possible with the ongoing behavior. In attempting to carry through this aim, instruments are often used to extend the range of events observed, to record them more reliably, and to provide permanent records.

In an effort to make more manageable the continuous flow of behavior, the observer selects categories of events to be observed. These categories are selected either on theoretical grounds, practical grounds (e.g., ease of observation), or empirically by grouping observations that have something in common (as is done by factor analysis). In addition, various sampling plans are used to condense the total flux into a workable portion. Time sampling and event sampling are examples of such plans.

Naturalistic studies are important in that they provide us with some idea of the nature of the world as it exists. As Barker and Wright (1955) point out:

> Geologists, biologists, chemists and physicists know in considerable detail about the distribution in nature of the materials and processes with which they deal. . . . In contrast, psychologists know little more than laymen about the frequency and degree of occurrence of their basic phenomena in the lives of men—of deprivation, of hostility, of freedom, of friendliness, of social pressure, of rewards and punishments. Although we have daily records of the behavior of volcanoes, of the tides, of sun spots, and of rats and monkeys, there have been few scientific records of how a human mother cared for her young, how a particular teacher behaved in the classroom and how the children responded, what a family actually did and said during a mealtime, and how any boy lived his life from the time he awoke in the morning until he went to sleep at night.

As such observations are made, the observer begins to suspect possible relationships between variables. These variables may sometimes be tried out in the laboratory. Knowledge of this sort will help decide whether the results of laboratory research can be validly generalized to the typical situation (Willems, 1967).

Another value of naturalistic studies is that they sometimes provide the basis for theories and broad speculations. The work of Freud was entirely clinical and his theories were based on inferences from observed behavior, yet there is little doubt that he has had considerable influence on modern psychology. Darwin's work was almost entirely descriptive, and yet evolutionary theory has become a firm basis for much of modern science. It seems to be true that theories affect people more than do facts, and bitter controversies are more likely to occur over differing theories than over differing facts. Perhaps it is because of the lack of control over variables or perhaps for other reasons, but observational studies seem more likely to engender broad theoretical speculations than do laboratory studies. To the extent that this is true, they provide a stimulant for further research.

One final point needs to be made. The distinction between naturalistic studies and laboratory studies is not always very sharp. For example, Piaget's naturalistic study of language development was done at a special private school for children where they were free to come and go and do whatever they pleased. This is certainly an "artificial" situation relative to the ordinary school classroom where the children are not free to talk or wander about and where classes are large in size. Similarly, Delgado's study of radio-controlled brain stimulation began with eight monkeys in a cage, certainly an unusual situation for most monkeys.

Within these limitations, it was assumed that "normal" social relations would develop.

These remarks serve to point up the fact that we do not have an unequivocal way of specifying what is natural and what is artificial since manipulations and restrictions of all sorts occur in everyday life. In a sense, experiments in nature occur all the time. There are disasters, floods, wars, concentration camps, prisons, slums, large schools and small ones, segregated schools and desegregated ones. These kinds of situations provide natural laboratories of a sort, with interacting variables. Imaginative investigators using experimental and observational techniques may yet produce rich yields of data and theory from the study of such situations, just as astronomers and geologists have advanced their sciences by carefully observing naturally occurring events. Scott (1955) has emphasized this point in relation to studies of development in animals:

> While experiments are designed to test new ideas, new ideas rarely come from them. Many of the important psychological ideas come directly from clinical observation, and the most original discoveries come from the observation of a curious fact and the inevitable question, why should this happen? As observation is improved there should be a corresponding improvement in the quality and depth of psychological research.

2

Experimentation as a Decision-Making Process

Science, as its name implies, is primarily knowledge; by convention it is knowledge of a certain kind, the kind, namely, which seeks general laws connecting a number of particular facts. Gradually, however, the aspect of science as knowledge is being thrust into the background by the aspect of science as the power of manipulating nature.

—Bertrand Russell

Four Reasons for Doing Experiments

Besides the general aims which all experiments share, that is, to increase our understanding of and our ability to control and predict events, there are a number of specific reasons why an experimenter might perform a particular experiment.

One basic reason experiments are done is simply to *determine the relations between two or more variables.* Sometimes this is referred to as exploratory research, or as research designed to determine the conditions under which certain events occur. Occasionally the impetus for beginning such a study is the appearance of new or improved technical instruments. If an investigator is interested in the effects of rewards on learning, or the effects of room color on mood, or the effects of the racial background of an examiner on the IQ of children, then the relation between two variables is being investigated. One may study such questions because of curiosity or because the answers may have practical importance, or for any other reason. The gathering of such data in systematic ways is the primary function of experiments and it provides the basic data of the science of psychology. A theory can only be developed in the light of well-established empirical generalizations which experiments provide.

The second reason particular experiments are performed is *to extend the range of study of a variable.* Frequently in psychology studies are done under limited conditions; a stress condition might be compared with a no-stress condition, a drug might be given to see if anxiety is produced, visual threshold might be determined for white light only, or transfer might be measured for just one level of practice. In most such cases a negative finding could conceivably mean that the magnitude of the independent variable was not sufficient to produce an effect. More stress, more of a drug, more practice might produce positive results or unexpected findings. The completion of any experiment almost invariably poses further problems for exploration, even if it only means going beyond the limits already studied.

Frequently, new phenomena are discovered as one pushes beyond the usual limits of observation. For example, with small increases of muscular tension, learning is facilitated; with large increases, learning efficiency drops. For short periods after learning a task, a "reminiscence" effect sometimes occurs; with longer intervals recall decreases. Changing the color of the light used in a threshold experiment shows that the eye is maximally sensitive to green light and least sensitive to red. Such examples could be multiplied. Thus one of the important reasons for experimenting is to explore beyond a range already tested.

Another reason for experimenting is *to increase the reliability of reported findings.* This simply involves the exact replication of previously reported experiments. This is common practice in any science. When, for instance, a physicist several years ago reported the discovery of a magnetic unit of matter comparable to the electrical unit of matter, a dozen investigators throughout the country quickly repeated the experiments and within a relatively short time had shown that a misinterpretation had occurred in connection with the original data. Replication is a very important function of experiments, since one can never be certain that all possible precautions have been taken to avoid bias. If different investigators, using different samples of subjects, are able to verify a reported finding, confidence in that finding is greatly increased. This is a function of the scientist that should not be underrated or looked upon with scorn, since lack of replication is a common enough occurrence in psychology.

A fourth general reason for doing experiments is well recognized and that is *to test theory.* Many studies have been done in an effort to test psychoanalytic propositions, the views of Gestalt psychologists, and the concepts of reinforcement theory, as well as many other hypotheses. Quite often, attempts to test broad theories of the type mentioned above do not produce clear-cut results. The reason is that such theories tend to be rather vaguely formulated so that no crucial experiments can be performed. This is not too surprising, since most theories have value as sources of stimulation for research rather than as exact predictors of new facts. In this context it is important to remember the point made by Conant (1947) in his discussion of the history of science. He wrote, "A theory is only overthrown by a better theory, never merely by contradictory facts."

Experimental Versus Correlational Studies

A great many studies have been done using what is called *correlational methods.* This means simply that the researcher tries to measure the relations between two or more phenomena that have been observed or measured. For example, a correlational study might determine the correlation between the IQs of identical twins or the relationship between success in college and certain personality traits. What these examples have in common is an acceptance by the investigator of whatever he or she finds. No attempt is made, as in experimental studies, to manipulate or change conditions.

A second characteristic of correlational studies is that the time sequence usually has no particular relevance. It makes no difference which twin's IQ is measured first, or whether the personality traits are measured before or after the college grades. By contrast, in an experiment the values of the independent variable (i.e., the one manipulated by the experimenter) are established and measured *before* the values of the dependent variable (i.e., the response measure) are determined. In order for an investigator to study the effects of drugs on mood, he or she must *first* administer specified amounts of drugs to the subjects and *then* measure the reactions.

A third point of distinction is the fact that a correlational study does not imply causation, whereas an experimental one does. The fact that cigarette smoking is correlated with frequency of lung cancer does not necessarily mean that it causes it. For example, it may be that people who smoke the most also live in the larger cities where smog and exhaust fumes exist in great concentrations, which in turn increase the chances of lung cancer. Perhaps heavy cigarette smokers have a diet which is different from that of nonsmokers, again affecting the probability of illness. Because a large number of hypotheses are possible, any correlation does not enable a direct statement of cause. In a good experiment, it is possible to say that the conditions manipulated by the experimenter caused the reactions which were obtained.

This raises a fourth point of distinction between the two kinds of studies. If the correlation between two variables turns out to be high and reliable, then we can use this for prediction. For example, some employee aptitude tests will predict with a high degree of accuracy how well a person will do on a given job. These tests can be of great help in selecting or rejecting individuals for those jobs. However, they do not tell us what variables influence good or poor performance. Thus, their use is limited to choosing the proper person for a job.

There is one further point that can be made with regard to the distinctions between experimental and correlational studies. To the extent that an experimenter can control the conditions under which an event occurs, he or she is prepared to make more accurate observations in contrast to an observer who simply records events as they occur.

The differences that have been described do not mean that correlational studies are of no value; on the contrary, in some areas of research they represent the only ways of getting reliable information. This is particularly true in clinical, educational, and industrial psychology where the most common approach is to collect tests, questionnaires, and rating data of various sorts and subject them to statistical analyses. In addition, correlational studies frequently suggest hypotheses that may be tested by means of experiments. This book, however, will be concerned primarily with experimental studies rather than correlational ones.

Independent and Dependent Variables

Two concepts frequently used by psychologists are the *independent variable* and the *dependent variable*. The independent variable is usually defined as that factor or variable which is manipulated by the experimenter, such as amount of drug administered, level of electric shock used, or amount of food reward given. The independent variable can also refer to the absence of external stimulation, such as the amount of time an animal is deprived of food. The dependent variable is defined as the measured changes in the subjects as indicated by their responses, for example, mood changes, frequency of avoidance responses, or speed of learning a task. These terms are widely used in the psychological literature in connection with the design of experiments, but the terms have been used in several different ways.

For example, in studies of maze learning, the subject learns to go through the maze to gain food reward. The subject reacts to such stimuli as the food object and the actual size and shape of the maze. But the animal's responses can be greatly modified by making it hungry, although the amount of hunger is not a stimulus in the same sense that the food reward is. Food deprivation is essentially the absence of stimulation, and yet the time of deprivation can be thought of as a variable. The food reward is a directly manipulated stimulus to the subject. In current usage, both the food and the deprivation time are conceived as independent variables.

It should be noted that the independent variable is only one sufficient condition among many which can affect the phenomenon being studied. For instance, maze learning will be affected to varying degrees by the size of the maze, as well as the amount of food reward that is given. In any experiment it may be possible to manipulate more than one variable at a time, and in such a case we would refer to two or more independent variables.

All experiments also require that certain conditions be kept constant. This is done, of course, for the very reason that these conditions might affect in some way the responses being measured. In most experiments, timing is carefully kept constant, apparatus is checked or calibrated, environmental conditions are kept fairly uniform, and any definitely known variables (other than those under study) are kept fixed at some value. It should be evident that the factors kept constant may all potentially change the response being measured, and, therefore, may all be thought of as *potential independent variables*. These variables that are kept constant are called *parameters*.

In recent years, there has been a tendency to extend the terms independent and dependent variable to relatively broad, complex social situations. In such cases, it is often very difficult to specify in any detail the particular parts of the situation to which the subject is responding. There have been studies, for example, concerned with the effects of psychotherapy in which "type of therapy" has been called the independent variable. Since therapy may go on for years and involve a continuous interaction between the patient and the therapist, it is almost impossible without many detailed studies to talk about the specific conditions which bring about changes.

In conclusion, it may be said that the concepts of dependent and independent variables are useful, so long as we all learn to use the terms in the same way. As science progresses we discover more of the independent variables affecting and modifying the events with which we are concerned. At the same time we are enlarging our conceptions about the applicability of those ideas in a regular progression from the simple stimuli of the psychophysical world to the complex patterns of social interaction.

Decision Making in Experimentation

Experiments are generally performed in order to find out what causes events to happen as they do. If we can determine causes, we can often learn to arrange conditions so that the events we are interested in will occur whenever we wish. Successful experiments therefore increase our control over events.

The aim of establishing cause and effect connections is simple and clear, yet in practice it is often very difficult to be sure that we have been able to do this. Let us take a simple example from the folklore of psychology. Does a bull really get angry when he sees the color red? In order to answer such a question quite a few decisions have to be made. For example, we have to decide whether we mean all bulls or only certain breeds, and then we have to decide how many of each type to measure. Then we must choose some red objects. Should they be red sheets waved at the bull, colored pieces of cardboard, a red fence, or perhaps colored lights? The words "red" and "angry" have to be clearly defined. If an animal being tested reacts to a waving red cloth, we still have to make sure that he does not react the same way to a white cloth or a blue one, and obviously we cannot compare a blue fence with a red cloth. Furthermore, we have to match the colors for intensity so that we do not inadvertently compare light blue with dark red since a difference in brightness rather than in color could be the reason for a difference in behavior. It should be evident that a great deal of work and care would be necessary before we could unequivocally answer the question that was posed.

There are some general lessons that may be learned from this example. In any experiment whatsoever, an experimenter must make a series of decisions. These decisions concern such matters as how to define the key concepts connected with the problem, how to select subjects to be used, how to measure their behavior, what factors to keep constant, what kind of statistics to use, and how widely to generalize the results. *All experimenters must make these kinds of decisions, explicitly or otherwise, in carrying out any experiment.*

Sometimes these decisions are made with full recognition of the implications; sometimes they are made simply as a matter of convenience, or by rules of thumb; and sometimes they are made implicitly without recognition of the implications. This is true whether the research deals with the influence of different schedules of reinforcement on behavior or with the problem-solving ability of small groups. What makes a person an expert in one field rather than another is a greater awareness of what factors to control, what variables are most effective, what kinds of definitions are most likely to be fruitful, and what kinds of measurements are most meaningful.

The preceding decisions have been given only for illustration. In the next section we shall look more closely at the general types of decisions that are implicit in every experiment.

General Classes of Decisions in Experimentation

The following descriptions are meant as a bird's-eye view of the kinds of decisions experimenters make, from the time they conceive of a problem until they write their final reports of the research. The sequence listed here does not necessarily imply that the decisions are made in this exact order; there is a complex interaction between the different classes of decisions, and those made at any time automatically restrict or affect those made later.

Decisions about Definitions. Most of the theoretical terms of psychology have been defined in a number of different ways. For example, changes of motivation or drive are defined sometimes by the operations used to produce them, such as hours of deprivation, or by their effects on behavior, such as rate of bar pressing to acquire food. Motivation means one thing in a school situation, another in an industrial plant, and something else in a study done with lower animals. The use of different definitions sometimes prevents the different situations from being comparable and limits the generalizations possible from experiments.

It has occasionally been suggested that the use of "operational definitions" and "intervening variables" will solve some of these problems. However, many criticisms have been leveled at these philosophic points of view. Some interesting questions concerning the philosophy of science are implicit in this whole matter of choice of definitions and some of these will be examined briefly in Chapter 3 in order to clarify the issues involved.

Decisions about Sampling. In all experiments, decisions must be made about the number of subjects to be used and the number of measurements to be made. Is taking 100 measurements from one subject the same as taking a single measurement on 100 subjects? Why is it that in some areas of psychology such as vision and audition research, generalizations are based on just a few subjects, while in other areas of psychology such as personality research, reliable conclusions often require the use of dozens or even hundreds of subjects? What are the considerations that enable us to decide to use 2 or 200 subjects, 20 or 2000 measurements?

Decisions about the Type of Experiment. A great many of the experiments reported in the literature are concerned simply with a comparison of two conditions. Is school A better than school B in the teaching of reading? Does group discussion affect consumer buying more than formal lectures? Will psychotic behavior be decreased more by reserpine than by a placebo? Is the eye more sensitive to blue light than to red? Studies of this sort compare two conditions or compare an experimental with a comparison or control condition (or control group). They provide a limited insight into the question of whether a factor or variable is or is not affecting the behavior or event measured.

A second type of experiment attempts to extend the kind of study described above by comparing several different conditions instead of only two. Thus it might involve a study of the effect of different dosages of a drug on bar-pressing behavior, or the effect of different amounts of punishment on learning. A great deal more information is obtained from this type of experiment, and a functional curve or graph may usually be plotted showing the relation between the variables which are studied.

A third type of experiment extends the functional study described above by systematically varying one of the other factors which had previously been kept constant. This produces a family of curves rather than a single one. An example of this type of experiment might be a study of the effect of different dosages of drugs on skilled performance for various age groups.

All of these types of experiments have different properties with regard to (a) the possibility of making generalizations, (b) the applicable mathematical techniques, and (c) the appropriate design method. Chapter 4 will be devoted to this analysis.

Experimental Design Decisions. In all research, decisions have to be made about the number of groups to use and in what sequence to study them. Sometimes groups or individuals are matched and then exposed to different conditions; sometimes random groups are used; and sometimes one group is studied under a variety of conditions. Each method that is used requires that certain assumptions be met. These assumptions vary for the different design methods. The explanation of these methods and assumptions is necessary, since different design methods do not always yield the same results.

Decisions about Measurement. There has been increasing recognition in recent years that the conclusions we draw from an experiment depend on what and how we measure. In learning and memory experiments, for example, the different measures used have different properties; theories which may be developed to account for one set of relations would therefore be unable to account for another set. This means that different experiments frequently are not directly comparable. For example, one investigator may measure learning in terms of the number of errors a subject makes, another by the speed or rate of response. The results of experiments using different measures of the same concept (such as learning) do not generally correlate in any simple fashion. Therefore, interpretations will vary. How one might choose the most adequate measure from a set of alternatives is a basic problem in doing experiments.

There is also the problem of the units of measurement. The kinds of statistical analysis permissible with a given set of numbers depend upon what sort of scale they represent. But how is an investigator to know whether a set of measurements that is made represents a scale with equal units, and if it does not, how might one be constructed?

Another important issue related to the problem of measurement concerns the properties of the instruments and apparatus used. Psychologists have come to depend to an increasing degree upon the instruments made for them by the engineers, particularly upon electronic equipment. These must be understood in order to be used properly. It is simply not sufficient to read numbers from a dial and assume that some psychological variable such as "emotionality" is being measured. The path from the measuring instrument to the person is a long one and must be carefully examined before meaningful conclusions may be drawn.

Statistical and Mathematical Decisions. In any study, the experimenter must make a decision on the way in which the specific information which has been gathered is to be handled. What kinds of statistical analyses are to be used? Are the assumptions of the statistical methods met by the data? Shall empirical curves be fitted, or is there a theory which predicts a specific kind of outcome?

Some methods of analysis are much more general, or useful, or sensitive than others. It is necessary to understand the specific assumptions, uses, and limitations of the various statistical and mathematical methods in order to be able to use them intelligently. There have been cases in the history of science where a later investigator reanalyzed the data of a previous worker and discovered unsuspected relationships. The proper choice of mathematical technique is very important.

Decisions about Generalizing. Once the data have been gathered and analyzed, it is necessary to draw conclusions and implications from the findings and attempt explanations. The kinds of generalizations that are made depend upon the type of experiment that has been performed, the design method used, the sampling procedures followed, and the adequacy of the instruments used for measurement. They depend also upon the experimenter's concept of what an explanation is, and what he or she means by the term *lawful.* Philosophic assumptions of this sort are inseparably linked to the conclusions drawn from experiments.

Summary

These seven broad classes of decisions implicit in experimental research provide a framework for considering the steps involved in research. Various chapters to follow will take up each of the major classes in turn and try to analyze the nature of the decisions to be made and their implications for research. Not all questions can be given a simple answer and some difficult and controversial problems will be raised. This is why experimentation today is partly an art.

3

Decisions Concerning Definitions of Concepts

Too great haste in defining is almost as much a fault as failure to define at all; and there is a peculiar fallacy which attempts to bar the way to all fruitful discussion by remarking that "it is all a question of definition, and if the terms had been first defined, all this argument would be unnecessary." The remark is perfectly true, but it overlooks the fact that any fully adequate definition is the product of thinking, not its point of departure.

—James E. Creighton

Although science may start from commonsense ideas, the gathering of new information quickly creates the need for new concepts. These new concepts introduced into the language of science serve various purposes.

For one thing, *new terms are introduced in order to make old ideas more precise or more general.* In the early 1930s, Skinner, for example, introduced the terms *operant* and *respondent conditioning* to distinguish more precisely between two types of conditioning situations. The term *respondent conditioning* was to refer to those cases where the unconditioned stimulus (e.g., the food or the electric shock) *elicited* a response which then became conditioned to a previously neutral stimulus. The term *operant conditioning* was to refer to those situations where the response to be conditioned was spontaneously *emitted* by the animal and then reinforced by some kind of reward (e.g., the presentation of food, or the termination of electric shock). In one type of learning situation, the unconditioned stimulus preceded the response being measured; in the other, it followed the response being measured.

A second reason for introducing new terms into the scientific language is for the *labeling of new observations.* Ethologists are biologists who are especially interested in behavior which is specific to each species of animal. Since the turn of the century they have known that in order to cross certain species of wild birds, it is necessary to have the young of one species reared by the adults of the other. When these birds reach maturity they prefer to mate with birds of the same species as their foster parents. It was also discovered that many birds reared from birth by humans develop social responses to the human caretaker which are normally reserved only for their own species. This phenomenon was given the name *imprinting* and was later reported to occur in insects, fish, and some mammals.

New terms are also introduced into the scientific language *to provide a theoretical explanation of some observed fact.* Psychologists have known for a long time that the apparent extent of certain visual illusions decreases gradually as an observer continues to look at the figure. More recently, a new phenomenon was discovered that was also related to the inspection of certain geometric figures. For example, if an observer looks at a bent arrowhead for a few minutes and then fixates on a straight vertical line, he or she usually sees the line bent slightly in the opposite direction. This phenomenon is called a *figural aftereffect.* Some of the Gestalt psychologists have suggested that both the decrease in the magnitude of certain illusions and the figural aftereffects can be explained by assuming the existence of so-called *satiation currents* in the brain. The new term is designed to provide an explanation, in some sense, of certain observations.

The fourth reason new terms are introduced into the scientific language is *to conveniently summarize in one word several related concepts.* One of the important learning theories of the present time, developed by Clark Hull, uses the term *excitatory potential.* The greater an animal's excitatory potential, the greater the chances are that it will respond to an appropriate conditioned stimulus. It is assumed in the theory that this variable depends on the number of rewards an animal has had and on its state of drive. However, the term excitatory potential does not mean anything more than these particular variables which are interacting. It serves simply as a convenient summary word for these variables and can be dropped at any time and be replaced by them. Such a term, which is used only as a summary for a group of other terms, is usually called an *intervening variable.*

Some psychologists (MacCorquodale and Meehl, 1948) have suggested that such summary terms be distinguished from other kinds of theoretical terms which are meant to imply something "real." For example, does the concept *gene* refer only to certain observations which are conveniently summarized by the word, or does it refer to some underlying reality? Similarly, does a word like *memory* function simply as a summary term for certain kinds of observations, or does it imply certain underlying brain mechanisms or even more fundamental biochemical structures? If a concept is used in the latter sense, it should be called a *hypothetical construct* rather than an *intervening variable.*

This kind of distinction has actually been part of the history of physics since the last century (Plutchik, 1954) and is still reflected in current psychological usages. For example, a word such as *drive* is sometimes used as a convenient summary word to describe certain procedures used in depriving experimental animals of food or water, but it is also sometimes used to refer to certain physiological changes inside the body. In the former sense it may be thought of as an intervening variable; in the latter, as a hypothetical construct. However, the essential criterion of the adequacy of any hypothetical construct is that its assumed properties can be measured and checked in several independent ways. For example, in the case of the concept of drive, it is possible to record changes in blood chemistry, stomach acidity, and muscular tension as independent measures of that state. If the independent measures corroborate the properties of the state being studied, this increases our confidence in the "reality" of the construct.

On Choosing a Definition

In this section we will examine several examples of decision-making problems associated with definitions. The first concerns the concept of *fear*.

In the many studies dealing with fear (sometimes labeled emotional response) there have been few attempts to specify its nature in general terms. Most investigators have simply chosen one particular method for producing or measuring this state and then performed all their experiments using the one method. Yet Miller (1957) has described eight different methods for producing or studying fear in animals. They are as follows:

1. *Avoidance conditioning.* In this method the animal is made to turn an activity wheel, or run from one box to another, or press on a bar in order to avoid a painful shock. The usual measures are the speed of response or the percent of avoidance responses made relative to the total number of trials.
2. *Strength-of-pull.* The animal tries to get away from a noxious stimulus and its strength-of-pull on a special harness is measured.
3. *Sidman technique.* The animal presses a bar in order to postpone the occurrence of a shock for a set period of time. Bar-pressing rate is measured.
4. *Approach-avoidance conflict.* A conflict is induced in the animal between the desire for food and the desire to avoid an electric shock.
5. *Conditioned-suppression.* A clicking sound is presented for a period and is immediately followed by the onset of electric shock. After some trials, the animal will decrease its rate of bar pressing during the clicking sound even though the shock is not given.
6. *Startle technique.* A signal is followed by a shock for a number of trials. On the test trials the shock is omitted and a sudden loud noise is given. The degree of startle measures the amount of conditioned fear.
7. *Physiological measures.* The animal's heart rate or skin resistance is recorded as a measure of fear.
8. *Naturalistic observations.* The spontaneous behavior of the animal is observed either under natural conditions or in a laboratory setting. Examples of flight and withdrawal behavior are noted.

In view of the existence of these many techniques for measuring or producing fear, which one should be used? In most cases, the key terms involved in any inquiry are usually general, theoretical terms. A concept such as *fear* is a theoretical term implying some general state or condition of the body. This is also true for such concepts as learning, memory, hunger, thirst, psychosis, emotion, and drive. Such general states *cannot* be measured completely by a single index any more than a person can be completely described by a single personality trait. The very essence of a general concept is that there are many different ways in which the various aspects of it can be measured. Any one method is simply one index, or indicator, but it never can provide a complete understanding of the concept. Different indicators may sometimes even give apparently contradictory results.

An example of this is seen in a study by Miller et al. (1950), who compared several different indices of hunger drive in rats with lesions in the part of the brain called the hypothalamus. Rats with such lesions had been found in the past to develop obesity when they had free access to food. It was therefore assumed that such brain lesions produced increased hunger or appetite. However, when four different measures of hunger were used, a different picture emerged. Rats with hypothalamic lesions pressed the bar for food at a slower rate than control animals who were without any brain damage. They also ran more slowly to get food, and they were stopped by lower levels of electric shock. They also worked less hard than the control animals in order to get food. All these measures seemed to imply that rats with hypothalamic lesions were less hungry than the controls, even though they ate more when given free access to food. These findings suggested that the brain lesions produced a more complex state than one simply connected with hunger.

We must be careful to recognize that results obtained by use of only one measure are always tentative. Thus, learning has been measured by speed of response, number of errors, trials to reach a criterion, rate of response, percent of animals responding on a given trial, and magnitude of response. These measures do not correlate with one another in any simple way, and in addition, very few attempts have been made to determine their interrelationships. Although any one measure may serve as an indicator of learning, at best it will provide insight into only one aspect of the hypothetical state we call *learning,* just as any one method for measuring fear provides limited insight into its nature. Ideally, studies should use multiple measures.

Operationism: Its Historical Background

In their attempt to understand the language of science, philosophers and logicians have suggested that there are many types of definitions that are actually used. To take a simple example, we may use a dictionary definition to define a word by giving other terms which may be used to replace it. Thus, someone might say that a definition of the word *drive* is "motive" or "impulse," and that we may use these terms interchangeably. Such dictionary definitions may be helpful in some cases and not in others, depending on the context.

Far more important in the thinking of psychologists are *operational* definitions. These definitions seem to play an important role in discussions of the philosophy of science, and the concept itself has an interesting origin and history.

In 1927, the physicist P.W. Bridgman wrote a book called *The Logic of Modern Physics* in which he discussed the philosophic significance of Einstein's theory of relativity. In his book, he indicated that physicists had been embarrassed by Einstein's theories because the theories had called for some fundamental revisions in thinking about old concepts which had been taken for granted. Bridgman then proposed a solution which he hoped would prevent such a revolution in our thinking in the future.

He proposed that our concepts should be defined by the operations we use to measure them. For example, he said, "The concept of length involves as much as and nothing more than the set of operations by which length is determined." This apparently simple idea actually has some far-reaching implications. It means, for example, that if we measure something in two different ways, we actually have two different concepts. This would imply that if we measured the temperature of an object by a mercury thermometer and also by an electric resistance thermometer, we would actually be measuring two different kinds of temperature. Similarly, it would mean that if we measured the intelligence of a person by two different tests we would be measuring two different kinds of intelligence. Furthermore, if someone requested a definition of intelligence, it would be sufficient simply to say "Intelligence is what my test measures."

This idea of Bridgman's, to define concepts by the operations used to measure them, seemed to appeal to psychologists. During the 1930s and 1940s they wrote about *operationism* (as this point of view came to be called) with great enthusiasm. They claimed that operational definitions of terms would help us avoid contradictory notions and hazy ideas and would lead to clarity and precision in our thinking.

After a number of such favorable reports had appeared, a reaction set in and several philosophers began to criticize this general point of view. Unfortunately, by this time operationism had already developed several different versions, and it was not always clear toward which one the criticisms were directed.

One point of view that developed proposed that operationism meant that the statements of scientists are valid only insofar as we can verify their truth by means of certain operations. Later on Bridgman himself (1950) decided that the word *operation* could refer not only to actual physical measurement procedures, but also mental, or paper-and-pencil operations; in other words, to the theoretical and computational procedures scientists actually use. What this means, simply, is that the physicist does not take his raw data at face value. In most instances, the raw data consist of numerical readings on dials. These readings are then assumed to measure the properties of certain unobserved structures such as electrical charges or nuclear forces, usually on the basis of complex theoretical or mathematical procedures. Raw data are often entered into equations which provide new hypothetical quantities.

A sociologist, Lundberg, in 1939, enthusiastically stated that by using only physical operations in defining concepts we could avoid "metaphysical problems" in science. In 1945, at a symposium devoted to the problem, Skinner proposed that "Operationism may be defined as the practice of talking about (1) one's observations, (2) the manipulational and calculational procedures involved in making them, (3) the logical and mathematical steps which intervene between earlier and later statements, and (4) nothing else." He also added, "Operationism is not regarded as a new theory or mode of definition." This last note was echoed by Feigl, a philosopher who participated in the 1945 Symposium on Operationism. He wrote, "Operationism is not a system of philosophy. It is not a technique for the formation of concepts or theories. It will not by itself produce scientific results." This sample of comments on operationism suggests that it has become a somewhat ambiguous idea to psychologists.

Another variant of operationism has centered around the question of whether an operational definition describes operations needed to *measure* a concept or operations needed to *produce* a phenomenon. How, for example, can we operationally define a "chocolate cake"? Using Bridgman's original ideas we would describe the operations used to measure the properties of the chocolate cake: its texture, color, taste, and so on. However, some writers on the subject have suggested that an operational definition can be given by simply providing a recipe for baking the cake. To take a psychologically relevant example, the word *drive* may be operationally defined by some measures of the behavior of a hungry animal, such as its restlessness, its bar-pressing rate to get food, etc. On the other hand, it might also be defined in terms of the procedures that have been used to produce a state of hunger, such as keeping the animal deprived of food for a certain number of hours. Now, although these two kinds of procedures may be related, they are not necessarily equivalent. One philosopher (Benjamin, 1955) has objected to the latter method of defining on the grounds that "operationism is a device for creating and defining *concepts,* not for producing *things.*"

During the past few years, a number of criticisms of operationism have been advanced (Plutchik, 1963). Some of the more important of these will be briefly summarized here.

Critique of Operationism

Measurement Presupposes a Concept

Operational definitions have often been illustrated by examples of the following sort, "Intelligence is what an intelligence test measures." Actually, this is a very inadequate way of defining any concept, because it can produce results which are obviously meaningless. This was shown by Adler (1947) in terms of his so-called C_n test, which he operationally defined by the answers to a series of questions, as follows:

1. How many hours did you sleep last night? _____

2. Estimate the length of your nose in inches and multiply by 2. _____

3. Do you like fried liver? (Mark 1 for Yes and −1 for No.) _____

4. How many feet are there in a yard? _____

5. Estimate the number of glasses of ginger ale the inventor of this test drank while inventing it. _____

Add the above items. The sum is your crude C_n score. Take the test daily at the same hour as long as you can. Then calculate your refined C_n rate by . . .

It is obvious that such a test does not make sense, regardless of the statistical formulas used or methodological refinements involved in the statement of items or categories of analysis. The statement that "C_n is what the test measures" is not satisfactory on the two grounds that we are unable to form any meaningful concept of it, and that all criticism is excluded, since "The test measures C_n and C_n is what the test measures." It is also clear that an infinite number of such "tests" could be formed in this arbitrary way. Operationism provides no basis for distinguishing between meaningful and meaningless concepts.

Before we can adequately measure anything, we need to know, at least in general, what we want to find out, even if there is some vagueness to our concept. Science develops its measuring tools, typically, by a series of successive approximations in which the concept gradually achieves greater precision, the ambiguities are eliminated, and the relations between the concept and other concepts are more clearly formulated. Observation and measurement presuppose objects with properties as well as previous theory. We never start from operations.

This means, for example, that before we can measure the length of something we need to have some idea that a ruler is appropriate for such measurement rather than, say, a magnet. Similarly, we form an idea of what we mean by a concept like *habit strength* before we measure it, and then we recognize that several different kinds of indicators, such as number of errors made, or speed of response, can all measure habit strength. Sometimes these different indices do not correlate very well, but operationism does not provide any basis for selecting which is a "better" measure.

The Problem of Generality

Several critics have raised the question of whether operationism does not make all general concepts impossible since even the smallest variation in the procedure of measurement would imply a new concept. Does the concept of *length* change if we measure the length of an object by a micrometer rather than a wooden ruler? Is *heat* different if it is measured by a mercury thermometer rather than a thermocouple?

Such variations in procedure are commonplace in science, and yet it is generally believed that these different procedures or operations are designed to measure the same concept. It is also recognized that certain sources of error may operate for one measuring procedure that do not operate for another. These sources of error are gradually discovered and eliminated, and the different measurement procedures converge to produce a single consistent answer.

Operationism literally interpreted would imply that the use of many different methods to determine the properties of the synapse, for example, means that many different and unrelated concepts are being studied. This, of course, is contrary to the spirit of the whole series of observations made in connection with this problem. If there are many independent operational definitions, how is it possible to arrive at general constructs? The fact is that most scientists are interested in finding general explanations and general concepts that will account for a large number of apparently isolated or unrelated observations in terms of a small number of terms or constructs. Operationism, literally interpreted, would move science in the opposite direction, greatly increasing the number of unrelated concepts and actually providing a new concept for each new kind of measurement. Such a situation would make scientific teaching and prediction very difficult.

The Problem of Error

The fact that in actual scientific practice there are often several ways of measuring a given phenomenon poses several problems for the operationist. One concerns the issue of the equivalence of operations, but a second question which arises is whether one measure is in some sense "better" than any other. To be able to judge the relative value of measurements or of operations requires criteria beyond the operations themselves. If a concept is nothing but an operation, how can we talk about being mistaken or about making errors? If *heat* stands for certain measurement procedures, there is no sense in talking of better ways of measuring it or of being mistaken in such measures. Similarly, from a definition such as "intelligence is what the IQ tests measure," one cannot construct a new test or judge how good the old one is.

One of the facts of science is a continuous tendency to modify existing methods of measurement so that certain properties can be evaluated with greater and greater precision. New instruments and new designs are continuously being developed, yet we do not identify the concept being measured with the measurement procedure or instrument being used. If we did, then improvements and changes of method would produce new concepts, which they generally do not.

Over the past half century, skin resistance, or the galvanic skin response, has been measured with dozens of different instruments using different circuits, designs, and procedures, and although many of these operations have had various sources of bias associated with them, the common element which binds all this research together is the fact that the particular concept *skin resistance* is being measured. As science develops the sources of error are gradually eliminated. Operationism has never adequately taken into consideration this problem of the improvement of measuring procedures and the elimination of error. Feigl (1945) has pointed out that thermometers and IQ tests did not arise in an historical vacuum, but that there were repeated redefinitions. "It makes perfectly good sense to ask whether a mercury thermometer measures temperature adequately." The same, of course, may be asked of psychological measurements.

The Problem of Theoretical Terms

The criticisms raised against operationism under this general heading are of three sorts: (a) very few terms have in fact been operationally defined, (b) some theoretical terms *cannot* be operationally defined, and (c) some terms can be operationally defined which are not usually thought to be included in the scientific universe of discourse.

Considering the first point, it has been noted that there is actually a dearth of illustrations in the literature of operational definitions of terms, and that the few examples usually given, such as "Intelligence is what the intelligence test tests," are not fair samples of the terminology of psychologists. Very few, if any, attempts have been made to define operationally such currently used terms as *field, synapse, emotion, cognitive map, Oedipus complex, drive, superego,* etc. Almost none of the terms in any dictionary of psychology are defined operationally.

That there are some meaningful concepts which are not operationally definable is also clear. Many of the terms used in science refer to ideal states such as perfect gases, point masses, frictionless engines, instantaneous velocities, etc., which represent the limiting condition of an infinite series of approximations. Mathematical concepts used in science also often refer to conditions not realizable in the actual world; this is illustrated by the concepts of the calculus which use notions relating to infinity. In addition to this, there are concepts employed in science which cannot be measured by currently available techniques; for example, the earth's core, the neurophysiological basis of memory, the fossil link between man and the higher primates, yet these concepts are not meaningless or invalid (Ginsberg, 1955).

In relation to the third point, it may be said that the way operationist thinking has developed, it is possible to "operationally define" almost all the terms of our language, even those usually called metaphysical. Operationists have extended the term to include paper and pencil, mental, and logico-mathematical operations, which dilutes operationism to such a degree that almost anything a scientist does to get knowledge can be included. Even a metaphysician uses mental operations, and *God* and the *soul* can be defined in these terms. Feigl also notes (1945) that such a broad definition of operationism can be applied to the speculations of theology and metaphysics. It is not evident that operationism can avoid or solve metaphysical questions as has sometimes been claimed.

Implications

The preceding remarks have been meant to indicate some of the problems implicit in the classical operationist position which has undoubtedly claimed too much. It is possible, however, to accept an important idea contained in this view, and that is that *all experimental and theoretical reports should be as explicit as possible in describing the methods used to obtain and analyze the data.* The methods section of any experiment should be clear enough and complete enough so that the experiment can be duplicated from that description alone (or with the aid of other published references). That the description of the experiment is clear and unequivocal does not mean that the concepts used in the experiment are nothing but the measurement operations. The concept always comes first, and then certain procedures (or operations) are selected from a larger possible number and used as *indicators* of the concept.

It is not consistent with actual usages in science for a particular investigator to simply say that his method of measuring something provides an operational definition. If this were done, then each investigator might have his own private operational definition of each concept and communication between researchers would completely break down. *In practice, each scientist's procedures for measuring concepts must relate in some reasonable way to the work of other investigators as well as to the history of that idea.* Science is basically a highly social enterprise in which new developments in knowledge are almost completely dependent upon the existing state of knowledge. This is why scientists are always eager to disseminate their findings and why they continually maintain communication with other scientists through journals and other channels.

The actual definitions used in psychology, or any other science, may be any one or more of a large number of types, because scientists introduce concepts into the scientific language by a variety of procedures. Textbooks of logic often distinguish a whole variety of types of definitions, for example, verbal, heuristic, operational, genetic, real, classificatory, extensive, intensive, systematic, circular, coordinating, dictionary, and literary.

Scientific dictionaries do not generally use operational definitions; they more often define concepts by the use of theoretical terms or by listing properties associated with the concept. The desire to be precise and restricted may unnecessarily limit the productiveness of research. It is interesting to note that early in the present century, Sigmund Freud made a statement that is quite relevant. He wrote:

> The view is often defended that sciences should be built up on clear and sharply defined basal concepts. In actual fact no science, not even the most exact, begins with such definitions. The true beginning of scientific activity consists rather in describing phenomena and then in proceeding to group, classify and correlate them. . . . It is only after more searching investigation of the field in question that we are able to formulate with increased clarity the scientific concepts underlying it, and progressively so to modify these concepts that they become widely applicable and at the

same time consistent logically. Then indeed, it may be time to immure them in definitions.

Summary

Just as there are many different reasons for introducing new terms into the language of science, so there are many different types of definitions. In most cases, the key concepts involved in experiments (e.g., learning, motivation, attitudes, etc.) are theoretical terms referring to general states of the body or inferred conditions. Such general states cannot be measured by a single indicator, but require many separate indices in order to provide a fairly complete understanding of the concept which has been defined.

Some psychologists have stressed the importance of operational definitions. Although some important ideas are implied by this notion, many criticisms have been directed at *operationism* and its claims. The major criticisms were presented and the point was emphasized that although the measurements used in any experiment should always be clearly stated and explained, it is not the case that the concepts used in the experiment are *nothing but* the procedures of measurement. Measurements are usually partial indicators of theoretical constructs. The use of different indicators of a concept often provides increased insight into its nature.

4

Types of Experiments

The uniformly certain and completely universal laws of science can be realized only in the carefully guarded conditions of the laboratory and are never found in the world outside.

—Norman Campbell

One of the decision-making problems any scientist faces when starting an experimental investigation concerns the type of experiment to be performed. The expression *type of experiment* refers essentially to the number of variables manipulated and to the number of values of each variable to be used. For example, it is possible to perform an experiment designed to compare two methods for learning French verbs or, in contrast, to develop a functional relation between two variables, such as is illustrated by Weber's law. Weber's law simply states that the sensitivity of a sense organ is approximately the same at all intensities of stimulation. Differences in the type of experiment performed lead to different design methods used and different analyses of the data, as well as to differences in the possibility of generalizing. This chapter will describe three types of experiments, their functions, properties, and limitations.

Bivalent Experiments

A type of experiment frequently performed in psychology is one in which two conditions are compared. The effects of "success" on a task may be compared with those of "failure," reinforcement with nonreinforcement, drugs with the absence of drugs, electric shock against no shock, "authoritarian" families with "democratic" ones. All such studies involving a comparison of two conditions, or two points, may be called *bivalent* (i.e., two-valued) experiments. It has been suggested that such experiments are most useful at the beginning of a series of studies in that they help identify important variables or factors which may be examined more systematically later on. There are, however, certain serious shortcomings in this type of experiment which greatly limit the kind of conclusions that may be drawn from them. These points will be illustrated by some examples.

Suppose a bivalent experiment is contemplated dealing with the effect of food deprivation on speed of performance. Assuming everything is done carefully, the results may look somewhat as shown in Figure 4–1. The bar graph shows quite clearly that 24 hours of food deprivation leads to an increase in speed of performing some given task. If the difference is significant, the result may be quite reliable. The experimenter is often tempted in such a case to say, "Speed of performing increases with amount of food deprivation."

Suppose, however, that another investigator unknown to the first tried this experiment in exactly the same way except for one slight modification: 48 hours of food deprivation was used instead of 24. The results might look somewhat as shown in Figure 4–2. If the difference is significant, this investigator would be tempted to conclude, "Speed of performing decreases with amount of food deprivation."

Both investigators may be said to be guilty of *overgeneralization.* The data may be reliable for each limited set of conditions, and yet both investigators could arrive at opposite conclusions. Such a situation might occur any time the relation between two variables is *nonlinear;* that is, when it cannot be represented accurately by a straight line. Figure 4–3 shows such a nonlinear relationship.

A number of interesting facts may be determined from Figure 4–3. If a food deprivation period of about 36 hours had been chosen instead of the other values, then *no* difference between the two conditions would have been found. Any deprivation time up to 36 hours produces an increase in speed of performing whereas any deprivation time after 36 hours produces a decrease in speed of performing. Thus, the conclusions drawn from the experiment depend on the arbitrary choice of the particular comparison conditions. Since, in any exploratory study, the experimenter does not know the shape of the total curve, any decision about conditions must be an arbitrary one. Quite obviously, if the re-

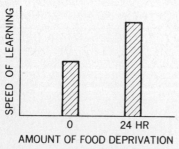

Figure 4–1. A hypothetical illustration of a bivalent experiment: speed of learning a task under two conditions of food deprivation.

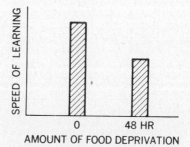

Figure 4–2. A hypothetical illustration of a bivalent experiment: speed of learning a task under two conditions of food deprivation.

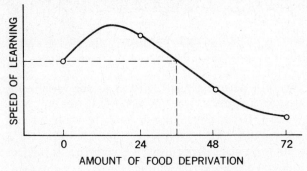

Figure 4–3. A hypothetical curve showing the relation between speed of learning a task and amount of food deprivation.

sults show no significant difference between the two conditions being compared, this does not necessarily mean that there is no relationship between the two *variables.* In any U-shaped or inverted U-shaped curve, there are many pairs of points which are at the same height. This means that there are many possible comparisons that would show no differences. Therefore, negative findings in bivalent experiments are never conclusive; positive findings are usually ambiguous.

There is another aspect of the problem. In many studies a comparison is made of a high condition with a low condition, for example, a high anxiety group with a low anxiety group, a high shock condition with a low shock condition, highly permissive parents with slightly permissive parents. The same general problems exist here as before, but in addition the following problem may arise. Many relations between variables show a plateau or *asymptote.* This is indicated by the portion of the curve between *B* and *C* in Figure 4–4. If the high and low anxiety conditions in our example happen to fall along the asymptote, no difference between the two conditions will be found. If they happen to fall somewhere

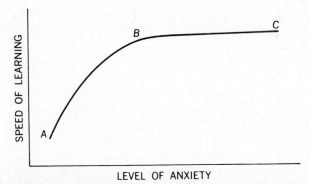

Figure 4–4. A hypothetical curve showing the relation between speed of learning and level of anxiety.

between *A* and *B,* then the experimenter will be tempted to conclude that an increase in anxiety leads to an increase in speed of performing.

Thus it may be seen that bivalent experiments are particularly subject to two dangers: (a) concluding that no relation exists between two variables being compared when in fact all that has been demonstrated is that no difference exists between two conditions; and (b) concluding that the effect of one variable on another is to cause an increase (or a decrease) when, in fact, this is true only over a small portion of the total curve. The actual relationship may be nonlinear and asymptotic. Both these dangers relate to the tendency to overgeneralize.

Another important point to be made about bivalent experiments is the fact that they give limited information about the relationship between two variables. If we discover that students of school A tend to get better grades than those in school B, or that a person can learn a poem faster with 10-minute rest periods than with 1-minute ones, there is very little else that we can add. Such findings will presumably indicate that the condition tested affected the dependent variable, but accurate interpolations are hardly possible. In other words, since one of the aims of science is to develop a body of laws or principles and theories which cover as wide a realm of phenomena as possible, we try to use the specific findings of any one experiment as a basis for *generalizing* to conditions and values not yet tested. We try to *predict* the outcome of untried experiments. In order to be able to do this with some hope of success, it is necessary to go beyond the simple bivalent experiment and to determine the functional relation between the two variables. This can be approximated more satisfactorily by means of a multivalent experiment.

Multivalent Experiments

The term *multivalent* experiment is used synonymously with the term *functional* experiment. Such experiments are designed to determine the relation between two variables and require that at least three values of the independent variable be used. This is because at least three points are necessary to determine the shape of a curve. The more points that are employed, however, the more reliable the resulting curve is likely to be, although only five to seven values of the independent variable are typically used.

Figure 4–5 is a graph illustrating a functional or multivalent experiment showing the relationship between learning time and amount of material to be learned. In this experiment, seven values of the independent variable were used: 8, 12, 16, 24, 32, 48, and 72 syllables in a list. These seven values actually represent a sample taken from a potentially unlimited range of values of the independent variable. Thus it would be possible to repeat the experiment with lists of 4 items, or 14, or 55, or 155. The experimenter is generally as interested in these other values as he is in the particular ones he selected. Since we assume that there is a continuous relationship between the independent and dependent variables, a continuous line can be drawn connecting all the points in the simplest way

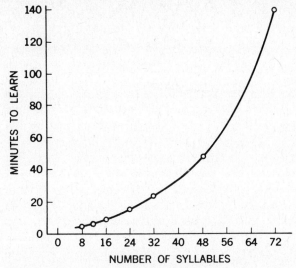

Figure 4–5. The relationship between learning time and number of syllables to be learned. (Adapted from T. G. Andrews, 1948.)

possible. From such a continuous curve it is possible to *interpolate* an estimated learning time for any amount of material, including those values not directly tested. It is also possible to make an estimate or prediction of the value of learning time for a syllable list either shorter or longer than the original range of values. Such estimates are called extrapolations.

Figures 4–6 and 4–7 present two illustrations of multivalent experiments taken from the psychological literature. Figure 4–6 shows the mean number of errors in learning a discrimination problem made by groups of monkeys differing in age. The curve is quite smooth and regular and would enable an interpolation for any other age group that has not been tested. For example, a group of monkeys 75 days old would be expected to make an average of about 22 errors in learning this task. In fact, from the curve it is possible to estimate (or interpolate) the mean errors for any group between the ages of 60 and 360 days.

It is possible to go one step further. The curve is so regular that an estimate of performance of 40-day-old animals can be made, as well as that of animals 400 or more days old. These *extrapolations* beyond the range of data originally tested must be made with some caution, but they can be made. In general, the further the extrapolation the greater the possibility of error.

Figure 4–7 shows the reaction time to each of the targets in a task having 16 alternatives. The curve that is drawn is called a best fitting curve for the obtained data. This best fitting curve is usually drawn in such a way that there are as many points on one side of it as on the other, and the sum of the distances from the points to the line on both sides are equal. This idea will be discussed in greater detail in Chapter 8. On the basis of this multivalent curve, interpolations and extrapolations may be made just as was done in the previous case.

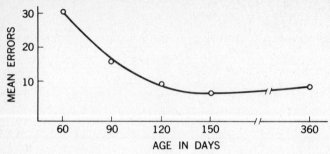

Figure 4-6. Learning as a function of age in terms of errors before attaining the learning criterion on initial discrimination problem. (Adapted from H. F. Harlow et al., 1960.)

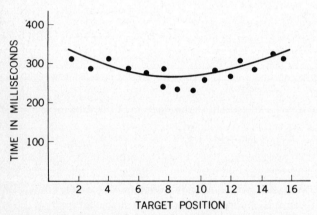

Figure 4-7. Reaction times to each of the targets in a 16-alternative task. Data are for one S. The curve is fitted by eye. (Adapted from P. M. Fitts, 1954.)

Multivalent or functional types of experiments are of fundamental significance to experimental psychology. When we compare a whole series of conditions, we are, in essence, sampling the independent variables over a wide range of values. This usually enables us to draw a smooth, continuous curve connecting the obtained points which in turn allows us to interpolate and extrapolate values that have not been directly tested. Our capacity to predict new observations is greatly increased as is the possibility of increased control. In addition, reliable functional relations provide the kind of quantitative material necessary for theory construction.

The importance of this type of experiment was recognized later in psychology than in some of the other sciences, but its importance is now widely accepted. Arthur W. Melton, in 1962, on retiring as editor of the *Journal of Experimental*

Psychology, wrote the following in connection with the question of how articles are selected for publication in that journal:

> . . . The investigation should not merely identify the effect of a variable, but should move beyond that simple demonstration to either the determination of a *function* relating levels of the variable to levels of the effect or the assembly of further information about the demonstrated effect. . . . We believed that the day of the archival report based on a simple experiment with an experimental and control group or with a 2 × 2 design was past in many mature areas of psychological research, and that each published report should make a more substantial contribution to the problem. In particular it seemed desirable for experimental psychology to move toward the determination of quantitative functional relationships between independent and dependent variables, especially since so many of these quantitative relationships in behavior turn out to be nonmonotonic.

In the light of these various considerations and comments, it seems that in many areas of psychology bivalent experiments are rarely defensible and should, if possible, be avoided. The extra time and effort needed to do a multivalent experiment is amply repaid by the gain in unequivocality and by the increased prediction that is made possible.

Parametric Experiments

This type of experiment is a further extension of the multivalent experiment. If the latter is conceived of as two-dimensional because it relates two variables, then the parametric experiment may be described as three-dimensional because it interrelates three variables. The term *parameter* is borrowed from the field of mathematics, where it refers to a constant in a given equation, but one which may take on different values. The different values of the parameter produce a family of curves.

In order to apply this concept to psychological research, it must first be recognized that all experiments keep some conditions constant while the relation between the independent and dependent variables is explored. For example, to study the relative sensitivity of the eye at different intensities of light, the duration of the flash of light used is kept constant at some value (e.g., half a second). To study the relation between serial position of a group of nonsense syllables and the speed with which each one is learned, the amount of trials used is kept constant. At any one flash duration or for any given number of trials, a functional relation will be obtained. However, at a different flash duration or for a different number of trials, a different functional relation will be obtained. This will usually produce a family of curves as shown in Figures 4–8 and 4–9.

Each family of curves shows the connections between three variables. In Figure 4–8, the variables are relative sensitivity of the eye (the dependent variable), intensity of light used (independent variable) and duration of light flash

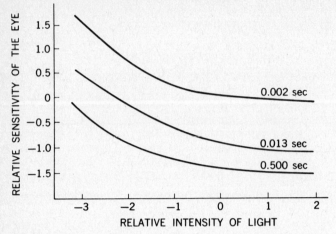

Figure 4-8. The relative sensitivity of the eye as a function of the intensity of light used (logarithmic units). Each curve is based upon a different duration of the flash of light. (Adapted from C. H. Graham and E. H. Kemp, 1938.)

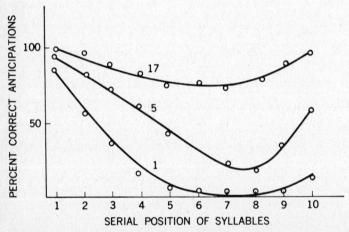

Figure 4-9. The learning of nonsense syllables as a function of the serial position of the syllables. Each curve is based upon a different number of trials used. (Adapted from E. S. Robinson and M. A. Brown, 1926.)

(independent variable plotted as a parameter.) In Figure 4-9, the variables are percent correct anticipations (dependent variable), serial position of the nonsense syllables (independent variable), and number of trials (independent or parametric variable). These relations may also be represented by a three-dimensional type of figure as illustrated in Figure 4-10. This graph is based on the classic study by Lashley in which he destroyed various amounts of cortical tissue in rats and tested

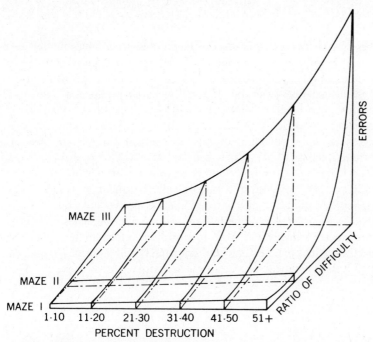

Figure 4–10.   A three-dimensional graph showing how the errors made in a maze depend upon both the difficulty of the maze and amount of cortical damage that has occurred. (Adapted from K. S. Lashley, 1929.)

them on mazes of different degrees of difficulty. The dependent variable was the number of errors made, while the two independent variables were the percent of the cortex destroyed and the relative difficulty of the maze. Figure 4–10 should be thought of as a three-dimensional solid. It shows at a glance how the three variables are interrelated. It shows that performance on easy mazes was about the same for all degrees of cortical damage, but that performance rapidly grew worse (increased errors) as the maze became more difficult. The effects of brain damage were therefore evident on difficult tasks, but not on easy ones.

Parametric experiments are still relatively uncommon in certain areas of psychology. They presuppose a knowledge of the most important variables affecting a given phenomenon, and they require a great deal of time and effort, but gains are proportionately greater. In the sciences of physics and chemistry, parametric experiments are relatively commonplace. As the science of psychology develops, there is no doubt that more and more parametric studies will be performed.

Summary

This chapter has described three types of experiments which are carried out in all sciences including psychology. These types differ generally in terms of the purpose of the investigation, the possibilities for generalizing, and the mathematical analyses which are used.

The types of experiments differ also in the number of variables related and in the number of values of each variable used. The *bivalent* experiment tries to *identify* a relevant variable by comparing the effects of two values of the independent variable on the dependent variable. If a change in one produces a significant change in the other, then a factor has been located. Generalizations from bivalent experiments are greatly restricted. A further extension is the *multivalent* experiment utilizing three or more values of the independent variable in order to determine the functional relationship between two factors. This greatly increases prediction by allowing more meaningful interpolations and extrapolations. When one of the conditions held constant in a multivalent experiment is systematically varied, that is, kept constant at a new value, while the multivalent experiment is repeated, a family of curves is obtained. Such a three-dimensional structure is called a *parametric* experiment and from it maximum information is obtained with which generalizations can be made. Other chapters will describe the specific experimental and mathematical procedures used with each of these types of experiments.

5

Sampling in Experimental Research

Proper sampling of situations and problems may in the end be more important than proper sampling of subjects, considering the fact that individuals are probably on the whole much more alike than are situations among one another.

—Egon Brunswik

One of the most important aims of the research scientist is to be able to make general statements about the events he studies. This is simply another way of saying that the scientist is usually interested in finding "laws." Although rats may be used as subjects, the researcher will usually say that he is interested in the "laws of learning," and although college sophomores are frequently used in social psychology experiments, the aim is often to find out about how attitudes may be developed or changed in the general population. How is it possible to do a limited experiment and come to a general conclusion?

In principle, the answer is simple. Generalizing depends upon adequate sampling. Only when the conditions of an experiment can be considered an adequate sample of a larger set of conditions can generalizations be made. Although this notion of sampling as a basis for generalizing is well recognized with regard to the subjects of an experiment, it has not always been made clear that it applies also to many other aspects of an experiment as well. For example, it applies as well to the variables which are studied. If a "high anxiety" group of subjects is compared with a "low anxiety" group, it is not at all evident that the results, whatever they are, apply to a "moderate anxiety" group or a "very high anxiety" group, or in fact, to any conditions other than the ones actually tested. This is one of the reasons for the emphasis, in earlier chapters, on multivalent and parametric types of experiments which greatly increase the validity of generalizations.

The present chapter is concerned with a more detailed description of the many ways that sampling issues arise in experimental research.

Populations and Samples

At one time the word *population* referred only to people. Later it was used to describe any large group of objects that could be counted. As mathematical statistics developed, the word became progressively redefined so as to refer to any group of numbers, finite or infinite, which usually referred to real or hypothetical objects or events. The term now is used to refer to such varied things as the number of school children in a given class, the entire set of records of mental hospital admissions in a given decade, or the total range of auditory frequencies which human beings can hear. "The term population implies that in principle one can catalog, or display, or index all possible members, even though the population is infinite and the catalog cannot be completed" (Loevinger, 1965). The important aspect of all populations used in research is that it is possible to select samples from them.

A sample is simply part of a larger population and, when appropriately chosen, can be used to describe the larger population with a high degree of accuracy. Although it might seem desirable to count or measure all members of the population whenever possible, yet there are a number of reasons why samples are not only adequate, but necessary.

For one thing, counts of an entire population may sometimes be so costly that the gain in accuracy they provide over a sample may not be worth it. During presidential elections, polls based upon less than 1% of the population typically provide estimates that are within 1% or 2% of the actual vote. Secondly, there are situations where the measuring process requires the destruction of the items of the population which are tested. If we want to find out how long radio tubes will last, a certain number of tubes will have to be used up. If we want to find out how long reptiles can live without water, a certain number have to be allowed to die.

There are also many situations in which the population is essentially infinite so that all the members cannot be counted. This is the case, for example, where we might wish to describe the laws of learning which are true for *all* species. In such a situation samples must be used. Similarly, in studies of personality, we cannot record every possible manifestation of a given trait, but must rely on samples of behavior.

Finally, there are many situations in which the data collected from a sample are more accurate than those based upon a complete survey. This is simply due to the fact that attempts to measure large populations may produce errors due to inadequately trained personnel, omitted data, and misrecorded information, whereas small samples may be thoroughly studied by highly trained people.

It is thus evident that samples are not only useful but also often necessary. The question arises, however, of how samples should be selected in order to allow generalizations to be made about a population. The answer given by the statisticians is simply that the samples must be *random*. This means that every member of the actual or hypothetical population must have an equal chance of being included within the sample.

In the remaining sections of this chapter a number of different kinds of sampling issues in research will be described.

Sampling of Subjects

The criticism is sometimes made that a good deal of what passes as psychological fact is based upon either the white rat or the college sophomore. This criticism, unfortunately, has a good deal of truth because much research by psychologists is done using subjects who are convenient and accessible rather than subjects who are random samples of defined populations.

In 1950, the comparative psychologist Frank Beach gave a paper in which he showed that in one of the leading journals there had been a year by year decline in the number of species studied and in the types of problems investigated. Most research was being done with rats, and more and more experiments dealt with learning. Based on this and other considerations, Beach later (1960) concluded that "nearly all so-called 'animal psychologists' are primarily interested in, and draw their problems from, the area of *human* behavior. They use members of lower species as substitutes for human subjects."

If this is true, the question arises of how similar the behavior of the rat is to the human being. Although there are psychologists who will argue for one or the other side of this question, the fact remains that at present there is very little of a comparative psychology of behavior that is in any way like the comparative physiology or comparative anatomy of the biologists. For example, before diphtheria antitoxin is used on humans it is standardized on mice, guinea pigs, rabbits, and horses. Typhoid vaccine is first tested on mice, guinea pigs, and rabbits. For much research the dog is used because its anatomy and physiology closely resemble those of man and it also suffers from a number of diseases known to affect humans.

Verplanck (1955) has reported that some of the "laws" of learning for the guinea pig are quite different from those for the rat, and that we have tended to unduly restrict the behavior of our experimental animals in order to obtain reproducible findings. To the extent that these things are true, it becomes difficult to use samples of animal behavior to generalize about human behavior. Only by working with many species of animals in comparable situations will the limits of our ability to generalize become evident.

The problem of generalizing from one group of humans to another is also a difficult one. Most academic research is done either with students in introductory psychology classes who are requested to participate, and sometimes given rewards, or with volunteers who may or may not be paid. The kind of problem that may arise in the former situation is that the students may be reluctant to express their true feelings because of a fear of offending the teacher or losing the proffered reward. In one study, for example, dealing with emotional reactions of students while under the influence of adrenalin, the students were told they would receive two extra points on their final exam for every hour they served as experimental subjects. In one part of the experiment they were placed in an unpleasant situation designed to make them angry. Their self-reports, however, indicated that they were not angry at all. The experimenter discovered subsequently that

> The subjects, who had volunteered for the experiment for extra points on their final exam, simply refused to endanger these points by publicly blowing up, admitting their irritation to the experimenter's face or spoiling the questionnaire . . . only after the purposes of the experiment had been revealed were many of these subjects willing to admit to the experimenter that they had been irked or irritated (Schachter and Singer, 1962).

The other difficulty with college student volunteers is that they have been found, in several studies, to be different from nonvolunteers both in personality characteristics and in ways of reacting. In one study of the effects of drugs on healthy, young male volunteers, routine psychological interviews and Rorschach tests were given to all subjects. It turned out that 25 out of 56 of the subjects were considered to be maladjusted; for example, 3 were psychotic and 7 were in treatment or seeking treatment for psychoneurosis. The incidence of "serious maladjustment" was estimated to be twice that found in a general college population (Lasagna and von Felsinger, 1954). These same authors briefly report a study in which it was found that a group of medical students were five times as sensitive to the toxic effects of a certain quininelike drug than were prisoners at Sing Sing. These findings cited above suggest the need for a great deal of caution in generalizing from samples of college student volunteers to other populations, or even to a general college population.

The use of volunteers presents another kind of problem in certain situations. Sometimes subjects have to be tested twice; sometimes children or adolescents are studied and an attempt is made to interview their parents or to obtain information from the parents by mail. In many such cases only a part of the original group returns for retesting and mail responses are typically quite small. For example, in a study designed to measure the effectiveness of certain psychological tests for predicting sales effectiveness, 862 salesmen working for a large, national corporation indicated a willingness to participate in the research. When it came to actually taking the battery of tests, only two-thirds of the salesmen completed it. In order to hold age and experience constant, the sample size had to be reduced to 248, so that conclusions were based on only 29% of the original volunteer group (Kirchner and Dunnette, 1959).

In another experiment, the attitudes of 1,200 adolescents were measured by a questionnaire and an attitude test was then sent to their parents by mail. Only 16% of the parents responded, a result which is more or less typical of mail questionnaires and one which raises the question of the extent to which the parents who responded are typical of the whole group (Stott, 1940).

An illustration of random sampling of subjects from a large population is the Midtown Manhattan Study, a survey of the incidence of symptoms of mental illness in New York City (Srole et al., 1962). Some of the methods and problems of this study are worth describing. A part of Manhattan containing about 110,000 people was selected as the area of study. A map of the area was then consulted and a number of blocks were selected at random, and then a number of buildings on these blocks were randomly selected, and finally a number of occupants. This produced a sample of 1,911 people ranging in age from 20 to 59 years. The method used excluded people who were living away at the time of the survey, for example, people in nursing homes, in military service, or at college.

Trained interviewers were then sent to contact each of the subjects and to get information on a standard questionnaire. Eighty-seven percent of the people contacted completed it. The data were then examined separately by two psychiatrists who rated the respondents on the severity of their reported symptoms and on their degree of incapacitation. These measures were then related to social class level, age, sex, and other general variables. It is evident that random sampling from a large population is often difficult and expensive.

Some Sample Survey Methods

A number of techniques have been developed by polling experts designed to obtain random samples from larger populations. Some of the more important ones will be briefly described here.

A Systematic Sample

In 1953, a survey was conducted in a Maryland city of 36,000 people designed to estimate the number of people over 45 years of age, their amount of illness, and their availability for work (Woolsey, 1956). The decisions that had to be made were approximately as follows:

1. An interview questionnaire was constructed and pretested. It included questions on work attitudes as well as work experience, family background, and recent illnesses.

2. Since no list of persons over 45 years of age was available, a list of all street addresses in the city was obtained from the city directory. (A supplementary list of new construction had to be added.) All designated apartments were treated as if they were separate street addresses.

3. Since no information was available on the number of households containing a person over 45, an educated guess was made so that a sample size could be decided on. On the basis of census data it seemed that 1,000 households should be interviewed out of the 11,000 known households in the city.

4. Only one interview per household was to be made.

5. Using a table of random numbers, about 1,500 addresses were randomly selected from the city directory. The last 500 were to be used only if the first 1,000 did not yield a sufficiently large number of respondents.

6. A random sample of city blocks was selected on the basis of a detailed city map, and each address was checked. This was done to determine the accuracy of the listings in the city directory.

7. If a respondent in a household was not home at the time of the interviewer's visit, repeated calls were made until he was interviewed. Only 8 respondents refused to be interviewed in over 1,000 households contacted.

8. On the basis of the obtained sample data, estimates were made of the variability of sample responses, and an estimate (with an associated confidence interval) was made of the number of people over 45 in the total population.

To oversimplify, the essence of random sampling is to assign each member of the population a unique number and then to select a subgroup of the population using random numbers. This method has the advantage of requiring a minimum knowledge of the population in advance, but it has the limitation of producing larger errors of estimate for a given sample size than does stratified sampling (to be described in the next section). When there is some kind of order to the members of the population (such as an alphabetical list of names, or the consecutive numbers of streets), the selection of members at a fixed interval after a random starting point is called systematic sampling. This is a simple and useful method unless there happens to be some unsuspected regularity in the list of names or addresses. Table C in Appendix III provides a list of random numbers and indicates how it may be used.

Stratified Sampling

In many situations, the experimenter has some knowledge of the population which he can put to use. He may know the distribution of men and women in a given community, and he may know something about the age and racial distribution. These sex, age, and racial factors, among others, are referred to as strata of the overall population, and, if a random sample is taken from each strata in accord with its proportion in the total population, the resulting sample is called a stratified random sample. Thus, if in a university there are twice as many freshmen as seniors and a sample of the entire student body is desired, the eventual sample will include twice as many freshmen as seniors, all randomly selected.

The advantage of stratifying a population before taking the sample is that the chances of picking a very deviant sample are less and estimates of population values are therefore more precise than would be the case with a simple random sample of the whole population. The major limitation of stratified sampling is that it requires advance knowledge of the strata within the population.

Cluster Sampling

Another sampling technique in common use is called cluster sampling. It relies on the existence of natural groups such as houses on a block, people in a family, or children in a classroom. If a large university wanted to obtain a sample of 100 students for a survey of attitudes, it could do this by at least two methods. Simple random sampling would require that each student on the enrollment list be assigned a number, and then 100 students would be selected on the basis of a table of random numbers.

The other method would rely on the existence of natural clusters. In this case it would be classes. Each class would be numbered, and then a random sample of (say) 10 classes would be selected. From each of the 10 classes, 10 students would be randomly selected. (For this example to be similar to typical cluster surveys, we would have to assume no overlap of students in the different classes.) Although the use of clusters to form the samples may lead to larger errors than equal-sized simple random samples, it often is cheaper from the point of view of costs. The random selection of city blocks, as in the Midtown Manhattan Study, is an example of the use of cluster sampling. From each block, of course, a random sample of families is then taken.

It should be clear from these examples, which do not include all the different sampling methods, that (a) they are all based on the principle of random selection of units, (b) they are necessary for valid generalizations about populations, and (c) they may be combined in various ways to achieve an optimum balance between precision and cost.

Experimenters as Samples

Many investigators have reported that the personal attributes of the experimenter such as sex, age, race, personality or prestige, may affect the kinds of results obtained from experiments (Johnson, 1976). One illustration of this problem was reported in a study of verbal conditioning in which the experimenter said "good" to the subject every time the subject used a sentence with a hostile word in it. However, two experimenters were used: one was a 5-foot, 90-pound, soft-spoken young lady, and the other was a 6-foot 5-inch tall, 220-pound former Marine. Results showed that the number of hostile words used was greater for the female experimenter's subjects than for the male experimenter's (Binder, McConnell, and Sjoholm, 1957).

A second illustration of this same kind of point was provided by Farina et al. (1976). These investigators wanted to find out if physicians would provide medical care to former mental patients that is different from that provided to normal patients. In order to examine this question, a 23-year-old male graduate student carrying a motorcycle helmet and knapsack made appointments with 32 physicians. To 16 of them, he described symptoms suggestive of ulcers that were reported to have occurred 9 months earlier while he was traveling around the country. The other 16 physicians were told that the symptoms began 9 months earlier when he was being treated in a mental hospital. It turned out that the medical care given by the physicians was the same under both sets of conditions.

The two experiments described above suffer from the same fault; that is, it is impossible to generalize about sex, personality, or mental status as relevant variables on the basis of a sample of one person. Obviously, each person has a whole group of special, personal characteristics that are unrelated to the variable supposedly being investigated and it is simply impossible to make any generalizations on the basis of a sample of one. "If we wish to generalize to populations of stimuli, we must sample from them" (Maher, 1978).

Stimulus Sampling

A number of years ago, Brunswik (1956) brought to the attention of psychologists the idea that sampling procedures should apply not only to the selection of subjects, but also to the selection of the stimuli to be presented to these subjects. He pointed out that in studies of the judgment of personality from photographs, it was necessary not only to use adequate samples of judges, but an adequate sample of photographs as well. He also suggested that the stimuli used should, in general, be as much like the "natural" environment as possible to maximize the possibility of generalizing. He called this way of thinking *representative design*.

During and after World War II, a number of experiments were done, dealing with form perception, which used some of these ideas. One of the aims of this research was to develop stimuli that could be considered to be representative of larger populations of stimuli. With ordinary geometric figures such as triangles and squares, there are no obvious populations which they represent except other triangles and squares. How then can different shapes be constructed which can be considered representative samples of a population of shapes?

The basic method used is to establish a stimulus domain defined by a set of explicit rules. These rules, when followed, will produce an infinite population of shapes. Any set of shapes formed by the rules may be considered a representative sample of the entire population.

A simple example of a set of rules for generating shapes may be taken from the paper by Attneave and Arnoult (1956).

1. Start with a sheet of graph paper, with 100 by 100 lines.

2. Use a table of random numbers and select successive pairs of numbers between 01 and 99. Each pair will determine a point which can be plotted on the graph paper.

3. Pick a two-digit number randomly to determine how many points to plot.

4. Use a straightedge to connect the most peripheral points to form a convex polygon. This will leave a few points inside the polygon.

5. Number the sides of the polygon and assign letters to the points inside it.

6. Use a table of random numbers to decide which central points are to be connected to which sides.

Using this method, "random figures" of the type shown in Figure 5–1 may be constructed.

Figure 5–1.   A random figure constructed by use of the
rules given in the text.

Many other sets of rules may be used to produce different populations of
shapes, some of which may have contours. The value of this kind of approach
is that the stimuli used in the research are random samples from defined populations and thus enable generalizations of known accuracy to be made.

Defining a Population of Colors

There are some situations in which the stimulus domain is not an infinite one,
but it is not clearly or completely specifiable. One example of such a case is color.
The question to be considered is: How many color names do people need to
describe all the colors they can see? Another way of saying this is: What is the
total population of color names needed to describe color "space" or color experience? If we could determine this, we could then sample this population for any
research involving color.

An interesting attempt to answer this question was made by Chapanis
(1965), and the following discussion is based upon his study.

The English language contains thousands of color names, and new ones are
constantly being added for the purposes of advertising. A survey of the language
of some best-selling novels, on the other hand, revealed only about a dozen
different color names in use. Somewhere between these two extremes there should
exist a set of color names that are rarely confused and which cover all the
important distinctions that humans make about color.

Chapanis approached this problem by selecting a large list of color names
based on the National Bureau of Standards' dictionary of color terms and
added a number of modifiers such as "strong," "pure," "dark," and "pale." All
basic color names were paired with all modifiers to produce a total of 233 color
names. Then, a large number of colored papers taken from the Munsell Book of
Color were put out on a table. These 1,359 color samples were designed to
represent every variation of hue, brightness, and saturation. The subject was
then given a color name such as "light purple" and asked to find the colored

paper on the table which best matched the name. Forty judges were used, 20 males and 20 females.

The analysis was designed to determine the degree of consistency between judges for all the color selections. It was found, for example, that purple and violet showed considerable overlap, and that compound colors such as greenish-yellow and yellowish-green could not be distinguished.

For all practical purposes, the modifiers pure, strong, and vivid turned out to be synonymous as did the terms deep and dark, and the terms pale and light. Finally, when an estimate was made of the total number of color names needed to represent all the 1,359 colored pieces of paper of the Munsell system, the figure turned out to be about 55. Thus one kind of stimulus domain has been established from which samples may be taken for any research on color perception. The basic ideas involved in setting up such a population can be applied to other problems as well.

The Sampling of Conditions

This is an issue which has already been discussed in some detail in Chapter 4, so that only a brief recapitulation will be presented here. When an experimenter chooses particular values for the independent variable, this is, in essence, taking a sample. If one wishes to compare a group of subjects given massed practice on a motor task with a group given distributed practice, one must select two intertrial rest times to represent two conditions out of a very large number of potential rest intervals. The massed practice group might use a 5-second interval between trials while the distributed practice group might use a 60-second interval. Theoretically, rest intervals might be chosen ranging anywhere from zero to infinity. From this perspective, it becomes obvious that a sample of two conditions out of an infinite number of possible ones is a very poor sample indeed and little generalization is possible.

It thus becomes obvious why the multivalent and parametric types of designs are much more desirable than the bivalent ones: they increase the sampling of the independent variables and thus increase the generality of the results.

The Problem of Response Sampling

In this chapter we have considered the notion of sampling and shown its relevance to the selection of subjects, experimenters, stimuli, and conditions in any study. Now we shall examine its relevance to the problem of measuring the subject's responses.

There are at least two aspects to this problem: (1) what responses to measure and (2) under what conditions to measure them.

For a long time there has been a tendency among psychologists to choose a single measure of a phenomenon as a basis for generalizations about it. For example, learning might be measured by the number of trials to reach a criterion, arousal might be measured by heart rate changes, or motivation might be measured by the rate at which an animal stimulates his own brain with small electrical currents. However, as information accumulates in each of these areas it usually becomes evident that there are many possible ways in which a phenomenon can be measured. Very often, as new measurement methods are tried, unexpected results are obtained and new insights gained. This is related to the fact that any theoretical term such as *learning, arousal,* or *motivation* will have many indices which do not correlate in any simple way because they measure different aspects of a theoretical state. A few examples will make this point clear.

In psychophysiological research the measures most often used are the galvanic skin response (GSR) and the heart rate, although, occasionally, skin temperature, blood pressure, or electroencephalic waves (EEG) are also recorded. It has been gradually discovered that the correlations between most physiological indices are quite low and that different organ systems react in essentially independent ways to imposed stimuli. Therefore, any one measure is generally a poor sample of the states of the various physiological systems of the body. Lacey and Lacey (1958) have pointed out that ". . . no single measure can serve as an index to the state of other measures or to the total 'arousal' of the organism."

In an attempt to measure the strength of the thirst drive in rats, Miller (1961) used three different measures, each of which had obvious face validity or relevance. One measure was the amount of water the animal drank; a second was the amount of quinine that had to be added to the water to prevent the thirsty animal from drinking; and a third was the rate at which the animal would press a bar in order to obtain licks of water. Miller found that this last measure did not correlate very highly with the others and that conclusions based on it alone were at variance with those based on the first two.

In studies of the effects of electrical brain stimulation the same sort of problem arises. It had been assumed that the rate at which an animal presses a bar to deliver electric shocks to its own brain was a direct measure of the degree of "pleasure" it felt. To test this assumption, Hodos and Valenstein (1962) set up a situation in which a rat was given a choice between two bars, one of which provided a low intensity shock to the brain and the other, a high intensity shock. They found that the rats chose the bar providing the high intensity shock, even though their rate of response on it was much lower than on the other bar. Thus, rate of self-stimulation did not appear to be an unambiguous measure of strength of reward.

A somewhat related finding was obtained by Plutchik, McFarland, and Robinson (1966) when several different measures of reward strength were compared. The rate of self-stimulation for electrodes implanted at various locations in the brain was compared with the escape-from-stimulation latency at the same sites. In the latter situation the experimenter turned the current on and the monkey turned it off whenever it wanted to and the time to do this was measured. It was discovered that for most electrode locations, the monkey turned off the current relatively quickly, even though it would self-stimulate if given an opportunity.

Since it had been assumed that animals that would self-stimulate a part of their brain would also not turn off (escape from) current introduced by the experimenter at the same location, the results appeared inconsistent. These findings further supported the notion that different measures of motivation do not necessarily measure the same thing.

These examples have been given to emphasize the fact that single measures of complex states such as motivation, neurosis, or learning will be so limited as to produce conclusions of doubtful generality. Another way of saying this is that a single measure of a complex state provides a poor sample. To the extent that it is possible, multiple measures should always be used and compared. Sometimes the inconsistencies of different measures create problems that eventually lead to new insights.

Response Sampling Methods

Once the decision has been made of what responses to measure in any given case, other issues arise. If a rat is learning a maze, how many trials should it be given? Each run through the maze may be considered a sample of the animal's behavior and the obvious question arises of how large a sample of the animal's responses should be chosen.

Unfortunately, no general answer can be given because the size of the sample of responses depends upon the purposes of the experimenter and the consistency of the responses. There are some situations where certain rules of thumb can be given with regard to sample size (Chapter 11) so that only a few general considerations are mentioned here.

One of the factors determining the number of responses to record is the anticipated statistical analysis that will be applied to the data. For various arbitrary levels of desired reliability, sample sizes can be estimated. Secondly, there will usually be a point of diminishing returns beyond which new data contribute very little to the stability of the responses. Thirdly, certain design methods require the subject to reach a stable level of response before the independent variable is introduced. Such stable levels are reached after different numbers of responses on different tasks. Finally, some design methods require the subject to begin the experiment at a very low (or poor) level of performance so that very few responses need be recorded. Thus many considerations are involved in a decision about the number of responses to record.

One further issue will be considered under the heading of response sampling methods, and that is, the observational techniques used for collecting information on complex sequences of behavior. In a situation where it might be desired to record some of the social behavior of a monkey or a child, it would obviously be impossible to try to record everything the subject does. A decision has to be made in advance about the categories of behavior the experimenter considers worth recording. This may range from something as simple as the number of times a monkey eats a pellet of food, to the number of aggressive attacks he makes on other animals. Once this is decided, a *time-sampling* plan can be instituted. This means that one or more observers make observations on the subject after either fixed or randomly selected intervals of time, and record the behavior being studied.

An example of time sampling can be taken from a report by Rheingold (1960) dealing with maternal care of human infants in institutions or at home. Observations were made on the babies for the first 10 minutes of each quarter hour for 4 consecutive hours. During each 10-minute period, 4 observations were made per minute in the following fashion:

> *O* looked at *S* for a full second and then recorded on the checklist what he was doing, if someone was caring for him, the nature of the care-taking act, where he was, and how many other people were in his environment. *O* could take as long as 14 seconds to complete the record, but in any case she did not look up again until the 15th second when she again observed *S* for a full second.

The results showed some interesting differences in child care procedures in the two types of settings.

One other illustration of time-sampling methods will be given based on work in the field of human engineering. The study was concerned with the activities and distribution of the work load of bus drivers. It was undertaken so that estimates could be made of the time the operator devotes to his various tasks, their order of performance, and possible and actual errors (McFarland and Moseley, 1954).

The drivers were observed during a 7-hour trip between Boston and New York and over 1,500 observations were made, some of which required motion pictures taken at intervals. Such behaviors as head, eye, hand, and leg movements were noted and related to specific vehicle traffic conditions. The percent of occurrence of a number of activities could then be tabulated (e.g., the right foot is kept on the brake during 13% of the observations). Knowledge gained in such studies has led to the introduction of automatic transmissions and improvement in the design and location of various controls.

These examples should indicate that time-sampling methods are quite general and can be used in a large variety of situations with either animal or human subjects (Plutchik, 1963).

Summary

In this chapter, an attempt was made to show the importance of sampling concepts in experimental research. If generalizations are to be made about various populations, research must deal with adequate samples of those populations.

The notion of sampling applies not only to the sampling of subjects, but also to the sampling of experimenters. In addition, it has relevance to the question of the stimulus objects used in research, since stimuli can also be considered to be samples selected from larger populations of stimuli. The concept of sampling applies also to the conditions of the experiment, that is, the values of the independent variable which are selected. If only two values are used, a high one and a low one, this is generally a poor sample of an entire dimension and multivalent studies are needed to enable generalizations to be made. Finally, the sampling notion is relevant to the responses of the subject. Complex states, such as motivations, cannot be unambiguously measured by single measures alone, and multiple indices are needed to sample the system. Various survey sampling procedures are described as well as time sampling as a method for sampling responses.

6

Basic Statistical Concepts

Acceptance of error and bias as unavoidable implies that we cannot rely upon a single experiment for the demonstration of a natural phenomenon, that we can never interpret the results of research, even when it is repeated, with absolute certainty, and that a knowledge of any phenomenon is always tentative and partial, never final and complete.

—William S. Ray

Statistics is a branch of mathematics which has great practical value as a tool in experimental research. Statistical methods are essentially ways of handling information obtained by repeated measurements. Probability theory provides the basic framework for statistical thinking, and its aim, generally, is to make predictions about the frequency with which certain results are likely to occur in the long run. Statistics helps make experimental conclusions seem plausible, not inevitable. It presents methods for making intelligent decisions in uncertain situations. Some statisticians have suggested that statistical analysis is like gambling or getting married since it involves making important decisions on the basis of incomplete information.

Historically, statistics had its roots in some very practical activities, the two major influences being the gathering of vital statistics or census data and gambling. The desire to compute current odds on gambling games led to the initial development of the theory of probability in France in the seventeenth century. Extensive development of this theory occurred in the nineteenth century, and it was applied to problems in astronomy, insurance, crime rates, and heredity. In the twentieth century there has been a huge increase in the collection of information for purposes of prediction and in the development of sophisticated mathematical procedures used to analyze such data.

During World War II a branch of applied statistics was developed called *operations research.* It helped solve such problems as optimum size of transatlantic convoys, optimum flight patterns used in hunting submarines, relative importance of different factors in the effectiveness of bombing missions, and other problems related to the war. Some of these same techniques are used today in connection with trucking operations, inventory decisions, and strategies in competitive games. Unusual current uses of statistics relate to the approximate dating of fragments of pottery or bones found in archeological research and to the study of literary styles in the Bible. There is no doubt that the use of statistical thinking in contemporary research will continue to increase.

Descriptive and Inferential Statistics

When the government collects census data every 10 years, an attempt is made to obtain information about every citizen living in the United States at that time. All members of the total *population* are to provide information. This kind of situation is to be distinguished from the more common one in which some part, or *sample,* of the total population is examined in order to be able to make estimates or inferences about what the total population is like. For example in presidential voting polls less than 5,000 people are interviewed throughout the country, and an estimate is then made of how 50 or 60 million voters will act.

A population includes all members of a defined group, but it is important to recognize that what is called a population depends on the purposes of the experimenter. Examples of populations are (a) all white rats of the Wistar Institute strain, (b) all students attending a particular university, (c) all elementary school children in a certain school district, (d) all people living in America in 1980, (e) all clinical psychologists in Indiana, (f) all scientists in government service in 1980, etc. In some cases the population being considered is a finite one with a single clearly specifiable number of people, for example, all persons who got married in 1981. In other cases, the population is an infinite or very large one, which does not have a single number to specify the total number of individuals. For example, the number of mice used each year in research is a very large number, with over 2 million being distributed from one major center alone. Even if we could conceivably test this huge population at any one time, within a few days there would be a large addition to the population. Since we are interested in the characteristics of all mice, those born next year as well as last, the population is essentially unlimited.

Many populations studied by psychologists are of this type. This means that it is essentially impossible to count every individual in the population, and therefore we must study representative samples. These samples are used to make *inferences* or *estimates* about the characteristics of the total population.

Because of the distinctions between a population and a sample, statistics is usually divided into two general branches. *Descriptive statistics* are concerned with ways of efficiently describing populations. This includes ways of summarizing census-type data for clarity of communication. *Sampling* or *inferential statistics* are concerned with the use of samples to make estimates and inferences about larger populations. Most psychological research is of this type.

Some Basic Statistical Concepts

This chapter will not attempt to describe all the procedures that are used in statistical analysis since there are many good textbooks that provide such information. There are, however, a few statistical concepts which are basic to an understanding of many of the procedures used in research; these will be described and illustrated here. These basic notions are (a) the frequency distribution and its measures, (b) the z-statistic, and (c) sampling distributions.

The Frequency Distribution

Since statistics is fundamentally concerned with information obtained by repeated measurements, it is obviously necessary that such information be described adequately. This is usually done by means of a frequency distribution, where the frequency with which an event occurs is plotted against the type or magnitude of the event. Figure 6–1 shows such a frequency distribution. It is based upon census data relating to the age at which males first marry. The distribution is not symmetrical, but skewed to the right with most marriages occurring between 21 and 24 years of age. A frequency distribution of this sort contains all the basic information obtained in any survey or experiment.

In many situations, the shape of the distribution changes somewhat as the number of cases is increased. Suppose, for example, that two dice are tossed a number of times and that a record is kept of the sum on each toss. This sum may range from 2 to 12. There is only one combination that can produce a 2 and only

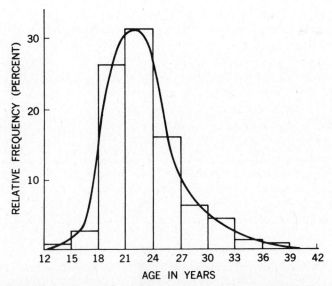

Figure 6–1. A frequency distribution showing the percent of the male population married at different ages.

TABLE 6-1 VARIOUS COMBINATIONS OF TWO DICE

Sum	Produced By	Expected Frequency (%)
2	1 + 1	$\frac{1}{36}$ = 2.8
3	1 + 2; 2 + 1	$\frac{2}{36}$ = 5.6
4	1 + 3; 3 + 1; 2 + 2	$\frac{3}{36}$ = 8.3
5	1 + 4; 4 + 1; 2 + 3; 3 + 2	$\frac{4}{36}$ = 11.1
6	1 + 5; 5 + 1; 2 + 4; 4 + 2; 3 + 3	$\frac{5}{36}$ = 13.9
7	1 + 6; 6 + 1; 2 + 5; 5 + 2; 3 + 4; 4 + 3	$\frac{6}{36}$ = 16.7
8	2 + 6; 6 + 2; 3 + 5; 5 + 3; 4 + 4	$\frac{5}{36}$ = 13.9
9	3 + 6; 6 + 3; 4 + 5; 5 + 4	$\frac{4}{36}$ = 11.1
10	4 + 6; 6 + 4; 5 + 5	$\frac{3}{36}$ = 8.3
11	5 + 6; 6 + 5	$\frac{2}{36}$ = 5.6
12	6 + 6	$\frac{1}{36}$ = 2.8

one combination that can produce a 12. There are two combinations that can produce a sum of either 3 or 11. The various possibilities are listed in Table 6-1. There is a total of 36 combinations, and it would be expected that *in the long run,* once in 36 times, we would obtain a sum of 2. Similarly, 6 times out of 36 we would obtain a sum of 7.

Figure 6-2 shows frequency distributions obtained by actually tossing two dice. The dashed line is based on 38 tosses and the thin solid line on 152 tosses. The ordinate, or vertical axis, gives the percent of times each particular sum was

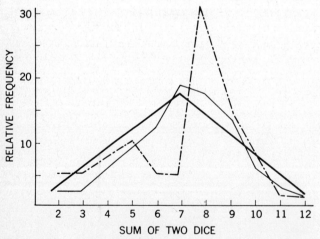

Figure 6-2. The dashed line is a frequency distribution based upon 38 tosses; the thin solid line is based upon 152 tosses. The heavy solid line shows the theoretical expectation.

obtained. The heavy solid line shows the theoretical expected frequencies based on the number of ways each particular sum can occur as determined by mathematical computation. It is evident that as the number of tosses (cases) increases, the distribution becomes smoother and, at the same time, begins to approximate the theoretical curve, that is, the one obtained by computation in Table 6–1. This process frequently occurs in experimental research as the number of cases or the number of measurements increases.

Central Tendency

In order to use the information presented in a frequency distribution for purposes of description or inference, it is necessary to summarize certain properties of the distribution. The two most important of these are the mean and the standard deviation.

It is very useful to find a single number to represent what is typical of a group of scores. Ideally, such a number should (a) be near the center of the distribution, (b) not weight extreme scores too much, (c) be computable by simple algebraic operations, and (d) be fairly stable from sample to sample. On the whole, the value that meets these criteria most adequately is the arithmetic mean, M or $\overline{X}$, defined simply as the sum of all the measurements, ΣX, divided by the number of cases, N, or in symbols

$$\overline{X} = \frac{\Sigma X}{N} \tag{1}$$

The symbol Σ is the Greek letter sigma and means "the sum of." The letter X refers to the individual scores.

It is important to remember that this is only one kind of average and that there are many other types, for example, the median, the mode, the harmonic mean, the geometric mean, and the root mean square. Which one is used depends on the nature of the problem, but the one used most frequently is the arithmetic mean defined above. This is partly because it is very easy to combine means from different groups, and because the mean multiplied by the number of cases immediately gives the total score, something which is not true for the other averages. In connection with sampling problems, the mean of a sample is the best estimate of the mean of a population.

Variability

Two frequency distributions may have the same mean yet differ greatly in the range of scores and in the shape of the distribution. Such differences may be revealed by measures of variability. As in the case with averages, there are many measures of variability, but the most useful is called the standard deviation. This measure is also a kind of mean, but it is a mean based on the deviations of each score from the arithmetic mean of the whole distribution.

For example, if four IQ scores, 102, 103, 107, and 112, are determined in a given sample, then the mean IQ is 106. The deviation d of the first score from the mean is -4, of the second score is -3, of the third score is $+1$, and of the fourth score is $+6$. The average of these four deviations, -4, -3, $+1$, and $+6$, is equal to zero. However, if each of the deviations is squared, then all negative signs are eliminated as follows: 16, 9, 1, 36. The mean of all these deviations (16 $+ 9 + 1 + 36$ divided by $4 = 15.5$) is called the variance. The standard deviation is the square root of the variance, or 3.9. The general equation used to compute the standard deviation s is

$$s = \sqrt{\frac{\Sigma d^2}{N}} \tag{2}$$

where Σd^2 is the sum of the squares of each of the individual deviations from the mean and N is the number of deviations, which is the same as the number of cases. Notice that this figure representing the standard deviation is roughly the same size as most of the deviations recorded in the first place. A second important point to notice is that, since the deviations are originally given in terms of IQ units, the mean of the deviations is still in IQ units. It is important to remember that the standard deviation is always given in the same units as the original scores. If we recorded the speed of a person's reactions in fractions of a second, the standard deviation of his scores would also be a value recorded in terms of fractions of a second.

There is a third important point that stems from those already mentioned. Since, in a frequency distribution, the score values are plotted on the horizontal axis, or abscissa, the standard deviation represents a certain kind of average distance along this abscissa. In fact, the standard deviation is often used as a kind of yardstick for comparing different distributions. It is especially useful if the different distributions are *normal* or approximately so. A normal distribution, roughly speaking, is one which is symmetrical around the mean, and bell-shaped. Many distributions obtained in research look this way and in addition many actual distributions seem to become increasingly normal as the number of cases increases. We must recognize, however, that the normal distribution defined by a mathematical equation is only a useful approximation to the kinds of distributions actually obtained in empirical research.

In computing the standard deviation it is sometimes very tedious to apply equation (2), particularly if the mean includes some decimal places and there are many deviations to square. As an alternative, it is possible to compute the standard deviation by using the original scores obtained in the experiment. Equation (3), although it looks longer, is actually simpler to apply in practice because there are usually tables available giving the squares of all numbers up to 1,000. The equivalent computational formula for the standard deviation is

$$s = \sqrt{\frac{N\Sigma X^2 - (\Sigma X)^2}{N^2}} \qquad (3)$$

where N refers to the number of scores, ΣX refers to the sum of all of the scores, and ΣX^2 refers to the sum of the squares of all the scores.

One of the important values of the standard deviation is that it can be used as a yardstick for locating the relative position of any score in a frequency distribution. This notion is fundamental to most applications of statistics, and it will be described in the following section.

The Z-Statistic

Suppose two boys in two different classes have each received an 80 on a mathematics exam. Does the same score necessarily mean that both boys did equally well? A moment's reflection will show that the meaning of a given test score depends upon how easy or difficult the test was. If the average score in the first class was 70 on the test, then the 80 is a fair grade, whereas if the average score in the second class was 85, the 80 is a poor grade.

The z-statistic attempts to take into consideration both an individual's score (i.e., position in the distribution) and the average performance of the group (i.e., the mean of the distribution). It does this by finding the difference between any given score (X) and the mean (M) of the distribution and then divides this distance by the yardstick, that is, the standard deviation (s). In mathematical notation it looks like this

$$z = \frac{X - M}{s} \qquad (4)$$

To take a simple example, if a student has an 80 on an exam in a class where the mean grade is 72 and the standard deviation is 8, then his z-value is $(80 - 72)/8 = 8/8 = 1.00$. This means that his grade is exactly one standard deviation above the mean of the class. If his score was an 88, he would be 2 standard deviations above the mean of the class. If his score was 84, he would be 1.5 standard deviations above the mean of the class, and if his score was 72, he would have a z-value of 0 and be 0 standard deviations above the mean of the class.

A z can also be negative. Thus in the second class mentioned above, having a mean of 85 and a standard deviation of 5, the student receiving a grade of 80 would have a z of $(80 - 85)/5 = -(5/5) = -1.00$. If his test score had been a 78, then his z would have been $(78 - 85)/5 = -(7/5) = -1.40$. Therefore, knowing a person's z locates him or her within a frequency distribution. When measurements are changed into z-scores, every distribution has a mean of 0 and a standard deviation of 1. In a sense, this converts all distributions into the same standard form and makes comparisons easier.

There is a second important idea connected with the use of a *z;* it also provides an estimate of the relative position of a score in terms of the percent of scores it exceeds in the distribution. Since the mean is exactly at the middle of a distribution, any score (i.e., a *z* of 0) which falls at the mean exceeds 50% of the scores of the distribution. Similarly a *z* of 1.0 exceeds approximately 84% of the distribution (50 + 34.1) and a *z* of 2.0 exceeds about 97.5% of the distribution (50 + 34.1 + 13.6). Figure 6–3 shows the relative percents of the distribution which are cut off by standard deviation units above and below the mean. It is possible to construct a detailed table showing what percent of a normal distribution is exceeded by every possible *z.* An abbreviated version of such a table is given in Appendix III (Table A).

Sampling Distributions

Another fundamental idea in statistical theory is the notion of a sampling distribution. This may be illustrated by the following example. Suppose we want to determine whether girls or boys, are brighter in a large public school system containing several thousand children. One way in which we might proceed is to get two alphabetical lists of names, one for all the boys and one for all the girls, and take every 100th name on each list. Assuming that there are 5,000 boys and 5,000 girls in the school system, this would give us a random sample of 50 boys and 50 girls. If we then determine the IQs of these children, it may turn out that the mean IQ for the girls is three points higher than the mean IQ for the boys. How shall we interpret this difference? Does it prove that the girls are brighter than the boys?

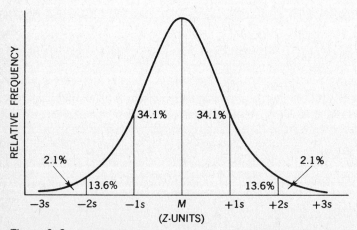

Figure 6–3.   An example of a normal distribution. *M* represents the mean and s the standard deviation. The numbers inside the distribution represent the percent of cases cut off by successively placing a length equal to a standard deviation along the abscissa.

The obvious answer is that we really do not know. It is quite possible that some other random sample of 50 boys and 50 girls could have given us a slightly different result. It is, in fact, possible to imagine repeating the experiment over and over again, each time selecting a different random sample of 50 boys and 50 girls. In some experiments (i.e., samples) the mean for the girls might be higher, while in others the mean for the boys might be higher.

These mean differences may be plotted in the form of a frequency distribution as shown in Figure 6–4. Such a distribution, based upon a very large number of samples, is called a *theoretical sampling distribution* of differences between means. It is called theoretical because rarely, if ever, are enough samples actually taken to determine such a distribution.

Fortunately, it is still possible to say a good deal about the theoretical sampling distribution on the basis of the sample of boys and girls *if certain requirements are met.* For example, the samples chosen must be selected randomly; that is, every student in the school system must have had an equal chance of being chosen. Secondly, we assume that all samples are of equal size, and, thirdly, we assume that the standard deviations (or variances) for the IQs of boys and girls in all samples are approximately the same. This last assumption is called the assumption of *homogeneity of variance.*

If these various requirements are met, it becomes possible to apply some simple equations to try to answer the question of whether the girls or the boys are brighter in this population of children. The first step requires *estimating* the standard deviation of the theoretical sampling distribution. The only information that is available to us is the mean IQs of the boys and girls in the samples, the standard deviation of the boys' (s_1) and girls' (s_2) scores, and the number *(N)* of

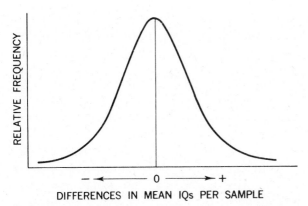

Figure 6–4.   A theoretical sampling distribution of differences in mean IQs between girls and boys for a large number of samples. This illustrates the case where the average difference between boys and girls is zero.

children in each of the samples. From this information an estimate may be made of the standard deviation of the theoretical sampling distribution by means of the following equation:

$$s_t = \sqrt{\frac{s_1^2}{N_1} + \frac{s_2^2}{N_2}} \tag{5}$$

This estimated standard deviation s_t is called the *standard error*. Once it has been obtained it can be used to determine a z. The difference between the mean scores for the boys and girls is divided by the standard error, as follows:

$$\tilde{z} = \frac{M_1 - M_2}{s_t} \tag{6}$$

The symbol $\sim$ over the z is used to indicate that this is an *estimated z* based on samples.

However, there is one important addition that is necessary to make this estimated z strictly analogous to a usual z. To determine a z, the mean of a distribution is subtracted from a particular score and then divided by the standard deviation yardstick. This means that in the comparison of the IQs of boys and girls, we need to know what the mean of the theoretical sampling distribution is so that we can compare it to the actual obtained difference in the sample. But here a problem arises. We do not know what the mean of the theoretical sampling distribution is. Therefore, the only way the statistician can proceed is to *assume* a particular mean for the theoretical distribution. For example, one can assume that the "true" difference in the mean IQs is four points in favor of the girls. Or one can assume that the "true" difference is seven points in favor of the boys. These assumptions, while possible, seem so arbitrary that the statistician usually makes the assumption that there is *no difference* in the true mean IQs of boys and girls in this population. This is at least reasonable if one has no other information available. This assumption of no real difference between the two groups in the total population is called the *null hypothesis*. It implies that the mean of the theoretical sampling distribution is zero. In equation form, therefore, the $\tilde{z}$ is then

$$\tilde{z} = \frac{(M_1 - M_2) - 0}{s_t} \tag{7}$$

The importance of this way of writing the z is that it always implies a null hypothesis. It reminds us that when we compare the mean scores of two samples, we are using as a convenient reference point the *assumption that the two groups are really equal in the total population.*

Another way of saying this is that the theoretical sampling distribution with a mean of zero (the null hypothesis) is what would be obtained if there was no difference between boys and girls in mean IQ and many hundreds of samples were taken. In some of them the difference would favor the boys and in some it would favor the girls, but in the long run most would be very close to zero. This sampling distribution would result if no real difference existed and only chance factors caused our samples to vary from experiment to experiment.

The basic strategy is to use this sampling distribution as our reference curve and then try to *determine whether an actual obtained difference was likely or unlikely* to have occurred on the basis of chance factors, that is, on the basis of variations in our random samples.

Let us explore these ideas using some actual figures. Suppose the girls had a mean IQ of 104 and the boys had a mean IQ of 101. Assume the standard deviation (s_1) for the sample of girls is 14 and the standard deviation (s_2) for the sample of boys is 15. We then compute the standard error (i.e., estimated standard deviation) of the theoretical sampling distribution by Eq. (5).

$$s_t = \sqrt{\frac{s_1^2}{N_1} + \frac{s_2^2}{N_2}}$$

$$s_t = \sqrt{\frac{14^2}{50} + \frac{15^2}{50}}$$

$$s_t = \sqrt{3.92 + 4.50}$$

$$s_t = \sqrt{8.42} = 2.90$$

We then use Eq. (7) to estimate a z for the difference of $104 - 101$.

$$\tilde{z} = \frac{(M_1 - M_2) - 0}{s_t} = \frac{(104 - 101) - 0}{2.9}$$

$$\tilde{z} = \frac{3}{2.9} = 1.03$$

What these computations have shown is that the difference of 3 IQ points in favor of the girls falls 1.03 z units (i.e., 1.03 standard deviation units) from the mean of the distribution. We can then look in Table A of Appendix III and discover that this score corresponds to a difference in means that is greater than approximately 85% of the differences found in the theoretical sampling distribution of differences. Therefore, about 15% of the theoretical differences are larger than the obtained one. These facts are shown graphically in Figure 6–5.

Now, we should recall that the distribution shown in Figure 6–5 is what we would get if (a) there was really *no* difference between the boys and the girls (null hypothesis), (b) we took many samples of boys and girls, and (c) only chance factors were operating to cause differences. This means that a difference in favor of the girls of three IQ points could occur about 15% of the time in random samples *even if there was no real difference between the boys and the girls in IQ.* Therefore, it is quite possible that this particular difference of three IQ points which was actually obtained in the experiment could have been a result of chance variations due to random sampling. We therefore conclude that the difference in IQ we actually obtained is a relatively frequent occurrence even when there is no

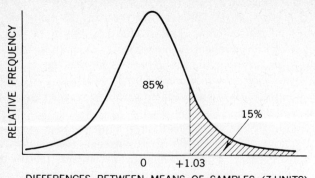

DIFFERENCES BETWEEN MEANS OF SAMPLES (Z-UNITS)

Figure 6–5.   The right-hand tail of the distribution shows the percent of cases which exceed a z of $+$ 1.03 in a normal distribution.

real difference in IQ, and so we say that the difference is not real or *not significant.* To say this still another way, we have found that the sample difference of three IQ points is consistent with the null hypothesis that there is really no difference between the boys and girls in IQ.

A new question should have occurred to the reader. If this difference of three IQ points is not considered "real" or "significant," how large does a difference have to be before it is considered significant? Unfortunately, there is no single or simple answer to this question. Many factors go into this decision, and they relate to such matters as the implications of a wrong judgment, the cost of doing the experiment, and the adequacy of the sampling procedure in the first place. However, a tradition has developed over the past 30 years stemming from the work of the British statistician Ronald Fisher, who first introduced many of these ideas. He felt that a difference which occurs by chance as infrequently as 5% of the time is a convenient guideline for deciding the significance of a difference. He argued, in essence, that if an experimenter finds a difference between two groups which could have occurred only 5% (or less) of the time as a result of chance fluctuations in repeated samples when there was no real difference, then the difference obtained is so unlikely that it must be "real." In other words, using the null hypothesis, unlikely outcomes are to be considered significant. This 5% figure mentioned above is called a *significance level.* It is, of course, possible for the experimenter to choose any significance level he or she wishes, although traditionally the 5% and 1% levels are most frequently used. This point will be discussed more fully in a later section.

One- and Two-Tailed Tests

The previous example actually represented an oversimplification. It is now necessary to qualify the conclusions. In our hypothetical example we assumed that the girls had a mean IQ three points higher than the boys. When we estimated the z, we took $M_1 - M_2$ and divided by the standard error. Now it is just as reasonable to take $M_2 - M_1$ and divide by the standard error. This would, of course, give us exactly the same z except that it would be negative, that is, -1.03 instead of $+1.03$. Graphically it would appear as in Figure 6–6. What Figure 6–6 shows is the percent of time a difference as large as three IQ points would occur if we took many samples and if there was really no mean difference between the boys and girls in IQ. This difference of three IQ points could be either in favor of the girls or of the boys. It appears that in 30% of the samples a difference as large as three IQ points could occur as a result of random variations in the samples. Therefore, the actual finding of this slight difference in favor of the girls is not significant.

When we consider both ends of the sampling distribution, as we did here, we are dealing with a *two-tailed test* of significance. This implies that for a 5% significance level we need 2½% of the cases in one tail of the distribution and 2½% of the cases in the other tail. Similarly, if we were interested in a 1% significance level, we would find an estimated z that corresponded to ½% of the cases in one tail and ½% of the cases in the other tail of the distribution. In general, *with large samples* the estimated z must be 1.96 or greater for a difference to be significant at the 5% level or better, and it must be 2.58 or more to be significant at the 1% level or better.

Significance Tests with Small Samples

The method described above for testing the significance of a difference between two samples is suitable if the samples are large in size, but it becomes less suitable as the sample size decreases. Although there is no sharp line of distinction between what is considered a large sample and what is considered a small sample, the usual rule of thumb is to consider small those samples whose combined N is less than 40 or 50. When such a situation exists, several modifications are necessary in the method of testing hypotheses.

The first change is in the method for computing the standard deviation of

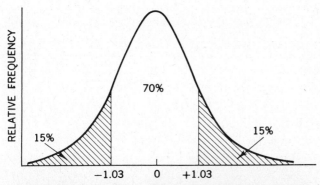

Figure 6–6. The two tails of the distribution show the percent of cases which exceed a z of $\pm$ 1.03 in a normal distribution.

the sampling distribution. A "pooled" estimate of the standard error is used which is slightly more complicated than before. The second change is in connection with the use of a z-table. A special table has been developed which gives the estimated values of z, except that the zs are now usually referred to as t-statistics. When this t-table is used (Appendix III, Table B), we find that the interpretation of t depends on the number of subjects in the sample. This number, called *degrees of freedom,* is actually computed by treating the samples as if they each had one less subject than they actually have. Thus, if one group has 8 subjects and the other 6 subjects, the degrees of freedom looked up in the t-table are $7 + 5 = 12$.

The actual equation used in computing a t-value for small samples is

$$t = \frac{(M_1 - M_2) - 0}{\sqrt{\dfrac{\Sigma X_1^2 - N_1 M_1^2 + \Sigma X_2^2 - N_2 M_2^2}{N_1 + N_2 - 2} \left(\dfrac{1}{N} + \dfrac{1}{N_2} \right)}} \tag{8}$$

N_1 and N_2 refer to the sizes of the two samples, M_1 and M_2 are the means for the samples, and ΣX_1^2 and ΣX_2^2 refer to the sum of the squares of the individual scores in each of the samples. The zero, of course, implies the testing of a null hypothesis.

Let us now take a specific example and work a problem through. Suppose we selected randomly five boys and five girls from a large school system and determined the mean IQ of each group, and let us assume that the mean for the girls is seven points higher than for the boys. The actual scores for the individuals are given in Table 6–2.

If we substitute the appropriate values from Table 6–2 into Eq. (8), we get

TABLE 6–2 A SET OF HYPOTHETICAL IQ SCORES FOR RANDOMLY SELECTED SAMPLES OF FIVE GIRLS AND FIVE BOYS

Subject	Girls IQ (X_1)	X_1^2	Subject	Boys IQ (X_2)	X_2^2
1	114	12996	1	103	10609
2	106	11236	2	101	10201
3	103	10609	3	111	12321
4	107	11449	4	100	10000
5	115	13225	5	95	9025
	$\Sigma X_1 = 545$ $M_1 = 109$	$59515 = \Sigma X_1^2$		$\Sigma X_2 = 510$ $M_2 = 102$	$52156 = \Sigma X_2^2$

$$t = \frac{109 - 102}{\sqrt{\dfrac{59515 - (5)(109)^2 + 52156 - (5)(102)^2}{5 + 5 - 2} \left(\dfrac{1}{5} + \dfrac{1}{5}\right)}}$$

$$t = \frac{5}{\sqrt{12.30}} = \frac{5}{3.50} = 1.43$$

This value of t of 1.43 may be looked up in Table B of Appendix III with an N (or degree of freedom) of $5 + 5 - 2 = 8$. The table indicates that t would have to be 2.3 to be significant at the 5% level, and we can therefore conclude that the girls are not significantly different from the boys in IQ when using a 0.05 significance level. The difference between the means obtained in the samples can reasonably be attributed to a chance difference related to the random sampling.

The correct use of the t-test, like all other statistical tests, depends upon certain requirements being fulfilled. The first and most important requirement is that the members of the sample be selected randomly from some defined population. The second requirement is that the standard deviations of the two groups be equal. This is the requirement of homogeneity of variance. The third requirement is that the populations from which the samples have been drawn be normal.

These may seem like very stringent requirements, and they are. Fortunately, however, it has been demonstrated that even where these requirements are not met very well, the t-test provides an accurate answer to the question of the significance of the difference between two means. For example, one psychologist (Boneau, 1960) deliberately established three very different distributions, one normal, one rectangular, and one J-shaped, and then drew samples of size 5 or size 15 from them to be compared by means of a t-test. (This, of course, was done with a computer since thousands of samples were drawn.) Boneau also arranged that some of the samples have variances (i.e., the square of the standard deviation) four times the others, thus violating the requirement of equal variability in the samples.

After analyzing his results, he concluded that *so long as the sampling is random,* lack of normality of the populations has little influence on the t-test, *so long as the sizes of the samples were the same.* In fact, he concluded that "samples of sizes of 15 are generally sufficient to undo most of the damage inflicted by violation of assumptions," so long as sampling is random. These findings are well worth remembering.

Some Statistical Issues

The statistical ideas and techniques that have been described are part of the "classical" tradition; they represent the more commonly used notions in experimental research. In recent years, however, there have been various criticisms made of these ideas, and some tentative alternatives have been proposed. Although some of these alternatives require considerable mathematical sophistication for a full understanding, it is possible to present the issues in a general way.

Levels of Significance

In the early part of this century the British mathematician Ronald A. Fisher developed the concept of tests of significance and showed how they could be applied to practical problems. The particular problems he was concerned with were biological—for example, whether the use of a certain type of fertilizer would increase the yield of corn. With variability in rain, soil characteristics, and seed properties, it was obvious that results were seldom clear-cut. Therefore Fisher proposed a rule of thumb that seemed reasonable to him. He assumed that if a certain outcome could have occurred by random sampling from a single population 5 times out of 100, and that if in the one sample he took it had actually been found to occur, then it was a rare enough event to consider significant. The concept of significance was thus closely tied up with the notion of rarity of occurrence of a phenomenon. Fisher pointed out that there is always a risk of error in making a decision. He decided that 5 mistakes in 100 repetitions was a reasonable risk to take, and therefore proposed the 5% level of significance as a dividing line.

When the psychologists began to use these statistical ideas, this rule of thumb gradually began to dominate their thinking too, and it has almost become elevated to the status of a principle at the present time. Textbooks of statistics usually caution the researcher to establish a level of significance in advance and to stick to it, but seldom do they question the general reasonableness of a 5% level for establishing significance of a difference between two groups.

There are, however, many factors that should affect the choice of a significance level as a basis for making a decision. If the experimenter is lenient in selection of a significance level, it is more likely that variables will be identified that should be studied more intensively, but at the same time, one will also discover more effects due simply to the operation of chance factors. If the experimenter establishes a very stringent criterion for significance, he or she will be reasonably certain of the reality of any difference obtained, but some promising leads may be missed.

At one time or another, statisticians have suggested possible considerations for selecting significance levels. For example, an analysis of 1,046 research articles obtained from 3 psychology journals was reported by Bozarth and Roberts (1972). In 86% of the articles, tests of significance such as t and F were used, and of these studies, 94% reported rejection of the null hypothesis at the 0.05 level or less. Only eight articles were replications of previously published studies. It appears that the finding of positive results in an experiment (i.e., the rejection of the null hypothesis) is related to the likelihood of publication.

When an investigator rejects the null hypothesis at the 5% level, it means a willingness to risk being wrong 5 times in 100 replications. In the light of this survey it appears that investigators do not generally publish experiments if they do not show significant differences at the 5% level or better, or they are not accepted for publication by journal editors. This means that the readers of experimental journals have no idea of how many times an experiment may have been replicated by some other investigators without their being able to reject the null hypothesis, since it is likely that many more experiments are performed than are actually published. Let us illustrate this point with an hypothetical example. Suppose 10 investigators at different times and places perform experiments to determine if praising children tends to increase their proficiency in arithmetic; assume that no clear-cut effects are found. No reports of this work are published. If another investigator then repeats these experiments and finds a significant effect and publishes a report of this research, how shall we interpret this?

It is obvious that even if there is no real difference between two groups or two conditions, if we take enough samples we will occasionally find what appears to be a real difference but which is due, in fact, to random sampling fluctuations. This means, most likely, that a certain number of the published articles describing a significant difference between groups are actually in error, and that the observed differences are chance effects of sampling. These people are making what is called a Type I error; that is, they are rejecting the null hypothesis when it is true. (A Type II error accepts the null hypothesis when it is false.) What this all means is that a Type I error has a good chance of ending up in print, whereas a Type II error does not. Since the reader does not know how many other related experiments have been performed with negative results (i.e., where no significant differences were found), one cannot accept at face value the risk stated by the author.

Some statisticians have suggested the need for conservatism in judging the significance of results. The statistician Cochran (1947) points out that when distributions are not normal, the use of the t-test, although fairly accurate, tends to err slightly in the direction of announcing too many significant results. In a similar vein, Lindquist (1953) points out that a good deal of research is concerned not so much with whether some condition affects some result (e.g., whether praise affects arithmetic performance), but rather with whether or not it is a relatively important factor. He writes:

> Having performed exploratory experiments with a number of possible factors, all of which may be real but not equally important, we would like to give priority in subsequent experimentation to the factors which are most important. If we always set a high level of significance for our tests at the exploratory level, we may be quite sure that we will not follow many completely false leads, and at the same time we will have some assurance that the true leads which we ignore (because of Type II errors) are probably among the less promising ones.

Another proposed reason for applying more stringent levels in evaluating the significance of differences relates to a recent development in mathematical statistics called *Bayesian Statistical Inference.* Although the details of the theory are quite technical, a few of the ideas and their implications may be summarized here. Bayesian statistics may be thought of as a set of methods for describing the opinions of ideally consistent people. Each person approaches a new situation with an expectation or "prior probability" estimate. This becomes modified by exposure to new data, but the new data are meaningful only in the context of the prior expectations. If, for example, a person who does not feel well takes his temperature and gets a reading of 110 degrees, he will most likely not rush off to the hospital but will assume that the thermometer is broken. A finding too inconsistent with prior opinions will normally lead to a reevaluation of the observed facts.

In most experimental situations, the investigator imposes conditions on subjects that there is some reason to believe will have an effect on them. They may be injected with a drug or exposed to a stress. In such cases the use of a null hypothesis which assumes no effect is really considered to be rather unlikely by the experimenter, and the prior expectation is that it has small chance of being correct. On the other hand, the prior expectation of an effect of some sort is quite high. In making a null hypothesis test, one is therefore typically comparing an unlikely, fairly precise, null hypothesis, against a likely, rather diffuse, expectation of some effect. When this idea is formalized mathematically, it turns out that many situations may arise where the usual t-test would imply rejection of the null hypothesis, whereas the Bayesian approach in the same situation would imply *acceptance* of the null hypothesis. This is partly related to the fact that most rejections of the null hypothesis are based on test statistics close to the borderline (i.e., 5% level). As the level used for the evaluation of significance becomes higher (e.g., 1 or $\frac{1}{10}$%, etc.) the usual t-test and the Bayesian approach tend to agree more and more. This therefore argues for greater conservatism in evaluating null hypotheses.

One- or Two-Tailed Tests

Another statistical issue that has arisen in the evaluation of experimental data concerns the question of whether to use one or two tails of the theoretical sampling distribution. Suppose, for example, that two groups of randomly selected schizophrenic patients are picked for a study designed to determine if a new drug is an effective tranquilizer. An experimental group takes pills containing the drug, the control group takes pills containing a placebo (e.g., sugar). The general behavior (on the ward) of members of both groups is then rated and compared. The null hypothesis is that there is no real difference between the groups.

Now it is at this point in the analysis that some investigators have argued that the only difference of interest to them is a difference in favor of the experimental group, for example, an increase in cooperativeness on the ward. In such a case, they say, it is possible to use only one tail of the sampling distribution (as shown in Figure 6–5) to evaluate the significance of any difference that might occur. They would, in essence, be asking the question, "What are the chances of finding an increase in cooperativeness of a given amount in favor of the experimental group as a result of chance fluctuations alone?" They ignore the possibility that the experimental group might actually get worse as a result of the drug.

The advantage of such an approach is that a smaller difference between the experimental and control groups will be identified as a significant difference. This is because the z or t necessary to indicate where 5% of the cases fall in one tail of a normal distribution is smaller than the z or t needed for 2½% of the cases in each tail (see Figure 6–6). Using a one-tailed test, a z of 1.64 is significant at the 5% level, while in the two-tailed distribution a z of 1.96 is necessary for significance at this level. Therefore, experimenters who use a one-tailed test find it easier to get a significant difference between their groups and thus to reject the null hypothesis.

A number of articles have appeared criticizing the use of the one-tailed test. Burke (1953) has objected to it on the grounds that the discovery of new phenomena will be impeded if we tend to neglect differences in the unexpected direction. Second, by making it easier to find significant differences, relatively unreliable effects will be accepted as important. Third, it becomes easier to abuse the statistical tools we have, since an investigator who does not find a significant difference using a two-tailed test might then think up a reason for switching to a one-tailed test in order to reject the null hypothesis. Cochran (1947) has also pointed out that if a distribution is not normal, the one-tailed test is more vulnerable to error. These are all strong reasons against the use of one-tailed tests in psychology.

Eysenck (1960) presents his objections to the one-tailed test in a different way. He points out that the results of statistical evaluations are generally stated in terms of the probability of rejecting the null hypothesis. It is usual to pick a certain probability value such as 0.05 (i.e., 5% significance level) and use this to divide the range of probabilities into two parts, a significant and an insignificant part. Although this is customary, it has little advantage, since it divides a continuum into a dichotomy, losing information, and determining in an arbitrary way which research is to be considered successful and which unsuccessful. On the contrary, the results of a particular experiment achieve meaning only in a broad context and depend upon such things as their relation to previous research, their predictability from theory, and the number of cases involved. If, for example, a study of extrasensory perception produced a result significant at the 5% level, it would be of questionable meaning in view of the many previous failures to find significant effects. Two similar experiments finding significant differences at the 4% and 6% level respectively are actually in good agreement even though one is arbitrarily called significant and the other is not. Eysenck goes so far as to suggest that the concepts of significant and nonsignificant as determined by an arbitrary rule of thumb be dropped entirely and that each experiment must be interpreted in the light of all available background information. There should be a clear separation of the objective statement of the probability of disproving the null hypothesis by means of a two-tailed test and the subjective evaluation and interpretation of the results.

The comments by all these authors show again the need for careful evaluation of experiments, not only in terms of simple statistical rules, but also in terms of other kinds of information. Statistics is a tool of research and not an end in itself, and it cannot guarantee meaningful conclusions simply by virtue of its application to experimental findings.

One vivid illustration of this point occurred in a Canadian hospital many years ago when diphtheria vaccine was first introduced. Over a period of several years the diphtheria vaccine was administered to several hundred people admitted to the hospital with diphtheria, while a control group of patients in the same hospital were treated in the fashion that had been in common use up to that time. It was found that 16% of the patients given the diphtheria vaccine died, while only 8% of the patients who were treated in the usual way died. The difference turned out to be statistically significant at better than the 5% level. The vaccine was apparently a menace to health, yet today this same vaccine is used routinely as a preventive measure. Why?

The answer is simply that the hospital authorities had been administering the vaccine only to patients who were very seriously ill (like trying a new drug on a terminal cancer patient), while they gave their usual treatment to those patients with milder symptoms. The groups were not comparable, and this resulted in a higher recovery rate for the older method. The moral of the story is that a significant difference does not prove anything unless the experiment is well designed. Even under ideal conditions there are limitations to what can be discovered from a single experiment.

There is an important implication that follows from the preceding discussions. One of the fundamental characteristics of scientific data is that the results of experiments are reproducible by any competent investigator in another laboratory, or by the same investigator on subsequent occasions. Rather than rely exclusively on statistical tests to confirm the reality of an obtained effect, researchers should rely more on independent replication of results. This is particularly important when differences appear significant at some borderline significance leve , regardless of what that level is. To paraphrase an old Chinese proverb, "One replication is worth a thousand t-tests."

Nonparametric Methods

In the last few years, a number of statisticians have provided tests of significance which do not require as many assumptions as the t-test and the z-test already described. The major characteristic of these so-called "nonparametric" tests is that they do not generally make any assumptions about the shape of the distributions from which the samples have been selected. They do not assume, for example, that the distributions are normal.

This characteristic, which makes such tests more generally applicable, is only one advantage among several. In addition, they may be used with scores which are only rankings as well as with more sophisticated forms of measurement. Rankings of two groups of officers on leadership ability may be compared using nonparametric tests, whereas the use of a z- or t-test with the same data may introduce an unknown degree of bias. Another advantage of these techniques is that the use of ranking systems greatly simplifies the computational detail.

These are all important advantages, and they justify the increasing frequency with which such tests are being used in research. They do have some disadvantages, however, which limit their value. The major limitation is that they are usually less sensitive to differences than the usual t-test would be. In other words, these tests are less likely to detect a significant difference between groups, if it is present, than the classical tests. This is simply due to the fact that the nonparametric tests usually reduce a set of measurements to ranks and manipulate only the ranks. This actually causes a loss of information concerning the absolute differences between the measurements.

To take an example, suppose eight dogs, representing two different breeds, are tested to determine the number of trials each animal takes to learn a signal necessary to avoid an electric shock. Assume that four beagles take 5, 8, 20, and 35 trials, and that four terriers take 3, 6, 14, and 21 trials. The mean number of trials for the beagles is 17 and for the terriers 11; therefore, a breed difference is suggested. However, if these values are reduced to rankings and all 8 measures are ranked, we get rankings of 2, 4, 6, and 8 for the beagles and rankings of 1, 3, 5, and 7 for the terriers. The mean ranks are 5 and 4 respectively, thus making the possibility of a significant breed difference less likely. In the language of the statistician, the nonparametric tests have less *power efficiency* than the classical tests. They are more likely to accept the null hypothesis, even when it is false, than the classical tests would.

Another limitation of nonparametric tests when used for the analysis of variance is that they are generally unable to test for certain aspects of the relationships between two or more variables (namely, interactions) without making some of the same kinds of assumptions that parametric tests make.

It is important to emphasize that *both* the classical and nonparametric tests assume that the members of the sample are drawn randomly and independently from whatever populations are being studied. If the sample is biased and the selections are not independent, there are no tests which give valid conclusions.

An Example of a Nonparametric Test: The Mann-Whitney U-Test

This is one of the better known of the nonparametric tests and is useful when two groups are to be compared and when the populations are believed to be markedly nonnormal.

Suppose two strains of mice are to be evaluated for exploratory activity. Five mice of each strain are randomly selected and allowed to wander through an enclosure marked with grid lines. The number of lines crossed in a 10-minute period is the index of exploratory drive. The scores for the mice, recorded as the number of grids crossed in a 10-minute period, are as follows:

$$\text{Strain } A \quad 210 \;\; 282 \;\; 256 \;\; 270 \;\; 234$$
$$\text{Strain } B \quad 190 \;\; 203 \;\; 220 \;\; 252 \;\; 242$$

It is now necessary to arrange the scores in order of size, but in doing this the sample from which each score comes should be identified.

$$190 \;\; 203 \;\; 210 \;\; 220 \;\; 234 \;\; 242 \;\; 252 \;\; 256 \;\; 270 \;\; 282$$
$$B \quad B \quad A \quad B \quad A \quad B \quad B \quad A \quad A \quad A$$

The statistic U is obtained by counting the number of A-scores preceding each B-score, as follows:

$$U = 1 + 2 + 2 = 5$$

This value of U may be looked up in a special table, developed by Siegel (1956) and reproduced in most statistics texts. It will be seen that a sequence of this sort is significant at approximately the 7% level; that is, it is not significant by the usual 5% criterion. Another way of saying this is that on the assumption of the null hypothesis of no difference between these two strains of mice, a sequence of the kind obtained will be found 7 times in 100 on the basis of random sampling fluctuations using sample sizes of 5.

In order to utilize any kind of statistical test intelligently, we must consider the reasonableness of the assumptions that underlie its use. Nonparametric tests are helpful in certain situations in which there is marked nonnormality and where the data are essentially rank-order type information, but they are no substitute for careful planning of experiments and random selection of subjects.

Measurement of the Size of an Experimental Effect

It is probably unfortunate that statisticians have attached the word *significant* to the results of certain statistical tests because of the inappropriate connotations of the word. A significant difference is simply a relatively rare event; it is one that occurs infrequently as a result of random sampling from a population. The use of the word *significant* does not indicate that a difference that has been found is important, large, meaningful, or valuable. In fact, "it is possible for a highly significant result to contribute nothing to our ability to predict behavior, and for a nonsignificant result to mask an important gain in predictive ability" (Hays, 1963).

During the past few years a number of investigators have pointed to a common misinterpretation of the concept of significance level. For example, Rosenthal and Gaito (1963; 1964) asked a group of faculty members and graduate students in psychology to rate their degree of confidence in results of experiments reported to be significant at various probability or *p*-levels. They found that the average degree of confidence was "great" when results were reported at the 0.05

level. When results were significant at the 0.10 level, the degree of confidence was "mild" or "minimal," and for a significance level of 0.20 or greater, belief was nearly absent. It thus appears that some investigators use the probability of Type I errors as criteria for belief.

Lykken (1968) has expressed a view opposing this use of p-values as criteria for belief. He writes: "A single experimental finding of the usual kind (confirming a directional prediction), no matter how great its statistical significance, will seldom represent a large increment of corroboration for the theory from which it was derived to merit very serious scientific attention." To support this position he cites a published report in which it was found that psychiatric patients who see frogs on the Rorschach show a higher incidence of eating disorders than patients not giving frog responses. This difference was highly significant, and the results were reported to be consistent with an interpretation that assumed that some psychiatric patients had an unconscious belief in a "cloacal theory of birth."

Lykken asked a group of 20 clinical psychologists to estimate the probability of the truth of the theory before being told the results of the investigation. The average probability was close to zero, indicating a general lack of belief in the theory. When the psychologists were informed of the results of the experiment and the apparent significant confirmation, their degrees of belief in the theory were essentially unchanged. It thus appears that in situations where a theory or hypothesis is initially unlikely or unconvincing, a significant finding in a single study does not necessarily increase one's degree of belief in the hypothesis. Lykken concludes that only multiple corroboration, through the use of many independent predictions and measurement procedures, should change the degree of belief in a theory. "The value of any research can be determined, not from the statistical results, but only by skilled, subjective evaluation of the coherence and reasonableness of the theory, the degree of experimental control employed, the sophistication of the measuring techniques, [and] the scientific or practical importance of the phenomena studied" (Lykken, 1968). The issue of statistical significance is thus obviously only one factor among many that needs to be considered in evaluating the adequacy, the generality, and the importance of an experimental finding.

A factor that has been given relatively little attention in the evaluation of experimental data is the magnitude of the experimental effect. An estimation of this magnitude is of considerable importance when one considers that there is no necessary connection between the significance of a finding and the strength of association between two variables. The reason for this is that when a t-test is employed, the larger the N, the greater will be the significance level of a given difference between two groups. Another way to say the same thing is that even very small differences between groups can be found to be "significant" if large enough numbers of subjects are used.

For example, significant differences have been reported between the mean IQs of boys and girls in cases where thousands of subjects have been compared. With such large Ns, even a fraction of an IQ-point difference can be statistically significant, yet the ability to predict sex from a knowledge of IQ may not be meaningfully enhanced by such a finding.

Dubious "significance" when large Ns are employed may be found for correlational data as well. For example, Meehl (1967) has reported that he computed correlations between all pairs of variables on 55,000 Minnesota high school seniors. The variables reflected such diverse contents as birth order, religious preference, number of siblings, vocational choice, mother's education, ability to dance, interest in woodworking, etc. Over 90% of the correlations were found to be highly significant, yet the magnitude of the correlations were so small that no meaningful predictions could be made.

Two Indices of Magnitude of Experimental Effect

These examples suggest that the accuracy of the prediction one can make from one variable to another is just as important as the statistical significance of a difference. This idea of whether prediction is improved as a result of an experiment is usually described by the expression "the proportion of variance in Y accounted for by X." Another way of saying this is that knowledge of the value of X (the independent variable) decreases by some amount, our uncertainty of the estimated value of Y (the dependent variable). In the typical two-group design, X simply refers to group membership, that is, control group or experimental group. The basic issue is whether knowledge of which group a subject is in decreases our uncertainty of what his scores will be on the dependent variable.

Omega Squared. Hays (1963) presents a simple equation that can be used to provide an estimate of the amount of uncertainty that is reduced by knowing X, or, to state it in other terms, the proportion of variance in Y accounted for by group membership. The equation is

$$\text{est } \omega^2 = \frac{t^2 - 1}{t^2 + N_1 + N_2 - 1} \tag{9}$$

where est ω^2 (read "estimated omega squared") is the proportion of variance in Y accounted for by X, t is the t-value obtained in the usual test of significance, and the Ns refer to sample sizes.

Using this equation, Hays shows that in two different experiments the same approximate level of significance may be associated with very different magnitudes of difference between the means of the groups. For example, suppose that two experiments, one using 10 subjects (Ss) per group and the other 100, find differences between the means of the experimental and control groups that are significant at the 5% level. Despite the equivalence of the significance level in both cases, the results of the experiments are quite different in meaning. With 100 Ss per group, the actual difference will be quite small and trivial in a practical sense. With 10 Ss per group, the actual difference between groups is much larger. In the case where N is large, the improvement in prediction is much less than in the case where N is small. Hays concludes: "Statistical significance is not the only, or even the best, evidence for a strong statistical association . . . it seems far more reasonable to decide to follow up a finding that is *both* significant *and* indicates a strong degree of association, than to tie this course of action to significance level alone."

The use of ω^2 provides one way of estimating the magnitude of experimental effect. Several other methods have been proposed and will be briefly described here.

d as a Measure of Effect Size. Cohen (1969) has developed an index of the size of an experimental effect which he calls *d* and which is defined simply as a kind of standard score. The equation is

$$d = \frac{M_1 - M_2}{s_p} \tag{10}$$

where M_1 and M_2 are the two sample means and s_p is the pooled estimate of the population standard deviation. This latter value is obtained by the following equation:

$$s_p = \sqrt{\frac{(N_1 - 1)s_1^2 + (N_2 - 1)s_2^2}{N_1 + N_2 - 2}} \tag{11}$$

N_1 and N_2 refer to the number of observations in each group, and s_1 and s_2 refer to the standard deviations of each sample. (It should be noted that the value of s_p can be roughly approximated as the mean of the two separate standard deviations.)

Once *d* has been obtained, the problem arises of how to interpret it as a measure of the magnitude of an experimental effect. Cohen describes three different interpretations that are possible: *d* as an inverse measure of population overlap, *d* as a measure of correlation, and *d* as a measure of proportion of variance accounted for. There are simple mathematical relations between these three measures.

From the point of view of population overlap, if *d* is 0, then it is evident that the two means M_1 and M_2 are identical and that the two distributions of scores are superimposed on one another. We can describe this as 100% overlap. As *d* gets larger there will be less and less overlap between the distributions. The degree of overlap for various values of *d* can be seen in Table 6–3.

It should be kept in mind that the value of the pooled standard deviation, s_p, is used as a yardstick for evaluating the size of the difference between the means of the two groups. This procedure is similar to that used when calculating a *z*-score. A *z*-score is the difference between two numbers (a raw score and the mean of a distribution) divided by the standard deviation, *s*, of the distribution. Similarly, a *t*-score is obtained by dividing the difference between two means, M_1 and M_2, by the standard deviation, s_p, of a theoretical sampling distribution. The *d*-statistic is obtained by dividing the difference between the two means, M_1 and M_2, by the pooled standard deviation, s_p, of the two sam-

TABLE 6-3 THE DEGREE OF OVERLAP OF EXPERIMENTAL AND CONTROL GROUP DISTRIBUTIONS FOR DIFFERENT VALUES OF d WITH CORRESPONDING PERCENT OF VARIANCE ACCOUNTED FOR ("OMEGA SQUARED")*

d	Degree of Overlap (%)	Omega Squared	d	Degree of Overlap (%)	Omega Squared
0	100.0	0			
0.1	92.3	.00	1.6	26.9	.39
0.2	85.3	.01	1.7	24.6	.42
0.3	78.7	.02	1.8	22.6	.45
0.4	72.6	.04	1.9	20.6	.47
0.5	67.0	.06	2.0	18.9	.50
0.6	61.8	.08	2.2	15.7	.55
0.7	57.0	.11	2.4	13.0	.59
0.8	52.6	.14	2.6	10.7	.63
0.9	48.4	.17	2.8	8.8	.66
1.0	44.6	.20	3.0	7.2	.69
1.1	41.4	.23	3.2	5.8	.72
1.2	37.8	.26	3.4	4.7	.74
1.3	34.7	.30	3.6	3.7	.76
1.4	31.9	.33	3.8	3.0	.78
1.5	29.3	.36	4.0	2.3	.80

*Based on Cohen (1969).

ples. In each case, some kind of a standard deviation is used as a yardstick, or unit of measurement.

Just as there are certain conventions for judging the significance of a difference between two means (e.g., 5% level), Cohen also suggests a convention for judging the magnitude of an "effect size." When d is around 0.2, he calls it a "small" effect. In such a case, approximately 85% of the two distributions overlap, and it is obvious that knowledge of a subject's group membership (i.e., experimental or control) will not allow an accurate estimate of his or her score on the dependent variable.

A "medium" effect size is represented by d values that are approximately 0.5. This value of d indicates 67% overlap of the two distributions. As an illustration of such an effect size, Cohen notes that it is "the magnitude of the difference in height between 14- and 18-year-old girls."

Finally, he suggests that "large" effects be considered to be associated with d values that are over 0.8. Such values represent an overlap of the two distributions of 52% or less. Such differences are usually fairly evident, and would be illustrated by the mean IQ difference between holders of the Ph.D. degree and typical college freshmen.

As is the case with all statistics, the accurate use of d as a measure of percent overlap depends upon certain conditions. These are equal sample size, equal variability (e.g., as measured by the standard deviations), and normality of the distribution. However, small variations from these conditions will not seriously bias the results.

Table 6–3 also presents the value of ω^2 that corresponds approximately to each value of d for the case where there is an equal number of Ss in the experimental and control groups. For example, an ω^2 that corresponds to a medium effect size (i.e., $d = 0.5$) is one in which only 6% of the variance in Y is accounted for by group membership. This ω^2 is associated with a 67% overlap of the control group and experimental group distribution of the Y variable. For a larger effect size (i.e., $d = 1.0$), 20% of the variance in Y is accounted for by group membership and there is a 45% overlap in the experimental and control group distributions. The table thus provides a way of relating two of the important measures of magnitude of experimental effect to each other.

The values of d have an important relation to the usual t-test, and they can be used to help estimate the sizes of samples needed for significance at various levels. The following discussion is based upon the work of Friedman (1968).

Friedman presents a table showing how various values of d require certain size groups for significance at the 5% and 1% levels. For example, if d is approximately 0.5, then the experimenter would have to use 2 groups of 38 Ss each in order to show that the difference was significant at the 5% level. For a d, or effect size, of 0.8, the experimenter would require only about 15 Ss in each group to demonstrate a significant difference at the 5% level.

Table 6–4 summarizes the total Ns required to achieve significance when d varies. This table is, in effect, what has been called a "power" table; that is, it may be used to indicate the size of a sample that is needed to detect a given effect.

To show its use, consider the following example. Suppose an investigator uses 10 subjects in each of 2 groups and finds a difference between the groups that is not significant. He or she then computes d for the data and finds that it is approximately 0.7. This indicates that a phenomenon that is associated with an effect size of this magnitude would require approximately 38 Ss (or 19 in each group) to detect a difference that is significant at the 5% level. The experimenter may then decide whether to repeat the experiment with new, larger groups, or whether to continue to study the phenomenon at all. He or she may decide that the magnitude of the experimental effect is too trivial to warrant any further expenditure of effort.

As an alternative possibility, the experimenter may conclude that the small size of an experimental effect that has been found is due to poor measuring instruments or faulty control of the independent variables. In such cases increased attention to sources of bias, or the introduction of alternative methods of measurement, may increase the sensitivity of the experiment without increasing the number of subjects. If the experimenter pays attention to the issue of the magnitude of the experimental effect, then a more rational decision can be made about an appropriate design and interpretation of his experiment.

Perhaps the most important point to be made is that experimenters should

TABLE 6-4 APPROXIMATE TOTAL NUMBER
OF SUBJECTS REQUIRED FOR SIGNIFICANCE
FOR DIFFERENT VALUES OF d

	Total Number of Subjects	
d	5% Level	1% Level
0.4	100	200
0.5	77	132
0.6	56	97
0.7	38	72
0.8	29	52
0.9	24	38
1.0	20	30
1.2	15	24
1.4	13	20
1.6	11	17
1.8	10	15
2.0	8	12
2.2	8	11
2.4	7	10
2.6	7	9
2.8	7	8
3.0	7	8

not become committed to an exclusive concern with significance levels in evaluating research. Of equal importance is the magnitude of an experimental effect that is produced by experimental manipulations of variables. If both factors are considered, we increase our ability to interpret rationally the data we collect and the theories we construct.

Combining the Results of Different Studies: Meta-Analysis

In recent years, the d statistic has been used to deal with the thorny problem of combining conclusions from different experiments. This has been most extensively described by Smith and Glass (1977) and by Smith, Glass, and Miller (1980) in connection with psychotherapy outcome studies.

Considerable debate has occurred during the past few decades over the question of whether psychotherapy works at all, and if it does, which form of psychotherapy is most effective. Most of the attempts to review the growing literature in the field have been narratives that arbitrarily exclude certain studies and retain others. Grounds for exclusion have varied but include such things as poor specification of treatment parameters and use of unreliable outcome measures. Once a subset of acceptable experiments has been defined, a "box-score" is then obtained of the number of positive and negative outcomes. The outcome with the most studies is declared the "winner."

Smith et al. (1980) point out that "the strategy of ex post facto impeachment of some studies based on design quality and outcome measurement is unsupportable. This strategy presumes an objectivity and distance from the problem that is rare among acknowledged advocates and adversaries. No study is above criticism. All studies vary on a number of dimensions of quality and rigor. Where any reviewer draws the line—assigning a study the status of acceptable or unacceptable—is purely an exercise in professional judgment. Any judgmental strategy permits the introduction of bias in the conclusions."

In view of these problems with the typical "box-score" review of studies, Smith and her colleagues have developed a technique called "meta-analysis" which is based on the concept of effect size. Their basic procedure is to calculate an effect size for each investigation in which an experimental group is compared with a control group. The equation they use is

$$ES = \frac{\overline{X}_E - \overline{X}_C}{s_X} \tag{12}$$

where $\overline{X}_E$ is the average score for the psychotherapy (or experimental) group on the outcome measure, $\overline{X}_C$ is the same, but for the control group, and s_X is the standard deviation of the control group.

This effect size measure provides an indication of the degree of overlap of the experimental and control groups, and the average effect size for all studies combined summarizes the results for the literature that has been reviewed. In the case of psychotherapy research, Smith et al. reviewed 475 controlled studies representing all schools of therapy and concluded that individuals receiving psychotherapy were 0.85 standard deviation units higher on the average than individuals, on the outcome measures. This is illustrated in Figure 6–7.

Another way of saying the same thing is that the average person in the

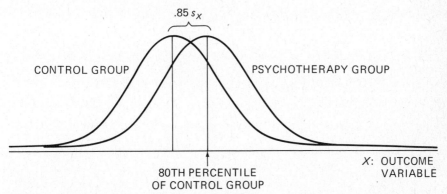

Figure 6–7.   This is an example of meta-analysis applied to psychotherapy research. Based on data from 475 controlled studies, it was found that the average score on the outcome variables was 0.85 standard deviation units higher in individuals exposed to psychotherapy than in the individuals who served as controls. (From M. L. Smith, G. V. Glass, and T. I. Miller, *The benefits of psychotherapy.* Baltimore: Johns Hopkins University Press, 1980. By permission.)

experimental groups has a higher outcome score than 80% of the subjects in the control groups. The same effect size analysis has been used to compare different schools of therapy as well as a number of other variables.

Summary

The statistical ideas that have been discussed in this chapter are important decision-making tools for the researcher. However, it should not be forgotten that statistical methodology is not synonymous with scientific methodology. The scientist is concerned with many decision-making issues that are not statistical issues per se, and he should not mistake "a low p value for the measure of the validity of his other inductions" (Bakan, 1967).

It should be kept clearly in mind that the t-test is of limited use and should be used only in the context of bivalent experiments. Even there it should be supplemented with measures of the magnitude of experimental effects, such as omega squared or d. Ideally, psychological research should move from the identification of variables to the precise measurement of these variables. Multivalent and multigroup experiments should then attempt to establish the nexus of relations between the important variables influencing behavior.

It is worth emphasizing that one of the leading figures in contemporary experimental psychology, B. F. Skinner, has made almost no use of formal statistical procedures. Both Skinner and his associates have instead emphasized the importance of good laboratory control of both subject and stimulus variables and have utilized simple but reliable response measures. In addition, their preoccupation with variables that have relatively large experimental effects means that subtle statistical methods are rarely necessary. Part of experimental sophistication is learning when and how statistical procedures usefully assist the experimental enterprise.

7

Analysis of Variance: Basic Concepts and Applications

The statistical test as a mathematical tool is absolutely neutral about what numbers measure, the level of measurement, what was or was not represented in the experiment, and most of all the cause of the experimenter's particular finding.

—William L. Hays

The *t*-test that has been described in the preceding chapter is used when the experimenter wishes to determine if the means of two groups are significantly different. However, in many experiments the investigator compares three or more groups and is interested in the differences among them. For example, one might wish to compare the effectiveness of three methods of teaching mathematics, or the emotional differences among four breeds of dogs, or the extent of avoidance behavior produced by five levels of electric shock.

One might think that in such cases one could simply compare all possible pairs of means using the *t*-test. Teaching Method 1 might be compared with Methods 2 and 3, and then Method 2 could be compared with Method 3, making three *t*-tests in all. If 5 groups were compared 2 at a time, then 10 *t*-tests would be performed.

If a 5% level of significance is chosen, then—because of random differences between the samples—in 5 comparisons out of 100 an obtained difference between two groups would be judged to be significant even if it was not. As the number of *t*-test comparisons increases, the chances of finding a significant difference by mistake also increases (Sakoda, Cohen, and Beall, 1954). In addition, multiple *t*-tests do not use all the available data in estimating population characteristics.

There is, however, another solution to the problem of comparing several different groups or conditions, and it involves the use of a technique known as *analysis of variance*. Before presenting the computational details, some of the general ideas behind analysis of variance will be presented.

Group Differences Reflected by Variability

Suppose groups of 50 boys and 50 girls are selected randomly from a school district and their mean IQs and the standard deviation of their IQs are calculated. Suppose also that there is no real difference in IQ between boys and girls in the general population. If this is true, then the mean IQ of the boys and girls should be approximately the same. If we combine both samples into one and compute a new standard deviation based on 100 students rather than 50, the standard deviation of the combined group should be approximately equal to that of either group alone, since the range of IQs has remained the same.

Suppose that we now add another group of 50 children, all of whom are known to be mentally retarded; that is, each child has an IQ below 70. If we now compute the standard deviation of IQs for all 150 children, we will obviously find an increase in variability since we have added a set of extreme scores. Thus, the variability of a set of scores may reflect the existence of different kinds of groups; the more different the groups, the greater the variability of their combined scores.

This basic idea has been formalized in the analysis of variance. For example, if we randomly select three groups of children from a given population we would expect them to be nearly the same. If one group is now praised for success in solving arithmetic problems, one group is punished (by misinforming them of their results), and one group is ignored, then we might expect differences in problem-solving achievement to appear. In this situation we have two major sources of variability; one reflects the differences between the groups because of the different ways they have been treated, and the second reflects the naturally occurring differences between the subjects who are treated a-like.

If praising or punishing the children had no effect, the variability between the means of the three groups would be nearly the same as the variability between the subjects within each group. Analysis of variance makes a formal comparison between the variability due to different treatment of groups and the variability due to random differences between subjects. The test used is called an F-test, and it involves a comparison of variances. When the first kind of variability is much larger than the other kind, the experimental treatments or manipulations are said to exert a significant effect on performance. Although the analysis of variance has many complex ramifications, most of them are "reducible to the single problem of testing whether one estimate of variance is significantly greater than a second such estimate" (Fisher, 1954). Conventional 5% and 1% levels of significance are usually used. If the F-test shows that the experimental treatments imposed on the subjects produce a significant overall effect, it is often still necessary to do a further analysis to identify the particular groups that are significantly different. One way to do this will be discussed later.

The Concept of Additive Variance

One of the important ideas central to the analysis of variance is that variability can be divided into parts, or, alternatively, that different estimates of variability can be summed. Since this property of additivity applies only to variances, it is the variance (s^2) of the groups rather than the standard deviation (s) that is employed in the statistical calculations. This concept will be illustrated by the following example, based upon the work of Chapanis (1951); the example is concerned with the interaction between the operator and the machine in radar systems.

Radar is used to locate the distance and position of targets moving at various speeds relative to the detector. The information that a human operator extracts from a radar depends upon at least two major factors: (1) the errors inherent in the radar instrument and (2) errors associated with the individual who must read and estimate distances and locations from a screen.

These errors are of two general types, constant and variable. Any constant overestimation or underestimation by the man-machine system is called a constant error, and it can be easily compensated for once such an error is identified. This is done in the same sense that a good marksman adjusts his sights if he discovers a constant tendency to shoot high.

Analysis has shown that constant errors in a system add algebraically. Suppose, for example, that a radar has been miscalibrated so that it reads 100 yards short. If the radar operator has a tendency to misread the target as 50 yards too far, this man-machine system will provide range readings that are on the average, 50 yards short.

In contrast, variable errors are an index of the inconsistency or instability of the readings and are usually measured by the standard deviation or the variance. Variable errors cannot usually be compensated for by any simple adjustments and are thus more important measures of system functioning than are constant errors. In fact, the reduction of variable errors is a major task of both instrument engineering and engineering psychology research.

If the reasonable assumption is made that the errors in the different parts of a man-machine system are independent, that is, uncorrelated, then it is possible to show that the total error (s_t^2), expressed as a variance, is simply the sum of the errors (variances) in the component parts (a, b, c, . . .) of the system. The equation is

$$s_t^2 = s_a^2 + s_b^2 + s_c^2 + \ldots \tag{1}$$

This equation can be used to provide some insight into the problem of how variable errors accumulate in a complex system. If we consider a realistic example, it might be found that the standard deviation of a large number of errors contributed by the radar itself is 10 yards. We may assume the not unrealistic likelihood that the standard deviation of errors made by the radar operator is 20 yards, that is, that the operator is twice as inconsistent as the machine. When both sources of error are combined in the man-machine system, the total variable error (standard deviation) is 22.36 yards ($s_t = \sqrt{10^2 + 20^2}$). Another way of stating this is that, even if it were possible to completely eliminate the inherent error in the machine, it would reduce the variable error of the system by only slightly over 10% [(22.36 − 20.00)/22.36]. Similarly, if the variable error of the operator was three times that of the machine, then the contribution of the machine to the total error would be only 5%.

These figures highlight an important implication: since humans are often more inconsistent than machines, maximum benefit, as measured by a reduction in errors, will be gained if attention is paid to the man rather than the machine. A knowledge of the characteristics of operators that make for variability will go a long way toward making the total system more stable.

One-Way Analysis of Variance

The example presented in the preceding section was concerned with the general concept of variance and the fact that it can be divided into components. In a fundamental sense, analysis of variance is concerned with identifying the components of variance in a population and comparing these components by means of statistical tests of significance. Although the details of these procedures are often quite complex (Winer, 1971), an example will be presented of the most common type of problem handled by analysis of variance. It is called *one-way analysis of variance.*

A good example of the reasoning involved in one-way analysis of variance is given in Wilson (1952), and the following discussion is based upon it. Assume that there is a population available with a mean of zero, a standard deviation of 10, and a variance of 10^2 or 100. Population values are usually represented by Greek letters so that the population mean (mu) is $\mu = 0$, and the variance (sigma squared) is $\sigma^2 = 100$. If nine scores are sampled from the population at random, the results obtained might look like those presented in Table 7–1.

The overall mean of these numbers $\overline{X}_T$ is 1.56, which is an *estimate* of the mean of the parent population. The variance σ^2 of the parent population may be estimated using the formula for the sample standard deviation.

TABLE 7–1   NINE SCORES RANDOMLY SAMPLED FROM A POPULA-TION WITH MEAN $\mu = 0$ AND VARIANCE $\sigma^2 = 100$

	14	− 4	8	
	− 5	1	8	
	− 18	8	2	
Sum	− 9	5	18	$\Sigma \overline{X}_T = 14$
Mean ($\overline{X}$)	− 3	1.67	6	$\overline{X}_T = 1.56$

$$s^2 = \frac{\Sigma d^2}{N - 1} \qquad (2)$$

where the Σd^2 is the sum of the squared deviations from the mean and N is the number of cases in the sample. Using this equation and all 9 scores in the sample produces a variance of 92.02, compared to the true population variance of 100.

Another estimate of σ^2 can be obtained by considering each column of three values as a separate sample, calculating s^2 for each column and then averaging the three results. Using this procedure, s for column one is 259; for column two, it is 36.4; and for column three, it is 12. Averaging these values produces a mean estimate of σ^2 of 102.46. This is called the within-groups (s_w^2) estimate of variance.

Still a third way of estimating σ^2 is by determining the mean of each column and treating these *means* as deviations from the overall grand mean of 1.56. Since the means vary less than do the individual measurements by a factor of N (the number of Ss in each group), we need to multiply this estimate by N (or 3 in this case) in order to obtain an accurate estimate of the population variance. The result of this procedure produces an estimate of the population variance of 60.78. This estimate is based upon the differences between group means and is symbolized as s_{Bet}^2. We thus have three estimates of σ^2, namely, 92.00, 102.44, and 60.78, with the true value of σ^2 being 100. The question arises: How large are such variations likely to be when we take random samples of different size from a single population?

If we imagine taking many samples from the population, from each of which independent estimates of σ^2 are made, we can then compare any two such independent estimates. We do this by computing the ratio of the variance estimate based upon the differences between group means, to the variance estimate based upon the differences between the subjects within groups, or s_{Bet}^2 / s_w^2. Since these estimates of variance differ only because of random fluctuations in the samples, they should, on the average, tend to be quite similar. This means that the most likely ratio of the s_{Bet}^2 / s_w^2 will be near 1.00, with a decreasing probability of obtaining large deviations from 1.00.

The distribution of ratios of variances is called the F-distribution; it shows the likelihood of obtaining any particular ratio of s_{Bet}^2 / s_w^2 as a result of random sampling. When unusually large ratios of s_{Bet}^2 / s_w^2 are obtained, it is assumed that they are probably not due to random fluctuations because of sampling from a single population. Instead, it is concluded that two or more separate populations are being sampled.

The same general rules of thumb apply here as in the case of tests of significance using t. If a particular ratio of s_{Bet}^2 / s_w^2 could have occurred only 5 or less times in 100 by chance, then we assume that chance was not the cause of the obtained ratio and that some other variable was acting. The F-table presented in Appendix III, Table D, lists the ratios of s_{Bet}^2 / s_w^2 that are needed for the 5% level of significance for degrees of freedom corresponding to different sample sizes. The degrees of freedom for the s_{Bet}^2 variance is 1 less than the number of groups, while the degrees of freedom for the s_w^2 variance is the sum of $N - 1$ for each group (or $2 + 2 + 2 = 6$ in this case).

In the example presented, a comparison of the between-groups variance estimate to the within-groups estimate produces an F-ratio of 0.59 (60.78/ 102.44). This value of F is not significant at the 5% level for the small Ns used in the samples. This indicates that all three samples did not come from different populations.

Programmed Learning: Does It Work? An Example with Computational Details

The procedures for calculating the variance estimates have become quite standardized, and there is a typical format for presenting the results. The following example will present in detail a typical one-way analysis of variance problem.

Suppose that three different publishers developed programmed textbooks for the teaching of statistics and that an instructor wanted to determine which program, if any, was superior as a teaching device. In order to do this, the class was randomly divided into four groups of six students each. Students in each of the first three groups used the three different programmed texts, while students in the fourth group used a nonprogrammed text. At the end of a month the same examination was given to all students; results are as shown in Table 7-2.

In order to do a one-way analysis of variance, the basic requirement is that we obtain estimates of the population variance in two independent ways, one based on the differences between the means of the four groups, and the other based upon the differences between the subjects within each group. The formula used is the one that defines the variance:

TABLE 7-2 HYPOTHETICAL TEST RESULTS OF STUDENTS USING THREE DIFFERENT PROGRAMMED TEXTS PLUS A STANDARD TEXT

	Programmed Texts			Standard Text	
	Group A	Group B	Group C	Group D	
	75	78	55	64	
	93	91	66	72	
	78	97	49	68	
	71	82	64	77	
	63	85	70	56	
	76	77	68	95	Total
ΣX	456	510	372	432	1770
X	76	85	62	72	73.75
ΣX^2	34,144	43,652	23,402	31,994	
$(\Sigma X)^2$	207,936	260,100	138,384	186,624	

$$s^2 = \frac{\Sigma d^2}{N-1}$$

The term Σd^2 is the sum of the squared deviations of each score from the mean, and $N-1$ represents the degrees of freedom.

For computation from the raw scores, the numerator of this equation for variance can be rewritten in its equivalent form.

$$\Sigma d^2 = \Sigma X^2 - \frac{(\Sigma X)^2}{N} \tag{3}$$

The term ΣX^2 refers to the sum of the squares of each raw score. $(\Sigma X)^2$ is the square of the number that is the sum of all scores. N refers to the number of scores. For the present data, the total sum of squared deviations, or $(\Sigma d^2)_T$, is

$$(\Sigma d^2)_T = (75^2 + 93^2 + 78^2 + \ldots + 56^2 + 95^2) - \frac{(1770)^2}{24} = 3654.5$$

Similarly, the sum of the squared deviations from the mean for the differences between the groups, or $(\Sigma d^2)_{\text{Bet}}$, is represented by the following symbolic equation:

$$(\Sigma d^2)_{\text{Bet}} = \left[\frac{(\Sigma X_A)^2}{N_A} + \frac{(\Sigma X_B)^2}{N_B} + \frac{(\Sigma X_C)^2}{N_C} + \frac{(\Sigma X_D)^2}{N_D} \right] - \frac{(\Sigma X_T)^2}{N_T} \tag{4}$$

The term $(\Sigma X)^2$ refers to the square of the number that is the sum of all scores for each of the four separate groups, A, B, C, and D. The terms N_A through N_D refer to the number of cases in each group, and N_T is the total N for all groups combined. $(\Sigma X_T)^2$ is the square of the number that is the sum of all scores. In the present example, the calculations are as follows:

$$(\Sigma d^2)_{\text{Bet}} = \left[\frac{(456)^2}{6} + \frac{(510)^2}{6} + \frac{(372)^2}{6} + \frac{(432)^2}{6} \right] - \frac{(1770)^2}{24} = 1636.5$$

Although equation (4) is most often employed in computing the between-groups variance estimate, there is an equivalent formula that is often useful. It is based upon the direct use of the means.

$$(\Sigma d^2)_{\text{Bet}} = N_A (\overline{X}_A)^2 + N_B (\overline{X}_B)^2 + N_C (\overline{X}_C)^2 + N_D (\overline{X}_D)^2$$
$$- N_T (\overline{X}_T)^2 \tag{5}$$

In this equation $\overline{X}_A, \overline{X}_B, \overline{X}_C$, and $\overline{X}_D$ refer to the means of each group, and $\overline{X}_T$ is the overall mean.

The third estimate of variance is based upon the variability within the groups. In order to calculate this variability, a term representing the sum of the within-groups deviations, or $(\Sigma d^2)_w$, must be determined. This sum is obtained as a sum of four terms in this particular experiment, where each term is based upon the deviations from the mean of each particular group. In symbolic terms:

$$(\Sigma d^2)_W = \Sigma d_A^2 + \Sigma d_B^2 + \Sigma d_C^2 + \Sigma d_D^2 \tag{6}$$

For purposes of computation, each of the Σd^2 terms is again represented by the same raw score equivalent form, as follows:

$$\Sigma d_A^2 = \Sigma X_A^2 - \frac{(\Sigma X_A)^2}{N_A}$$

$$\Sigma d_B^2 = \Sigma X_B^2 - \frac{(\Sigma X_B)^2}{N_B}$$

$$\Sigma d_C^2 = \Sigma X_C^2 - \frac{(\Sigma X_C)^2}{N_C}$$

$$\Sigma d_D^2 = \Sigma X_D^2 - \frac{(\Sigma X_D)^2}{N_D}$$

When the appropriate numbers are substituted, the $(\Sigma d^2)_W$, or within-groups deviations from their means, is found in the following way:

$$\Sigma d_A^2 = 35,144 - \frac{207,936}{6} = 488$$

$$\Sigma d_B^2 = 43,652 - \frac{260,100}{6} = 302$$

$$\Sigma d_C^2 = 23,402 - \frac{138,384}{6} = 338$$

$$\Sigma d_D^2 = 31,994 - \frac{186,624}{6} = 890$$

$$\Sigma d_W^2 = 488 + 302 + 338 + 890 = 2018$$

Unnecessary detail has been presented in order to clarify the first phase of the computation. A simple calculation will show that the total sum of the squared deviations from the mean is actually equal to the sum of the between-groups and the within-groups squared deviations.

$$(\Sigma d^2)_T = (\Sigma d^2)_W + (\Sigma d^2)_{Bet} \tag{7}$$

In this case

$$3654.5 = 2018.0 + 1636.5$$

It is customary to compute the total sum of squares $(\Sigma d^2)_T$, and the between-groups sum of squares, $(\Sigma d^2)_{Bet}$, and then to calculate the within-groups sum of squares from equation (7).

It is important to emphasize that the calculations presented thus far have only obtained the numerator, Σd^2, of the equation for variance

$$s^2 = \frac{\Sigma d^2}{N-1}$$

In order to obtain a variance estimate, the numerator, Σd^2, must be divided by the appropriate degrees of freedom. The appropriate N for the between-groups estimate of variance is 1 less than the number of groups, or 3 in this case. The appropriate N for the within-groups estimate of variance is obtained by subtracting 1 from the N in each group, and then summing for all groups. In this example, it would be $5 + 5 + 5 + 5 = 20$. The total degrees of freedom is 1 less than the total N, or 23 in this case. Just as the sum of the squared deviations for between- and within-groups estimates add to the total sum of squared deviations from the mean, so too do the degrees of freedom for the between- and within-groups estimates sum to the total degrees of freedom.

All these various computations can be conveniently summarized in an analysis of variance table (Table 7–3).

The variance estimates are obtained simply as follows:

$$s_{Bet}^2 = \frac{1636.5}{3} = 545.5$$
$$s_{W}^2 = \frac{2018.0}{20} = 100.9$$

If the null hypothesis of no differences in population means among the four groups is valid, then these two variances should be similar, and the ratio of variances, or $F = s_{Bet}^2 / s_W^2$, should not deviate greatly from 1.00. The obtained ratio is actually 5.41. When this figure is looked up in the table of F-values (Appendix III, Table D), it is found that an F-ratio of 5.41 for these particular groups occurs as a result of random sampling only about 1 time in 100. An F-ratio of 5.41 is therefore a rare event, and it is concluded that the differences between the groups leading to such a ratio were probably not due to random sampling fluctuations. In other words, the F-ratio is said to be significant and the null hypothesis is rejected. It appears that different textbooks do influence the amount learned.

TABLE 7–3 ANALYSIS OF VARIANCE TABLE FOR THE STUDY COMPARING PROGRAMMED TEXTS

Source of Variation	Degrees of Freedom	Sum of Squared Deviations	Variance Estimates*	F
Between Groups	3	1636.5	545.5	5.41
Within Groups	20	2018.0	100.9	
Total	23	3654.5		

*In many textbooks, it is customary to use the term "mean square" in this box; however, the term "variance estimate" seems more descriptive (Runyon and Haber, 1967).

At the beginning of this chapter it was pointed out that, in man-machine systems, total error expressed as a variance is the sum of the errors (variances) in the component parts of the system. In the analysis of variance the situation is somewhat more complex. The total sum of squared deviations is the sum of the between-groups squared deviations and the within-groups squared deviations. However, the total *variance* estimate is not equal to the sum of the between- and within-groups variances. Additivity in the analysis of variance applies only to the total sum of squares.

From a theoretical point of view it can be demonstrated that the between-groups estimate of variance can be conceptualized as the sum of two variances, one due to differences between groups and the other due to differences between subjects within groups. It is only in this sense that the variance estimate is the sum of two (or more in certain cases) other variances.

Group Comparisons After Analysis of Variance

For the instructor who is interested in deciding on which particular textbook to use for a statistics course, the results obtained by the analysis of variance are not very satisfactory. The instructor is not really concerned about the fact that textbooks influence the amount students learn; he or she is interested in identifying a particular "best" text from the ones used.

Several methods have been devised for determining which of the groups are significantly different from each other. The one to be described here was developed by Tukey, modified by Snedecor, and is fairly simple to use (Snedecor, 1956). The following steps are necessary:

Step 1. Make up a table of all differences between means. Arrange the means from high to low and subtract each mean from those above it, as shown in Table 7–4.

Step 2. Calculate a value called s_x (standard error of the mean) using the within-groups estimate of variance, s_w^2, and an N representing the number of subjects per group.

$$s_x = \sqrt{\frac{s_w^2}{N}} \qquad (8)$$

TABLE 7–4   THE TUKEY-SNEDECOR METHOD FOR DETERMINING SIGNIFICANT DIFFERENCES BETWEEN GROUPS AFTER AN ANALYSIS OF VARIANCE

Group	$\overline{X}$	$\overline{X} - 62$	$-\overline{X} - 72$	$\overline{X} - 76$
B	85	23	13	9
A	76	14	4	
D	72	10		
C	62			

In this case

$$s_x = \sqrt{\frac{100.9}{6}} = 4.1$$

Step 3. Enter the special Q-Table (Table E in Appendix III) for the number of groups used in the study and for the number of degrees of freedom associated with the within-groups estimate of variance. Determine a value of Q from the table. For 4 groups and 20 degrees of freedom, the Q-value is 3.96.

Step 4. Use the equation

$$D = Qs_x \qquad\qquad (9)$$

In this case, $D = (3.96)(4.1) = 16.24$.

Step 5. Compare this value of D with all the differences between means listed in your table (Table 7–4). It is evident that only one pair of means differ significantly at the 5% level. This indicates that programmed textbook B is associated with significantly better test grades than programmed textbook C, but it is not significantly better than the other texts.

In most applications of analysis of variance, the investigator is inter-ested in determining specific differences between groups and should therefore routinely use either the Tukey or some alternative method (Edwards, 1968).

Analysis of Variance: An Evaluation

Like all statistical tests, the analysis of variance is based upon certain assump-tions. One of these is that the population from which the scores are sampled is normally distributed. A second assumption is that the variances of the popula-tions from which different groups are sampled are equal, that is, that the variances are homogeneous. A third assumption is that the errors of measurement as-sociated with the different groups are equal. A fourth assumption is that the subjects used in the experiment are randomly selected from a given population. Hays (1963) has pointed out that the assumption of normal distributions can be violated with little effect on results, particularly if the Ns are large. The need for homogeneous variances can also be violated with little effect on results if the Ns are equal. The need for equal errors of measurement among the samples cannot be violated without seriously distorting the results. Such a situation usually occurs in learning studies in which some variable is measured as a function of trials and analysis of variance is used to demonstrate that practice has an effect on performance. As practice continues the mean score systematically changes, and the standard deviation typically gets smaller as well. In such a case the mean and variability measures are correlated, and various transformations of the data are needed to correct for the violations (Adler and Roessler, 1964), but caution is necessary in interpreting the results.

Finally, if the assumption of random selection of different subjects from a population for placement in the different groups is violated, the results of the analysis of variance are difficult to interpret. These facts underscore a point made in an earlier chapter in connection with the t-test. No statistical test ever has all its necessary assumptions fully met, so that all results obtained with its use are approximate. No statistical test can substitute for good planning of research, careful use of random selection methods, or elimination of sources of bias.

Since so many factors will influence the outcome of an experiment, results of borderline significance or lack of significance may be interpreted in many different ways. The independent replication of findings should carry greater weight in the justification of conclusions than the results of a single statistical test.

There are three other important points to be made about the analysis of variance. The first is that analysis of variance can become quite complex as more variables are added to the analysis. With 3 or 4 variables and with replications, as many as 10 or more variance estimates are possible with as many F-tests. Since the F-tests are not statistically independent (since the same value is used in the denominator in all cases), a certain number of significant F-ratios will be due to chance. This fact, plus the existence of multiple interactions, make complex experiments often difficult to interpret. In fact, the author of a statistical textbook has written that "other things being equal, the simpler the psychological experiment, the better will be its execution and the more likely will one be able to decide what actually happened and what results actually mean" (Hays, 1963).

The second point to be made about analysis of variance is that the F-values obtained by a comparison of variances are only an estimate of level of significance, not of magnitude of experimental effect. In other words, a highly significant F-value may be obtained in a given experiment if the N is large, even though the actual effect size (as measured, e.g., by omega squared or d) is small. Just as in the case of the t-test, interpretation of analysis of variance results will be more meaningful if both F and some measure of effect size are computed. Discussion of methods for evaluating the magnitude of an experimental effect using analysis of variance data may be found in Hays (1963), Friedman (1968), Cohen (1969), and Fleiss (1969).

The last important point to be made about analysis of variance is that there are certain types of situations for which it is inappropriate or inefficient. Such situations occur when we are dealing with groups of subjects who are used to systematically sample a dimension. Suppose, for example, that we wish to study the effect of electric shock as an incentive to learning. Five groups of animals are used in a multivalent experiment, with one group receiving no shock and the others 10, 20, 30, or 40 volts for incorrect turns in a T-maze. Let us further assume the reasonable outcome that there is a U-shaped function relating shock level to number of errors made (Figure 7–1). The group of animals given no shock and the group of animals given the maximum shock have

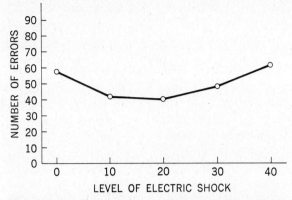

Figure 7–1.   Hypothetical data showing the multivalent relation between number of errors rats make in a T-maze as a function of level of electric shock for incorrect turns.

many errors, while the groups receiving mild punishment show the best relative performance.

In such a situation, it is quite likely that an analysis of variance of the data would show no significant effect of shock simply because there might not be any large differences between the means of the groups. Analysis of variance typically ignores the *pattern* of the scores, the U-shaped function, and treats the data as if the sequence of means is irrelevant.

A rearrangement of the data of Figure 7–1 is shown in Figure 7–2. This is done to illustrate the fact that one-way analysis of variance ignores the pattern

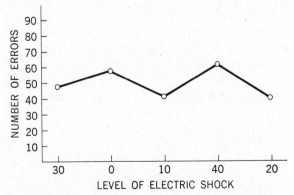

Figure 7–2.   A rearrangement of the data shown in Figure 7–1 to illustrate that a one-way analysis of variance ignores the pattern of data that is obtained. The data of both Figure 7–1 and Figure 7–2 would be treated in exactly the same way and any other sequence of the five means would also be treated identically.

of results. The data of both Figure 7–1 and Figure 7–2 would be treated in exactly the same way and would produce the same F-values. In fact, any other sequence of the five means would also be treated identically.

If the analysis of variance indicated a significant effect, the investigator could only conclude that shock level has some effect on the errors animals make in learning. Or the experimenter might erroneously try to find the pair of means that were significantly different and would ignore the sequential pattern of scores. The data, as obtained, already provide a fairly precise way of predicting errors from knowledge of shock levels. Analysis of variance is inefficient in the sense that it ignores this precise functional relation between the variables.

Analysis of variance, as it is usually used, is not the technique of choice for multivalent or parametric studies in which the experimenter is interested in the functional relation between variables. In such cases, curve-fitting techniques and mathematical equations are appropriate. The following chapter will serve as an introduction to such techniques.

8

The Treatment
of Functional Data

Although all science is fundamentally empirical, it is easy to put too much confidence in a curve or formula fitted to some observed points but unsupported by any conceptual scheme. . . . Purely empirical formulas should not be trusted too far from the data on which they are based. A good theory can help considerably.

—E. Bright Wilson, Jr.

The previous chapter has described some fundamental concepts, as well as some cautions, connected with the use of statistical procedures. Most of the techniques presented tend to be used in the context of exploratory research; they are generally concerned simply with determining whether a variable manipulated by the experimenter can produce a reliable effect. Such research is designed to determine, for example, whether time between trials is a factor influencing learning, or whether stress is likely to influence memory. The answer is typically given in yes-no or dichotomous terms. Yet it is a fact that most variables of interest to psychologists—intelligence, stress, learning, anxiety, motivation—are not dichotomies but are continuous functions which vary or can be made to vary over a range of values. Once we go beyond the simple exploratory study concerned only with identifying variables, we become interested in finding out how a systematic change in one variable affects another. In other words, we become interested in the precise relationships between two or more variables. Unfortunately, much of classical statistics, using methods such as *t*-tests, is concerned primarily with exploratory research and is not particularly applicable to the study of functional relationships. In view of this, what kinds of mathematical or statistical devices can be used in dealing with the resulting functional data? The purpose of the present chapter is to describe a few of the simpler mathematical concepts used in the analysis of such information.

The Search for Laws

Scientists typically seek generalizations. They are rarely interested in the results of single experiments except insofar as they relate to other studies and other sources of information. Although at an early stage of investigation of a problem they may use a qualitative statement of a relation, they aim toward eventually making the statement more precise. They attempt to go from a tentative generalization to a precise law.

Let us look at one classic illustration of this process. Well over 100 years ago experiments were performed to learn how people see and hear the world. One kind of study was concerned with *differential thresholds,* that is, how sensitive our sense organs are to small changes in the intensity of stimulation.

One of the first things discovered was that the sensitivity of the eye to a change in illumination depended on what the initial level of illumination was. In a dimly lit room only a small increment in light intensity was needed before a change was noticed, whereas in a brightly lighted room a larger change in light intensity was required for the change to be noticeable. Similar findings were also observed for other sense modalities. Such research was exploratory. It identified an important variable (i.e., the intensity of the stimulus) and a crude kind of generalization was possible: the greater the intensity of the initial stimulation, the greater the change in stimulus intensity that was needed before the change was noticed.

It was not long before attempts were made to extend these studies in order to determine in a more precise way the relation between initial level of intensity (symbolized I) and the change necessary to be just noticed (symbolized ΔI and pronounced delta I or "change in" I). Experiments showed that over a wide range of intensities the just noticeable change was directly proportional to the initial level of intensity. This fact could be summarized by a single mathematical equation

$$\frac{\Delta I}{I} = C \tag{1}$$

This means that the ratio of the just noticeable change to the initial level is always a constant, symbolized by the letter C. This simple equation is known as Weber's law, and it summarizes in a simple way a great many observations that have been made. In addition, it allowed *interpolations* and *extrapolations* to stimulus conditions that had never been tested before. It also provided some reliable information that needed explaining. In other words, theorists now had something to theorize about. As might be expected, however, this simple relationship turned out to be correct only for a part of the range of intensities, and as more extreme values were used, more complicated equations became necessary.

This general pattern of (1) identifying a variable, (2) determining precise functional relations between it and some measure of response, (3) extending the range of study of the variable, and (4) expressing the relationship in mathematical terms has been followed in many areas of psychology, particularly in connection with sensory psychology and learning.

Putting a set of observations into mathematical form has several advantages. For one thing, it enables interpolations and extrapolations to be made. This is extremely important since researchers are usually interested in the *relation* between two (or more) variables and *not* in the particular values they happened to pick for study. Thus, in an experiment in which the effects of 24 hours of deprivation are compared with the effects of 12 hours of deprivation, the investigator would ideally like to know what the effects of *all* deprivation times are and not just the effects of 24 and 12 hours. If a functional relation between deprivation time and speed of running a maze was established, then one could estimate what might happen if 18 or 23 or 32 hours of deprivation were used. If the results were reliable and consistent, they could be described by a mathematical equation and called a *law*.

A second important value of the mathematical statement of a relationship is that it often provides a clear-cut basis for theory construction. Theories are generally designed to explain results, and they can do this only if the results to be explained are clearly stated and unequivocal.

Third, the mathematical statement of relations sometimes helps clarify inconsistencies in previous research. When Weber's law was stated precisely, it was immediately recognized to be only an approximation to the facts. Several other mathematical formulations have since been tried with varying degrees of success in summarizing the experimental observations. This point will be elaborated later in this chapter.

Concepts of Curve Fitting

At the conclusion of the data collection phase of a multivalent (or parametric) experiment, the investigator usually has a set of measurements of some dependent variable at certain selected values of an independent variable. For example, the measurements may consist of the number of trials it took a group of animals to learn to jump over a partition in order to avoid getting an electric shock, the independent variable here being the intensity, in milliamperes, of the electric current. The usual first step in analyzing the data is to determine the mean values for each set of measurements and then to plot them on a graph as illustrated in the hypothetical data of Figure 8–1. The circles represent the mean values based on five animals per group. The problem now arises of how best to summarize the relationship by means of a mathematical equation. This is the problem of fitting a curve to the data. The aim is generally to find a single expression which represents the mean values as closely as possible. Unfortunately this is a more difficult problem than one might realize, and it is "in a sense an art; it cannot be reduced to a set of inflexible rules" (Lewis, 1960).

One reason it is difficult is that it is theoretically possible to fit an infinite number of different mathematical equations to a finite set of observations. There-

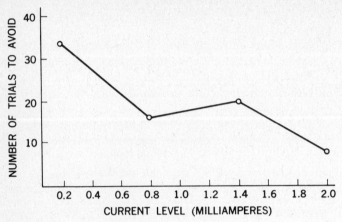

Figure 8–1. Hypothetical data illustrating the results of a multivalent experiment.

fore, some other criteria must be considered. The two criteria that are most important are the criteria of *continuity* and of *simplicity*.

The assumption of continuity refers to the belief that there is only *one smooth* curve that should be fitted through the obtained experimental points. The alternative would be to fit a series of straight lines from point to point as is illustrated by Figure 8–1. Such a series of straight lines is *discontinuous:* they imply several different mathematical relations. The assumption of continuity is made, on the other hand, for two reasons. It implies that a *single* equation is necessary for fitting the data, *and* it implies that the observed variation is partly due to the existence of errors of observation and sampling. It is assumed that if our observations were made with more precision and if the number of measurements was greatly increased, the apparent irregularities in the curve would disappear, leaving a smooth, continuous transition from point to point.

Another way of saying this is that there is an unknown amount of error associated with each measurement and that the smooth continuous curve we draw is designed to approximate the *theoretical outcome* under ideal conditions using large numbers of subjects and many precise measurements. Such a theoretical curve is usually called a *best fitting* curve. The expression "best fitting curve" is used in a general sense and can apply to straight lines as well as curved lines.

A problem still remains. There are many continuous curves that may be drawn through a set of points on a graph, and therefore, a further decision must be made. This decision is usually made on the basis of a desire for simplicity. What is simple for the layperson may not necessarily be considered simple by the mathematician, and so the term is used only in the mathematical sense. Some equations are mathematically simpler than others, and the researcher usually tries to select the simplest equation that fits the data closely. For example, a straight line is considered simpler than a curved line.

Mathematical Equations: A Common Language

If the investigator is interested in the simplest mathematical equation that fits closely to the data, then the range of choices is considerably narrowed. From a mathematical point of view there are only three or four types of simple equations that are frequently found to be appropriate to many types of empirical measurements. For example, the following is an *exponential* equation used in optics to estimate the intensity of light (I) transmitted through a filter, that is, a piece of dark glass.

$$I = I_o\, e^{-kd} \tag{2}$$

I_o is the intensity of the light source, d is the depth of the absorbing material, k is a constant, and e is a constant. The difference between k and e is that k is an empirical constant whose value depends on the particular type of glass used, while the e is a universal constant, like pi ($\pi = 3.1415\ldots$) which has the same value in all situations. The value of e is approximately $2.718\ldots$, and it is usually referred to as the base of the natural system of logarithms.

An equation used in meteorology is

$$p = p_o\, e^{-kd} \tag{3}$$

where p is the pressure of the atmosphere at a certain height, p_o is the pressure at sea level, and h is the height. The values k and e are again constants, k specific to the situation and e always the same.

The third example comes from the field of psychology. A well-known psychologist named Clark Hull formulated a mathematical theory of learning (1943). In the theory, he tried to relate the strength of a habit (H) to the number of trials of training (N) the subject had, and to the plateau (M) the performance would gradually approach. His equation was

$$H = M - Me^{-iN} \tag{4}$$

Here again, i is an empirical constant and e is the same universal constant used before. Although this equation is slightly different in form than those cited above, it is of the same general exponential type.

The point of these illustrations is that the same, or very similar, mathematical types of equations can be used in a wide variety of contexts to describe very different kinds of observations. These equations may be thought of as a kind of generalized language which enables us to talk about the common characteristics of different situations. Another way of saying this is that mathematical equations are general models, or analogies, that can be fitted to many different situations. Therefore, if we learn something about a few common models (i.e., equations) then it is likely that they can be used to describe many different situations we will encounter in research.

Some Simple Equations

The simplest equation with which the mathematician deals is one which represents a straight line. In symbolic terms the equation is

$$Y = a + bX \tag{5}$$

where a and b are constants. If we take any fixed values for a and b, such as 2 and 3, we get an equation $Y = 2 + 3X$ which can be graphically represented by the line in Figure 8–2a. Given the equation, the line can be plotted by substituting values for X and calculating the resulting value for Y. If X is 0, then Y is equal to 2. If X is 1, then Y is equal to 5, etc. Notice that the line crosses the Y-axis at $Y = 2$ and that the steepness or slope of the line is equal to 3. The slope is determined simply by seeing how much of an increase occurs in Y for each increase of one unit of X. In Figure 8–2b, the line represents the equation $Y = 15 - 5X$. Here we notice that the line crosses the Y-axis at 15, but that it slopes downward to the right; that is, it has a negative slope. For each unit increase in X there is a decrease of 5 units of Y.

It should be obvious by now that a simple generalization can be made about linear equations when they are put in the form $Y = a + bX$. It will always be the case that the constant a will determine where the line crosses the Y-axis, or to use a more formal terminology, it determines the Y-intercept. The constant b will always determine the slope.

Now we may understand what investigators mean when they say they want to fit a straight line (i.e., a linear equation) to a set of obtained points. The data

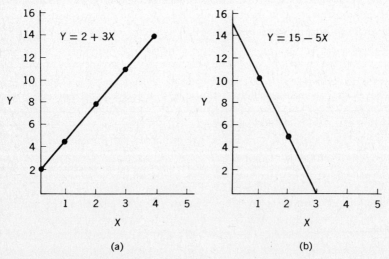

(a)   (b)

Figure 8–2. Examples of linear equations.

points actually represent the X and Y values; therefore, the job is to work backward, so to speak, and determine the constants of the equation, the as and bs. In general, *curve fitting is the determination of values of the constants that belong in equations assumed to apply to sets of data.*

There are several ways in which this can be done in connection with a straight line. The simplest method is to draw the line by eye so that it passes through the observed points. This is satisfactory if all the points clearly lie along the line but may lead to error if the points are irregularly spaced and a best fitting line is desired.

A second method is to pick two values of X and their corresponding Y values and substitute these into the equation of the straight line, producing two simultaneous equations. Thus, if the second and the fifth pair of points in Table 8–1 are selected the equations would be

$$0.18 = a + b(2)$$
$$0.47 = a + b(5)$$

These can be solved by simple algebraic methods to yield values for a and b. The difficulty with this procedure, however, is that the values of a and b depend on which pairs of points are selected. Therefore, the method used in practice follows this general pattern but uses all the information in the data.

This is done by dividing the data into two equal halves (odd versus even pairs would do as well) and getting the sum or means for each half. These values are then substituted into the two equations and solved. Using the data of Table 8–1, we select the first three points and determine the sums for the Xs and for the Ys. Then we do the same for the last three points. The sum of X for the upper half is $1 + 2 + 3 = 6$ and for the lower half it is $4 + 5 + 6 = 15$. The sum of Y for the upper half is $0.10 + 0.18 + 0.31 = 0.59$ and for the lower half it is $0.39 + 0.47 + 0.55 = 1.41$. For each half the as have been added three times. These values are now substituted into the equations of a straight line.

TABLE 8–1 HYPOTHETICAL DATA SHOWING THE RELATION BETWEEN THE INTENSITY (I) OF A STIMULUS AND THE MAGNITUDE OF THE JUST NOTICEABLE DIFFERENCE (ΔI)

X(I)	Y(ΔI)
1	0.10
2	0.18
3	0.31
4	0.39
5	0.47
6	0.55

$$0.59 = 3a + b(6)$$
$$1.41 = 3a + b(15)$$

These equations can be solved by subtracting the upper equation from the lower one to yield

$$1.41 - 0.59 = 3a - 3a + b(15) - b(6)$$
$$0.82 = b(9)$$
$$0.091 = b$$

By replacing this value of b in one of the above equations, we can solve for a.

$$0.59 = 3a + (0.091)(6)$$
$$0.59 = 3a + 0.546$$
$$0.590 - 0.546 = 3a$$
$$0.044 = 3a$$
$$0.015 = a$$

The equation of the straight line is therefore

$$Y = 0.015 + 0.091X$$

This method is called the *method of averages* and is a simple and convenient way of estimating the constants of a linear equation.

The Method of Least Squares

The technique generally considered most accurate for determining the constants of a straight line equation is called the method of least squares. It is the most frequently used method for determining the best fitting line for a set of observations.

When we draw a best fitting line by eye, we generally try to place the line in such a way that there are as many points on one side of the line as on the other. We also try to make the average distance (i.e., deviations) of the points from the line in both directions balance. These criteria, however, will not produce a unique placement of the best fitting line, and another criterion must be substituted. This criterion is that *the sum of the squares of the deviations of the observed points from the line must be a minimum.* When this criterion is met, a unique best fitting line is obtained based on all of the data of the experiment.

On the basis of this assumption it is possible to develop equations that enable us to determine the constants a and b of the best fitting line for a set of observations. The procedure again involves the establishment of a pair of simultaneous equations which are then solved for a and b. The solutions can be generalized in the following two equations.

$$a = \frac{\Sigma X^2 \, \Sigma Y - (\Sigma XY)(\Sigma X)}{N\Sigma X^2 - (\Sigma X)^2} \qquad (6)$$

$$b = \frac{N\Sigma XY - (\Sigma X)(\Sigma Y)}{N\Sigma X^2 - (\Sigma X)^2} \qquad (7)$$

In these equations a and b are the constants to be determined, N refers to the number of paired observations, ΣX is the sum of the values of the X (or independent) variable, ΣX^2 is the sum of the squares of the X values, ΣY is the sum of the values of the Y (or dependent variable), and ΣXY is the sum of the values obtained by multiplying each X value by its corresponding Y value.

TABLE 8-2 HYPOTHETICAL DATA SHOWING THE RELATION BETWEEN THE INTENSITY (I) OF A STIMULUS AND THE MAGNITUDE OF THE JUST NOTICEABLE DIFFERENCE (ΔI)

$X(\mathrm{I})$	$Y(\Delta\mathrm{I})$	XY	X^2
1	0.10	0.10	1
2	0.18	0.36	4
3	0.31	0.93	9
4	0.39	1.56	16
5	0.47	2.35	25
6	0.55	3.30	36
21	2.00	8.60	91
ΣX	ΣY	ΣXY	ΣX^2

The use of these equations may be illustrated by the data of Table 8-2, which is Table 8-1 rewritten and extended. To determine the Y-intercept a, we substitute the various sums from Table 8-2 into equation (6):

$$a = \frac{(91)(2.00) - (8.60)(21)}{6(91) - (21)(21)}$$

$$a = \frac{182 - 180.6}{546 - 441}$$

$$a = \frac{1.4}{105}$$

$$a = 0.013$$

We may proceed similarly with equation (7) to determine the slope constant b:

$$b = \frac{6(8.60) - (21)(2.00)}{6(91) - (21)(21)}$$

$$b = \frac{51.60 - 42.00}{546 - 441}$$

$$b = \frac{9.6}{105}$$

$$b = 0.091$$

The resulting best fitting linear equation determined by the method of least squares is therefore

$$Y = 0.013 + 0.091X$$

If this equation is compared with the one calculated by the method of averages, we see that there is a slight discrepancy but that the two methods are in very good agreement. The differences are due largely to the arbitrary way of dividing the data into two groups in the method of averages. Whenever a precise estimate is desired, the method of least squares should be used.

Uses of Linear Equations

There are at least three different kinds of situations in which linear equations are used. They are used to describe experimental data and are often a good first approximation for a set of observations. This was seen, for example, in our discussion of Weber's law.

Linear equations are also used in analyzing the appropriateness of more complex curve forms for given sets of data by providing a simple *transformation.* More will be said about this point later.

Finally, linear equations are at the basis of one of the important tools of statistical analysis—the correlation technique. We shall begin by briefly examining this last point.

Correlation as Linear Covariation

If two sets of measurements are collected, we may, if we wish, attempt to correlate them. The measurements may consist of such things as IQs and high school averages for a group of students, age and speed of learning scores in a group of rats, or length of reported breast feeding in infancy and frequency of cigarette smoking in a group of adults. In such cases it is not necessary to assume that one of the variables is, in any sense, the cause of the other. We look only at the covariation or the degree to which they vary together. If one of the variables increases when the other does, we speak of a positive correlation; if it decreases when the other increases, we speak of a negative correlation; and if there is no systematic relation between the two variables, we describe this as a zero correlation. The degree of correlation is indicated by a coefficient which may vary from $+1.0$ to -1.0. These general possibilities are illustrated in Figure 8–3.

The method that is actually used to obtain a specific numerical value of the correlation coefficient depends upon certain assumptions. One of these assumptions is that the relationship between the two variables, X and Y, can be adequately described by a best fitting *straight line.* The way the best fitting line is obtained is by using the method of least squares to determine the slope of the line. This is done after all the scores are converted to z-scores to make all distributions comparable. Then two best fitting lines are determined, one with the deviations

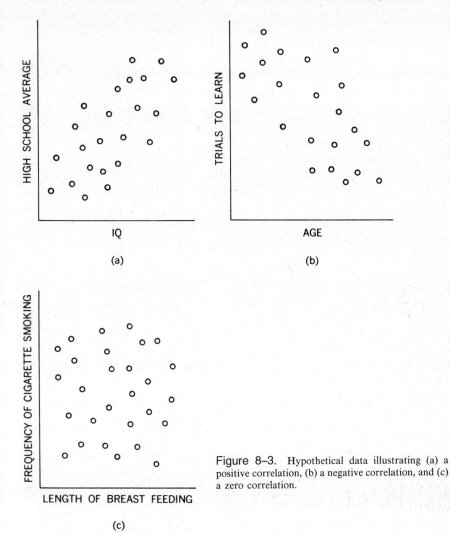

Figure 8–3. Hypothetical data illustrating (a) a positive correlation, (b) a negative correlation, and (c) a zero correlation.

minimized in relation to the X-axis, and the other with the deviations minimized in relation to the Y-axis. The correlation coefficient r is then simply the average of the two slopes (except that in this case, the geometric mean is used instead of the arithmetic mean).

The process described above would be quite tedious to compute, so several alternate, but equivalent formulas are used. If the data are conveniently arranged in z-score form, then

$$r = \frac{\Sigma z_x z_y}{N} \tag{8}$$

where N is the number of pairs of measurements and $\Sigma z_x z_y$ is the sum of the products of paired z-scores.

Unfortunately, data in z-score form are seldom available, so a computing formula based upon the original scores is typically used. This equation is

$$r = \frac{N\Sigma XY - (\Sigma X)(\Sigma Y)}{\sqrt{[N\Sigma X^2 - (\Sigma X)^2][N\Sigma Y^2 - (\Sigma Y)^2]}} \qquad (9)$$

N is again the number of paired measurements, ΣX and ΣY refer to the sum of the X- and Y-scores, ΣX^2 and ΣY^2 refer to the sum of the squares of the X- and Y-scores, and ΣXY is the sum of the products of all XY pairs.

The correct use of this formula, as well as most other correlation methods, depends upon the appropriateness of the assumption of linearity, that is, the extent to which a straight line is a best fit (as defined by the method of least squares) for the set of observations. Thus, concepts relevant to linear equations are basic to this important tool.

Linear Equations as Transformations

Another and equally important use of linear functions is in connection with the testing of theories and the evaluation of goodness of fit. This last expression means, among other things, that one kind of mathematical equation is more appropriate to observations than another; it describes them better because it "fits" the points more closely. To make this idea clearer, we shall examine a specific illustration.

Around the middle of the last century the German physicist G. T. Fechner proposed that there existed a simple relationship between the strength of a person's sensations and the intensity of stimuli that impinged upon his or her sense organs. Fechner suggested that the relation was logarithmic and that it could be expressed by the equation

$$S = k \log I \qquad (10)$$

where S was meant to represent the strength of a person's sensations, k was a constant which depended on the sense modality, and I was the intensity of the stimulus. The logarithm of a number is defined as the power to which the number 10 must be raised in order to produce that number. (The logarithm of 100 is 2 because $10^2 = 100$; the logarithm of 1,000 is 3 because $10^3 = 1,000$.)

If we examine Fechner's equation, we see that it implies that a person's sensations do not increase in strength in the same proportion as the external stimulus does. An increase in the external stimulus from 100 units to 1,000 units would only increase the strength of the sensation from 2 to 3 units (if k had a value of 1.0). If the external stimulus increased 1 million times, the sensation might increase only 6 times.

Although there was evidence that such a relationship might be true for some cases, there were enough discrepancies to prompt psychologists to look for other equations to represent the various findings.

One attempt along these lines has been made by Stevens (1957), who has suggested that the relationship between sensation S and the intensity I of the stimulus can be represented by a *power law* of the form

$$S = kI^n \tag{11}$$

where k is an arbitrary constant and n is another constant which depends on the sense modality and the individual subject.

Given these different equations, how does one go about deciding which is more appropriate to the experimental data? One of the major methods that is used is to transform the theoretical equation into the equation of a straight line and check for linearity of the observed data. This notion will now be explained.

The word *transformation* as used in mathematics refers to any procedure which systematically modifies a number or an equation. For example, if we have a set of numbers and we double each one, this is a simple transformation. Similarly, taking the square root or the logarithm of each number is a transformation. But this idea can be applied to equations as well as to numbers. If we have an equation such as $Y = 2X$, then we can transform the equation without altering its basic equivalence by performing the same operation on both sides. Thus $2Y = 4X$ or $\sqrt{Y} = \sqrt{2X}$ or $\log Y = \log (2X)$. So long as we use the same procedure on both sides of the equation, the equality remains.

Let us illustrate this point by reference to an equation of the form

$$Y = aX^b \tag{12}$$

This type of equation is referred to as parabolic or hyperbolic, depending on the value of the exponent b; it is also called a power function. Depending on the values of the constants, the curve may increase or decrease, but in all cases the curves gradually approach a plateau or *asymptote*.

It is possible to transform this equation into another useful form by means of a logarithmic transformation, that is, by taking the logarithm of both sides. This will yield $\log Y = \log (aX^b)$. This can be reduced still further on the basis of some rules governing the manipulation of logarithms, rules which are typically covered in any high school algebra course. For example, one rule says that the logarithm of a product ab is equal to the sum of the logarithms of each term, or $\log ab = \log a + \log b$. Another rule says that the logarithm of a number raised to a power ($\log X^a$) is equal to the power times the logarithm of the number, or $\log X^a = a \log X$.

We will now use these rules to simplify equation (12).

$$\log Y = \log (aX^b)$$

But since aX^b is the product of two terms a and X^b, we may write

$$\log Y = \log a + \log X^b$$

The term $\log X^b$ may be further reduced to $b \log X$ by the second rule governing the manipulation of logarithms. Thus the equation finally becomes

$$\log Y = \log a + b \log X \tag{13}$$

The equation $Y = aX^b$ when written in this form is actually the equation of a straight line. This will become evident if we substitute the letter Y' for log Y, a' for log a, and X' for log X. The equation may then be written

$$Y' = a' + bX' \tag{14}$$

This is quite obviously the equation of a straight line if we plot Y' against X'. In practice, this would mean plotting log Y against log X. The slope of the line which results is the constant b and the Y-intercept is actually equal to log a; from this a can be calculated.

To summarize the points made here: If we assume an equation of the form $Y = aX^b$, then we can transform this equation into a straight line form by taking the logarithms of both sides. If the experimental data actually conform to this equation, then by plotting the log of the X-values against the corresponding log of the Y-values, a straight line should result graphically. If it does not, then it means that the equation is probably inappropriate. This general procedure of transforming a complex equation into a straight line form is not limited to the one type of function described above but can be used with many different kinds of equations.

In the light of this discussion, it is evident that the equation suggested by Stevens is in a form which can be easily transformed into a straight line for testing. Given that

$$S = kI^n$$

then

$$\log S = \log k + n \log I$$

This means that if the so-called *power law* is true, when we plot the logarithm of the intensity *(I)* of the stimulus, against the logarithm of the subjective sensation S, we should find a straight line whose slope is n and whose Y-intercept is log k.

It is easy to measure the intensity of a physical stimulus such as a light or a sound, but how can we measure the intensity of a subjective sensation? Since this point will be discussed in detail in a later chapter, we simply note at this time that a rating scale method (magnitude estimation) can be used for evaluating the intensity of subjective sensations. In one study Stevens (1957) used a scale of 0 to 100 and required subjects to rate the intensity of their sensations. The physical stimuli were tones and lights of varying intensity. When the logarithms of both these sets of measurements were plotted, the results looked like those in Figure 8-4. The plotted values in both cases fall very nicely along straight lines, implying that the equation $S = kI^n$ is a very good summary of these data. Hence, the linear function plays a role in deciding on the appropriateness of complex theoretical equations for particular sets of observations.

We have thus seen that the straight line equation is a valuable tool (1) in summarizing data, (2) in correlational analysis, and (3) in testing the appropriateness of complex, theoretical equations for specific sets of data.

A Note on Constants

From a mathematical point of view it is always possible to calculate the constants that are used with a particular equation. Because the values of the constants depend upon the obtained data, they may vary from experiment to experiment. It is therefore always especially interesting when an investigator discovers the *same constant* appearing in several different situations. It suggests to him that there may be some common elements in the different situations that are worth exploring.

A long time ago chemists discovered that the product of the pressure and the volume of a gas is approximately constant if the temperature is fixed. Later it was found that the constant was itself the product of two other constants, one of which (Avogadro's) became a cornerstone of molecular theory. Similarly, the distance a body falls as a function of time t is given as $16t^2$. It was discovered that the constant 16 was actually one half of the gravitational constant g that appears in many different equations relating to the movements of physical bodies in space.

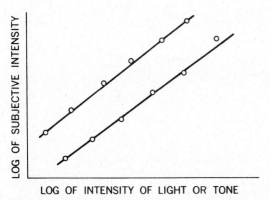

Figure 8–4. The logarithms of varying light or sound intensities are plotted against the logarithms of magnitude estimations of subjective intensity. (Adapted from S. S. Stevens, 1957.)

In Stevens' work, a wide range of values have been found for the constant n in the power law, ranging from 0.3 to 3.5. A study by Jones and Marcus (1961) has revealed large differences in the constants of the equation obtained from different individuals in the same test situation. They have therefore proposed that the constant n be considered as the product of two constants, one of which is to reflect the individual and the other the modality. If this program can be successfully implemented, perhaps a generalized constant will be found which is appropriate to many different situations.

A final point is that curve fitting is most useful in the context of a theory. This idea was stated in the quote introducing this chapter, and there is no better way to emphasize the point than to repeat part of it: "Purely empirical formulas should not be trusted too far from the data on which they are based. A good theory can help considerably."

9

Concepts of Causality in Experimentation

The scientific methodologies in the various sciences undergo continual change, and the mark of a successful investigator is that he can find novel methods of solving his problems.

—Alphonse Chapanis

The fact that there exist many different experimental design methods reflects the fact that there are many different kinds of problems. Experimental designs are basically ways of arranging the conditions of an experiment in order to identify relevant variables, and determine causes of events. Because causation is one of the key concepts involved in experimental design, it will be helpful to indicate briefly what is meant by this term.

The Concept of Causality

There have been many discussions by philosophers and scientists concerning the concept of causality and many subtle issues are involved. A few of the important notions will be described here.

In the eighteenth century, David Hume, a philosopher, presented a very important analysis of the concept of causality. He pointed out that there seem to be three important criteria that people use to judge (explicitly or implicitly) that one event is the cause of another. First, it is usually assumed that the cause and the effect are very closely related in space and time or are *contiguous.* One of the reasons that Newton's concept of gravitation was not immediately accepted is that his gravitational law seemed to imply some kind of action-at-a-distance. This idea was so completely inconsistent with the notion of causality accepted even by Newton himself that many physicists tried to develop modified gravitational theories that did not require this assumption.

Second, it is assumed that the *cause must precede the effect* in time. So strongly has this idea influenced scientists that the great French mathematician Laplace, early in the nineteenth century, claimed that if he could know the present conditions of the universe he could predict its future course for all time.

The third assumption often made in connection with the idea of causality is that there is a *necessary connection* between a cause and its effect. To understand this notion requires a definition of two important terms: *necessary* and *sufficient conditions.* When it is said that event A is necessary for event B to occur, it means that B cannot occur unless A has occurred, but it does not mean that B must occur whenever A occurs. This is because event A may be necessary for B but not sufficient; that is, other conditions must also be present. When it is said that event A is a sufficient condition for event B, it implies that A can cause B, but so can other events, C, D, E, etc. In other words, A is simply one "cause" among several possible ones.

To illustrate: suppose a man is injected with a drug which produces symptoms of hallucinations 30 minutes later. If this finding is a consistent one and can be shown to occur with great uniformity, then the drug is a sufficient condition for the production of hallucinations. It is, however, not a necessary condition, since other drugs could conceivably produce similar effects, and the effects may even occur in the absence of any known administrations of drugs, as in some psychotic patients. Is it possible to say what some necessary conditions are? In a general sense, this would mean such things as the fact that the subject is an adult who can verbalize his reactions, that he is in "normal" health, that the drug gets into the bloodstream so it may be distributed to various parts of the body including the brain, etc. Although each of these conditions may be necessary, none are sufficient in themselves to cause hallucinations. One may only *assume* that there is some basic biochemical reaction in the brain, which can be triggered by several different drugs or even by modifications of diet, or certain environmental conditions, which is both *necessary* and *sufficient* to cause hallucinations in an adult.

It should be obvious from this illustration that there is a big difference between finding some of the sufficient or necessary conditions which may affect some aspect of behavior and finding the one single necessary and sufficient condition. Typically, most research is concerned with finding sufficient conditions which affect various phenomena, while the so-called "basic, underlying cause," that is, the necessary and sufficient condition, is usually inferred, or developed, in a theory.

An interesting illustration of the ambiguity of the word *cause* is given by Morison (1960) in a discussion of the history of concepts concerning malaria.

Whatever the reason, medical men have found it congenial to assume that they could find something called *The Cause* of a particular disease. If one looks at the history of any particular disease, one finds that the notion of its cause has varied with the state of the art. In general the procedure has been to select as *The Cause* that element in the situation which one could do the most about. In many cases it turned out that, if one could take away this element or reduce its influence, the disease simply disappeared or was reduced in severity. This was certainly desirable, and it seemed sensible enough to say that one had got at the cause of the condition. Thus in ancient and medieval times malaria as its name implied was thought to be due to the bad air of the lowlands. As a result, towns were built on the tops of hills, as one notices in much of Italy today. The disease did not disappear, but its incidence and severity were reduced to a level consistent with productive community life.

At this stage it seemed reasonable enough to regard bad air as the cause of malaria, but soon the introduction of quinine to Europe from South America suggested another approach. Apparently quinine acted on some situation within the patient to relieve and often to cure him completely. Toward the end of the last century the malarial parasite was discovered in the blood of patients suffering from the disease. The effectiveness of quinine was explained by its ability to eliminate this parasite from the blood. The parasite now became *The Cause,* and those who could afford the cost of quinine and were reasonably regular in their habits were enabled to escape the most serious ravages of the disease. It did not disappear as a public health problem, however; and further study was given to the chain of causality. These studies were shortly rewarded by the discovery that the parasite was transmitted by certain species of mosquitoes. For practical purposes *The Cause* of epidemic malaria became the Mosquito, and attention was directed to control of its activities.

Entertainingly enough, however, malaria has disappeared from large parts of the world without anyone doing much about it at all. The fens of Boston and other northern cities still produce mosquitoes capable of transmitting the parasite, and people carrying the organism still come to these areas from time to time; but it has been many decades since the last case of the disease occurred locally. Observations such as this point to the probability that epidemic malaria is the result of a nicely balanced set of social and economic, as well as biological, factors, each one of which has to be present at the appropriate level. We are still completely unable to describe these sufficient conditions with any degree of accuracy, but we know what to do in an epidemic area because we have focused attention on three or four of the most necessary ones.

Research scientists in the laboratory constantly make interpretations about causes of things. How, in fact, is this done? Early in the nineteenth century John Stuart Mill, a British philosopher, described several general methods for establishing cause-effect relations. Mill tried to set down certain rules or canons that could be used as a basis for experimentally identifying causes. These methods should be understood since they provide a basis for understanding many of the currently used experimental design methods. Therefore, they will be briefly described and illustrated.

Method of Agreement

If several instances of some event being observed have only one circumstance in common, then that circumstance is the cause of the phenomenon. Thus, if a group of delinquent boys are all found to come from broken homes, it is sometimes said that the existence of broken homes is a "cause" of delinquency. This situation is like the frequently cited case of the man who wanted to find out in a "scientific" way, why he got drunk. The first night he drank rye and water and became drunk; the second night he drank scotch and water and became drunk; after getting drunk on bourbon and water the third night, he concluded that he had better give up water.

Obviously, in any complex situation there may be many more common factors present than the observer is aware of; and, in addition, a given effect may be produced by many different causes. Thus delinquency may be related not only to broken homes, but to economic status, value conflicts, possibilities of social mobility, or biochemical factors, any one or more of which may simultaneously be present.

The *method of agreement* is thus inadequate as a way of unequivocally identifying causes. However, it often provides a clue or suggestion about important variables to be looked at or examined in more experimental ways. Much of clinical practice, in both psychology and medicine, relies on this method, and at least in the case of psychoanalysis, a whole theoretical edifice has been erected on the basis of observations common to diverse patients. The existence of many rival schools and the frequent disagreements among practitioners attests, at least in part, to the unreliability of the method.

Method of Difference

If two situations differ in only one respect, and an effect is observed in one situation and not the other, then the effect is due to the factor which is different. In psychology this can be illustrated by experiments in which the investigator tries to equate two groups in as many respects as possible, and then subjects one of the groups to an experience or condition which is expected to influence some phenomenon being measured. For example, two groups of rats of an inbred strain may be established by separating litter mates randomly. One group is then required to learn a maze while under the influence of some drug; the other group learns the maze under identical conditions except that no drug is administered. If it turns out that maze-learning ability of one group is different from that of the other group, it is usually concluded that the difference is due to the drug (the one different factor).

Although this method is the basis for a great deal of experimental work in psychology as well as in the other sciences, it poses certain serious problems. For one thing, it requires that the two groups be equated, that is, equal in all respects at the start of the experiment. How can one know or justify this? Even a chemist working with two samples of a purified chemical knows that certain impurities exist in one that do not exist in the other, or do not exist to the same degree. This is much truer of complex biological organisms such as rats, monkeys, or humans, who differ not only in genetic endowment but in life experiences as well.

The answer usually given to this objection is that groups are equated not on all possible conditions, but only on *relevant variables,* that is, variables known or believed to influence the effect being measured. The problem then arises: how does one know what variables are relevant? This can only be determined by another experiment using the very method which one is trying to justify, and thus a vicious cycle is established.

A tentative answer to this dilemma can be given by pointing out that science develops only by a series of successive approximations. At any one point in the history of science, certain variables are judged to be of major relevance on the basis of experiments which are more or less limited. If at a later time inconsistencies appear or theoretical difficulties arise, it may require changes in the variables which are studied until a better approximation is obtained. This may be illustrated by the many studies of the *galvanic skin response,* or GSR. This term refers to the small electrical changes that take place in the skin under a variety of conditions. Two of the most outstanding characteristics of these reports are their inconsistency and variability. This is due not only to the great differences between subjects, but also to variations in instrumentation and methods of collecting and analyzing data. Such factors as electrode placement, type, size and pressure of electrodes, polarization effects, type of current (AC or DC), and amount of current, as well as the basal resistance of the subject, all have been found to affect the size of the GSR; thus the conception of what is a *relevant variable* has gradually been enlarged and may be taken into consideration in future research.

Similarly, it has been demonstrated that the effect of punishment on behavior depends upon such factors as the strength of the punishment, the time interval between the response and the punishment, and the strength of the response to be punished. It took a great deal of research to clearly identify even these factors and it is reasonably certain that there must be others as well. Thus, even if it were possible to take all of these factors into account in any one experiment, the results would still be tentative and conditional. It is in the nature of science to always proceed by successive approximations.

Joint Methods of Agreement and Difference

Sometimes, observations using the method of agreement will enable certain hypotheses to be formulated. An hypothesis is an assumption about a possible causal factor influencing some behavior. An experiment may then be performed using the method of difference in order to determine whether the hypothesized factor actually produces an observed change.

One of the contributions of the psychoanalytic movement was its emphasis on infantile determinants of later adult behavior. This hypothesis stemmed from clinical observations. Eventually, a number of studies using the method of difference were done with lower animals in an attempt to examine some of these hypotheses. Hunt (1941), for example, exposed a group of young rats to a feeding stress (i.e., limited access to food) during the first weeks of their lives, while another group of litter mates had unlimited access to food during the same period. In later adult life, when both groups were tested for hoarding behavior under a mild deprivation stress, the previously frustrated group was found to hoard significantly more. Many other similar attempts have been made to experimentally test hypotheses developed by clinical observations.

Method of Concomitant Variation

Mill stated this canon in the following way: "Whatever phenomenon varies in any manner whenever another phenomenon varies in some particular manner, is either a cause or an effect of that phenomenon, or is connected with it through some fact of causation."

In a sense, this method is an extension of the method of difference in that instead of two equal groups being used with a certain factor present or absent, three or more groups or conditions are used, and the factor being studied is varied over a range of values. Thus, in certain studies of learning, the length of a list of syllables is varied in order to determine the effect of length on recall, or changes in the brightness of a radar screen are made in order to determine its effect on the accuracy of identification of signals. All these kinds of studies are what are usually called functional or multivalent experiments.

Some writers have interpreted this canon as also including correlation studies in which "naturally occurring" variations in some condition are correlated against some other condition. This would be indicated by correlations between IQ and school grades, or childhood training practices and adult personality traits. Obviously, a simple correlation does not in itself give any adequate evidence for cause-effect relations. But, in general, when the method of concomitant variation is conceived as a functional type of experiment, it is more satisfactory than any of the other types thus far described. It is no surprise to discover that one of the signs of advancement in a science is an increasing use of this method in the form of multivalent experiments.

A review of this list of Mill's rules of experimental inference should make it evident that all are limited in one way or another and all involve certain assumptions which can never be completely met in practice. This is not a cause for despair; it simply reflects the fact that empirical science will *always* have an element of doubt in its findings and conclusions and will always be capable of extension and correction. As science progresses, however, we gradually move closer to an increasingly complete understanding of natural phenomena.

Other Methods for Identifying Causes

Since John Stuart Mill first formulated his canons, many extensions and developments have been made. The detailed application of these ideas to psychology will be the subject of a later chapter; at this point, however, one other general schema for identifying causes is pertinent. In a book dealing with research problems in the physical sciences, Wilson (1952) described various methods that can be used to identify causes of difficulty in equipment which does not work properly. These methods will be described here, using psychologically related illustrations.

Method of Artificial Variation

If a piece of equipment does not function properly, vary a *suspected* cause by an amount greater than normal and see if the troublesome effect correlates closely with these variations.

An example of this might be the following. Suppose an investigator wishes to determine the number of trials it takes to learn lists of nonsense syllables of a given length. He discovers that there is a great deal of variability in the results, not only from subject to subject but also from one list to another. After considering the matter, he suspects that a possible reason for the variability is that the nonsense syllables vary a lot in the degree to which they suggest actual words, a property called *association value.* Some lists seem to have many words with high association value and some have only a few such words.

Using the *method of artificial variation* as a guide, the experimenter makes up several lists with syllables which vary systematically in association value, and he then measures the number of trials it takes to learn each list. If he finds that this varies with association value, he concludes that it is possible that this factor produced the large variability in his original study.

This conclusion is at best tentative since there are several other alternatives. It is possible, for example, that although the large changes in association value that were actually tried may affect rate of learning, the smaller ones present in the original experiment may have had little to do with the variability of the findings. Even if association value is a real variable affecting learning, it may still be the wrong variable in this particular case.

Another problem that may arise with this method is that it is sometimes difficult or impossible to produce the artificial variations one believes are responsible for the effect. If it is suspected that changes of the weather affect moods or that childhood experiences of frustration affect an adult's frustration tolerance, it is extremely difficult to actually manipulate these suspected causes outside their normal range of variation in order to test the hypotheses. Thus, this method, although useful, is not without limitations.

Method of Stabilization

Another method for determining whether a suspected cause is operating in a given situation is to *reduce* the variation in the suspected cause. In the previously discussed example, if the experimenter suspects that the association value of the syllables varies from list to list, he might then prepare a series of lists which are deliberately made equal in association value. Of course, this has to be done by some independent method, using other subjects. If this can be done, and the variability in the data decreases, it is possible that this factor had originally produced the large variability. This, again, is not entirely certain, since other factors might have been varied in the new lists of syllables. The method, though useful, is never conclusive.

Method of Correlation

This method simply requires the recording of naturally occurring changes in a suspected variable and correlating them with changes in some observed effect. This kind of procedure is, of course, frequently used in psychology as well as in some other sciences. Some of the limitations have already been described, but a few additional comments will be made here.

One of the difficulties sometimes encountered in correlational studies is the existence of time lags between cause and effect which greatly obscure or minimize the correlation between them. This may be illustrated by studies concerned with the medical effects of new drugs. Not uncommonly the undesirable side effects do not occur immediately but only weeks or even years later, or they occur only under special circumstances. A case in point is thalidomide, one of the tranquilizers. A large number of people had used the drug without any apparent ill effects. Then it began to be noticed that pregnant women who had used it gave birth to defective infants. Subsequent research showed that the drug is relatively harmless for all users except pregnant women during a certain critical period. These complex relationships obscured any simple correlation between drug usage and side effects.

The other point to be made about correlation studies is an old one: correlation does not necessarily imply cause. If two events are causally related, then there will be a correlation between them, but a correlation between two events does not necessarily mean that they are causally related. In other words, a correlation is a *necessary* condition for causation but not a *sufficient* condition. However, correlation studies are valuable for suggesting hypotheses about possible causes which can be investigated by other design methods.

The Factorial Method

If several suspected factors are operating simultaneously to produce some observed change, it is possible to determine their relative contributions and interactions in the following way. Arrange to give each suspected variable a high and a low value. With three variables there are eight combinations possible. One observation is made under each of the eight conditions, and then the results for comparable high values and low values are averaged and compared.

To take a psychological illustration, suppose that an investigator studying the galvanic skin response (GSR) suspects that there are several sources of variability affecting the data: one is the size of the electrodes which are attached to the skin, another is the amount of current going through the subject, and the third is the subject's skin temperature. The experimenter then sets up an experiment in which eight observations are made as follows:

Conditions	Suspected Variables		
1	small electrode	low current	low skin temperature
2	small electrode	low current	high skin temperature
3	small electrode	high current	low skin temperature
4	small electrode	high current	high skin temperature
5	large electrode	low current	low skin temperature
6	large electrode	low current	high skin temperature
7	large electrode	high current	low skin temperature
8	large electrode	high current	high skin temperature

By averaging the four large electrode conditions and comparing the mean with the mean of the four small electrode conditions, the effect of electrode size on GSR may show itself in spite of fluctuations due to the other variables. The same can be done for the other two suspected variables. The evaluation can be carried out using the analysis of variance.

Although the factorial method is important and is being increasingly used in research, it does have some limitations. One kind of limitation concerns the choice of "high" and "low" values for each of the suspected variables. Since these terms are completely relative, the experimenter may make a choice which is not different enough to show an effect or, on the other hand, too different. This latter condition will occur if there is a U-shaped relation between the variable and the effect, as described in Chapter 4. In a sense the factorial method can be thought of as several bivalent experiments carried out simultaneously. It is a relatively efficient means for identifying relevant variables, but gives little information on the functional relation between the cause and the effect.

Summary

A number of different procedures have been suggested for identifying cause and effect relations. The basic ideas behind most of them were described over a century ago by John Stuart Mill, an English philosopher. These methods have been called: *the method of agreement, the method of difference, the joint methods of agreement and difference,* and *the method of concomitant variations.* Most experimental inquiry uses these methods in various guises. Each method has its limitations, and each provides only an approximation, more or less adequate, to the "truth."

10

Sources of Error and
the Nature of Controls

The study of error is not only in the highest degree prophylactic but it serves as a stimulating introduction to the study of truth. . . . We see vividly, as normally we should not, the enormous mischief and casual cruelty of our prejudices. And the destruction of a prejudice, though painful at first, because of its connection with our self-respect, gives an immense relief and a fine pride when it is successfully done.

—Walter Lippmann

Experimental design methods have the purpose of eliminating or minimizing sources of error or bias so that unequivocal causal connections can be established. It is therefore necessary to examine the nature and sources of bias in research before discussing the different kinds of procedures that have been developed to deal with them.

Since experiments are always performed to answer specific questions, a bias or source of error may be thought of as any fact or factor which contributes to an erroneous conclusion or which makes the conclusion ambiguous. Another way of describing error is to define it as any *unspecified* factor which affects one condition or one group of the experiment differently than others.

Errors may occur in connection with the overlooking of relevant variables, through inadequate analysis of data, through inadequate sampling procedures, through experimenter expectancies, and for other reasons. The following sections will illustrate some of the more important of these sources of bias.

Error Due to Overlooking Relevant Variables

A great deal of research in psychology, particularly in the field of learning, has been done using rats as subjects. Although certain important generalizations have been attempted, there have been many disagreements and conflicting reports concerning the findings of particular kinds of experiments. Some investigators have suggested that a possible explanation for the differing results is the fact that rats vary greatly in the experiences they have had before being used in an experiment. Many articles published in the literature dealing with learning do not mention the source of the rats used, the maintenance schedule, or the caging and handling procedures even though evidence has been accumulating that each of these factors has an influence on later learning performance. Thus it is possible that some of the contradictory findings in the literature are related to the variability of preexperimental treatment in different laboratories.

Another illustration of the need to identify and control relevant variables concerns the effect of early mother-child separation on the development of the child. Several clinical reports had appeared during the 1930s which remarked on the high frequency of delinquencies among children who had very disturbed relations with their mothers in their early years. Since retrospective clinical reports are subject to serious biases, several studies were begun to investigate this hypothesis. In the next two decades these studies reported that children raised in an institutional environment showed marked declines in indices of development during their first year of life and that children living in a residential treatment nursery showed more signs of behavior disturbance than a group in a day nursery. As research continued, however, it was seen that these findings were by no means consistently confirmed and that many children apparently show no signs of disturbance even though hospitalized at an early age. As a result, it was finally explicitly recognized that there are many relevant variables operating to affect child personality in addition to separation. The age at separation, the relationships to adults during the period of separation, the age at which substitution or replacement appears (if at all), as well as constitutional factors all seem to be relevant.

A final illustration comes from the recent research on the biochemistry of schizophrenia. In one experiment it was found that hospitalized schizophrenic patients tended to excrete less of a certain hormone in their urine than normal control subjects. It was hoped that this fact might provide a biochemical basis for distinguishing between them. A repetition of the experiment using control subjects on the same diet as a schizophrenic group showed no significant differences in the excretion of the hormone. Further observations seemed to indicate that control subjects, when on the same diet as schizophrenic subjects, did not differ from them in the amount of the hormone secreted.

What all this implies is that no research can be done adequately without knowing the relevant variables and taking them into consideration. Serious errors may enter into an experiment as a result of ignoring the influence of such variables. The more we know about the factors operating to affect a given phenomenon the more adequately can we plan research. This is why a literature review is so important *before* an experiment is done. Although at any time we may not know all the variables which may influence a measurement in which we are interested, we can still take into account those that are known and use design methods that tend to distribute unknown effects more or less equally. These methods will be described later.

Error Resulting From Inadequate Analysis of Data

It is surprising how often errors enter into an otherwise adequate experiment through errors in the analysis of data. There is first of all the more or less obvious matter of the need for computational accuracy. Until the 1940s there was a relatively infrequent use of statistical procedures beyond simple measures of central tendency and variability, and the clinical literature and even a sizeable part of the studies dealing with animal behavior tended to be largely descriptive. But as the science of psychology grew, more and more elaborate apparatus, experimental designs, and mathematical and statistical procedures were developed and put to use. With this increased sophistication has also come the greater possibility of computational errors. Computational and reporting errors are occasionally noted in the psychological literature. For example, Rosenthal (1978) reported on 21 published studies from which an estimate of the frequency of recording errors could be made. He found that about 1% of the observations were in error, and that two-thirds of the errors favored the hypothesis of the investigator. This important source of error can best be handled by having at least two experimenters analyze the data independently and check for consistency at each stage of the analysis.

Of far greater importance as a source of error associated with the analysis of data is the question of the adequacy and appropriateness of the statistical procedures used. Many published papers have demonstrated that statistical procedures are sometimes utilized incorrectly. For example, chi squares used to assess the significance of differences between expected and observed frequencies of events are often incorrectly applied, particularly when small numbers of cases are involved. In such situations, corrections for the small Ns must be made. Another problem that sometimes occurs is the determination of a large number of t-tests without adjustment of significance levels for chance findings. In other words, if 100 t-tests are computed, we would expect 5 of them to be significant at the 5% level simply on the basis of chance. In cases where many t-tests are obtained, the level required for significance should be made more stringent. Still another misuse of statistics occurs when three or more conditions are compared, and t-tests are used to evaluate the differences between each pair of conditions. In such cases an analysis of variance should always be computed first, and *ad hoc* comparisons made by appropriate procedures only if the F-test has been found to be significant. Other statistical misuses occur when factor analysis is computed with small numbers of subjects, or when less powerful techniques are used instead of more powerful ones (e.g., certain nonparametric tests rather than parametric ones). It is generally helpful for the less experienced investigator to consult with a statistician in order to avoid these kinds of problems.

Error Due to Inadequate Sampling

Since one of the aims of experimentation is to be able to make general statements on the basis of laboratory research, the question of adequate sampling naturally arises. If generalizations are to be made, then the subjects used must somehow represent in a known way the larger population to which data are to be related. This is often very difficult to do, and errors frequently enter into an experiment as a result of the sampling procedures. We may illustrate this point with several different kinds of examples. They will be kept brief since a detailed discussion of sampling problems has already been given in Chapter 5.

Many studies have reported that people who are willing to respond to mail questionnaires are usually different on a number of variables from those who do not respond. This has also been found in connection with the self-selection of male volunteers for the Kinsey study of sexual behavior (Maslow and Sakoda, 1952). Differences have also been reported between those who volunteer as subjects for hypnosis experiments and those who do not. At the National Institute of Mental Health, an evaluation of 83 subjects who had volunteered as normal control subjects for medical experiments showed that about half the members of the group had marked signs of psychiatric maladjustment (Perlin et al., 1958). Such findings have been reported with enough frequency in recent years to indicate that inadequate selection of subjects could become an important source of bias.

A related criticism has been raised about research in the area of propaganda. In a review of 34 attitude change experiments, one group of investigators found that 28 used college or other students as subjects. While this practice is quite common in psychological research, it may contribute error in studies of attitude change where the eventual aim is to apply the results to different social groups.

In 1969, Jung surveyed 52 universities about their practices and policies regarding the use of college students as subjects in psychological research. He found that of over ^80,000 students who participated in experiments, 80% were from introductory psychology classes. Only 2.3% of the students were from nonpsychology courses.

In addition, 93% of the college students participated in the research because such participation was required as part of course work or because it led to some special reward. Given the fact that volunteers differ from nonvolunteers on a number of characteristics (Bell, 1962; Jung, 1971), plus the highly selective nature of the subject population used in most research, it is evident that subject sampling biases exist and that generalizations to the general population are very limited.

Error Due to Experimenter Expectancies

In recent years, a number of experiments have been reported that have attempted to demonstrate that an experimenter's expectations may inadvertently affect the kind of results obtained. For example, in one study, psychology students in a laboratory course were themselves the unwitting subjects of the experimenter. Some of the students were told that the rats they would be experimenting with had been specially bred for intelligence as measured by maze-learning ability. Other students were told that their rats had been specially bred for dullness in maze-learning. The animals actually given to all the student experimenters were standard laboratory animals and were randomly assigned. The results seemed to demonstrate that those experimenters who believed their animals to be "bright" had rats who showed significantly faster learning than the other group (Rosenthal, 1963).

Most of the studies attempting to demonstrate experimenter expectancy effects have used the same task, one concerned with the judgment of facial expressions. The usual design is as follows: student experimenters, usually students taking a laboratory course in experimental psychology, are assigned the job of testing other students on a so-called test of empathy. The test consists of 20 photographs of different individual faces, and the Ss are to rate each photo, using a $+10$ to -10 scale, on the extent to which the person in the photograph has been experiencing "success" or "failure."

Unknown to the student experimenters, most of the photographs have been previously rated as neutral, or zero. An attempt is then made to bias the student experimenters by instructing half of them to expect their subjects (i.e., the other students) to produce a mean rating of $+5$. The other half of the student experimenters are biased to expect a mean rating of -5 from their subjects. Such biases are created presumably by telling the student experimenters that these findings have been previously obtained and are well established, and that this study is an attempt to replicate these findings.

In many of the studies using this technique, experimenter expectancy effects have been obtained, while in others they have not (Barber et al., 1969). In addition, such effects have not usually been found in studies using other types of tasks, for example, the Rorschach test, reaction time studies, and interviews (Jung, 1971).

These apparent discrepancies have led to an exchange of views between Rosenthal (1968), who has been most involved in demonstrating expectancy effects, and Barber and Silver (1968), who have been critical of the usual interpretations of most of the pertinent studies. In 1968, Barber and Silver critically reviewed 31 published studies supposedly showing experimenter expectancy effects and concluded that most did not clearly demonstrate the phenomenon. They further claimed that "in those instances in which the effect was obtained, it was apparently due to one or more of the following: the student experimenters misjudged, misrecorded, or misreported the results; they verbally reinforced their subjects for 'expected' responses; or they intentionally or unintentionally transmitted their expectancies and desires by paralinguistic or kinesic cues."

In a follow-up paper, Barber (1973) discussed the expectancy effect in a broader context and described a number of additional sources of error that should be seriously considered in the conduct of research. In this paper he distinguished between the role of investigator and experimenter; the investigator designs the experiment, trains the experimenters, analyzes and interprets the data, and prepares the final report. The experimenter is the person who actually tests subjects and records their responses. Sometimes the investigator and the experimenter are the same person, but often they are not.

It is important to recognize that some sources of error relate to the investigator, some to the experimenter, and some to both. The following list, based on

Barber's analysis, describes the various sources of potential error related to experimenter expectancies.

1. Sometimes the experimenter's expectancies are unintentionally communicated to *S*s by tone of voice, facial expressions, etc., so that they influence the responses of *S*s.

2. Even when the protocol, or procedures of an experiment, are clearly specified, the experimenter may not always follow these procedures exactly. Friedman (1967) has shown that experimenters vary in the way they greet their *S*s, in the way they read instructions, and in the way they carry out the experiment. In the study of "bright" and "dull" rats cited previously, it was found that some of the experimenters prodded the rats to get them to run faster (Rosenthal and Fode, 1963).

3. A number of studies have shown that experimenters sometimes make mistakes in recording their data or in summarizing or transcribing scores, and that such errors tend to be in line with the experimenter's desires.

In addition to these errors created by expectancies, Barber lists several other possible sources of error:

1. Sometimes the investigator fails to describe to the experimenter exactly what he is to do, so that different *S*s are not treated in a standardized way. If the experimenters interact with different *S*s in different ways, biased data can result.

2. Errors can result from inadequate analysis of data. A common error in this regard is to perform a large number of statistical tests, but to report only the few significant ones. Occasionally, gross errors are made in the computations or interpretations, as Wolins (1962) has shown.

3. The motivation to find "significant" results and to publish is sometimes so great that a few instances are known where investigators have fudged their results (DuShane et al., 1961).

4. Sometimes the personal attributes of the experimenter (such as his sex or skin color) may affect the responses of the *S*s.

5. Experimenters have also been known to falsify data. For example, Azrin et al. (1961) discovered, inadvertently, that when an experiment was almost impossible to carry out, a number of experimenters actually completed the study either by changing the procedures or by making up the data.

It is thus evident that there are many pitfalls or potential sources of error in experimental research. Barber suggests a number of remedies for these problems, including the following: (1) less emphasis on "positive" results in the training of researchers; (2) closer check by investigators to see that experimenters faithfully implement experimental protocols; (3) use of double-blind procedures as much as possible. This means, in essence, that the experimenter who does have direct contact with the subject should not know, if possible, what outcome is expected. In drug studies this is done through the use of coded but otherwise unidentified drugs and by use of placebos, that is, neutral materials such as plain water. Rosenthal (1964), in proposing remedies for these problems, also recommends that contact between the experimenter and the subject should be kept minimal, for example, by using tape-recorded instructions. In addition, he notes that replication of experimental results by different investigators is one of the best ways of dealing with inadvertent biases. Barber concludes: "There are so many pitfalls in any one experimental study, that we should not take any one study too seriously. The results of any one experiment should be replicated by a variety of investigators who hold different paradigms or theories, before they are accepted as an integral part of the area of inquiry."

Although these cautions should be taken seriously, it is worth remembering that there is little evidence that well-trained experimenters using well-structured experimental tasks produce results contaminated by their expectancies or other major sources of error (Stewart, 1971). In addition, to the extent that errors do occur, it is time that investigators went beyond the mere demonstration of this fact and tried to systematically measure the magnitude of such effects.

Errors Due to the Use of Secondary Sources

There is one other source of bias which is not often mentioned, and which occurs to an unknown degree. This bias is related not to the experiment itself but rather to the way it is reported and the way that information about the study is disseminated in the scientific literature.

An interesting illustration of this source of bias is the reporting of the famous Hawthorne research that led to the well-known "Hawthorne effect." In 1924 the Western Electric Company began a series of studies in its Chicago plant to determine the effect of a number of variables such as room illumination, rest periods, hours of work, use of fans in summer, piecework payment, and use of a friendly supervisor instead of an authoritarian foreman. The studies were continued until 1932. The results were first reported in a 12-paragraph news summary in 1927 and a Western Electric memorandum (now unavailable). Based on this limited information a description and interpretation of the results was published in 1939 and modified and repeated in hundreds of reports and textbooks since that time (Parsons, 1974).

The general description of the results of the Hawthorne studies is that the girls who were inspecting parts and assembling relays and coils worked progressively faster regardless of increases or decreases in illumination, and regardless of changes in most of the working conditions. Interpretations of these supposed findings usually relied on the concepts of "morale," "cohesiveness," "attention" and the like.

However, in two detailed reviews of the evidence that is available, Parsons (1974, 1978) has documented two basic conclusions that have been almost universally overlooked. The first is that the productivity of the workers did not *rise* under all conditions. The second is that the productivity *did* rise under two sets of conditions; namely, when the workers received daily feedback information on their productivity, and when the workers were rewarded with a new piecework system that allowed them to earn more money than most of the other workers in the factory. In the words of Parsons, "The unsuspected culprit at Hawthorne was information feedback, and its accomplice was differential monetary reward." It appears that incorrect information and interpretations were circulated for many years on the Hawthorne effect. The basis for this error is an uncritical reliance on secondary sources; one effect of it is to create experimental hypotheses which are not based on research findings.

The Need for Controls

The illustrations given have indicated how many different possible sources of error there are in connection with research. Problems of bias are by no means confined to psychology but are more or less general and are relevant to all sciences. Even a cursory examination of the history of science would show how many erroneous conclusions have been drawn as a result of unrecognized sources of error. In medical research we find the same problems. To illustrate: an analysis of 100 consecutive articles in a medical journal, dealing with a procedure or a type of therapy, revealed that 45% of the studies made no attempt to compare the results of the specific therapy with results obtained from a control group. In an additional 18% the control used was judged as inadequate (Ross, 1951). A similar review of the studies reported in 11 psychiatric journals led to the same conclusions.

To be able to draw meaningful conclusions from research, the source of bias must be dealt with in some manner. In general, the problem of bias may be approached in three possible ways: (a) sources of error may be *avoided,* (b) the effects of error may be *distributed* evenly among the various conditions being measured, or (c) the error may be *measured* and its relative contribution evaluated. *One of the purposes of experimental design methods and controls is to accomplish one or more of these aims.*

The Nature of Controls

The word *control* has come into use relatively late in the history of science and has already acquired several different meanings.

Examples of controlled experiments are recorded at least as far back as 1648 when Pascal showed that the height of a column of mercury in a tube was dependent upon the altitude. The controls he exercised in this case were examination of the height of a mercury column at several places along a mountain path, and regular checking of a similar tube at the foot of the mountain.

By 1843, John Stuart Mill had made implicit the notion of control, primarily in the sense of a verifying check. In the 1870s the word control began to be used in the sense of a standard of comparison in regard to which a difference may occur, and by 1893, the New English Dictionary defined control as "a standard of comparison used to check the inferences deduced from an experiment by application of the Method of Difference." Darwin had used the word control in an 1875 publication also in the sense of a standard of comparison to describe some of his experimental studies of insectivorous plants.

In psychology the word control was used in the sense of a calibration by Wundt in the 1870s, and several other investigators of psychological problems used controls in their experiments. By 1901 Thorndike and Woodworth had recognized the need for a control group in experimental studies of transfer of training, but it was not until 1908 that control groups began to be used for the first time. In 1933, 11% of the articles in psychological journals indicated that control groups had been used, and in 1951, 52% of the studies used control groups. Over the same period there has also been an increase (although less consistent) in the use of control observations.

This brief survey has shown that the word control has been used primarily in the sense of a basis of comparison between two or more conditions or two or more groups. Another way of saying this is that the control represents a reference point in relation to which a comparison is made. If, for example, an investigator is concerned with the effect of drugs on behavior or IQ, then a condition without drugs would represent a reference point or norm against which to evaluate a change.

Controls, however, have been used in at least two other senses in experimental research. One sense refers to the manipulation of variables or conditions; that is, we control the independent variable in an experiment by causing it to change in a specified and known manner. We might control the amount of deprivation in an experiment on drive, the meaningfulness of a list of syllables in a study of transfer, or the type of verbal reinforcement in a study of verbal conditioning.

The other meaning of the term control is in the sense of restraint of variables or the keeping of constant conditions. Just as we manipulate certain variables in an experiment, an attempt is made to keep all other relevant variables constant. In a study of visual sensitivity in humans, for example, the color and size of the light stimulus as well as the position of the eye are kept constant. Quite typically, head and chin rests are used to keep the head steady, sometimes even a mouth bite is used to further prevent movement, and a fixation point or circle is generally put into the visual field. All these procedures plus some constant (or control) period of dark adaptation are used to maintain all variables known to be relevant at constant values. In human learning studies, the variables kept constant in most cases include the type of material, the amount of practice, and the distribution and length of trials.

From these illustrations it should be evident that the factors kept constant or controlled are the very factors which can affect the variable being measured. But since it is not possible to know *all* the variables which can operate at any given moment, we can only control those factors which we believe are relevant to the research at hand and this, in turn, depends, at least in part, on the state of knowledge in the field. As the illustrations cited earlier in this chapter have shown, a frequent source of error in research is the overlooking of relevant variables and the failure to control them in the sense of keeping them constant. The use of controls, therefore, presupposes considerable knowledge.

In summary we may note that the word control has been used in at least three different ways: (a) as a reference or comparison point, (b) in the sense of manipulation of independent variables, and (c) in the sense of restraint or the keeping constant of variables not under investigation. Therefore, in the broadest sense, *controls are procedures used in research which are designed to limit probable sources of error.*

One further point should be made: the very fact that sources of error exist and that inadequate controls are used in research implies that it is not always obvious to the investigator what variables require controlling or how the control may be carried out. This depends partly on knowledge of the field under investigation, on general knowledge of research designs, on economy or feasibility in terms of time or money, and on the ingenuity and imagination of the investigator. It should be evident also that these problems are by no means limited to the field of psychology but apply to all experimental science.

Ways of Handling Error

This chapter will conclude with some illustrations of ways of dealing with error in research. As was pointed out earlier, there are three general approaches: (a) to avoid the source of error, (b) to distribute the error, or (c) to measure the amount of error.

If the problem being investigated, for example, is whether a certain type of drug produces a persistent drop in blood pressure in hypertensive patients, it is recognized that several possible factors may produce such an effect in addition to the drug being studied. One of these factors is the doctor-patient relationship. The importance of this relationship is demonstrated by a study which found that the attitude of the physician affected efficacy of the drug when the physician administered *known* hypotensive (i.e., blood-pressure reducing) agents. During the period when an observer classified the physician's attitude as enthusiastic, the drug produced a marked decrease in blood pressure, but when the physician's attitude was classified as unenthusiastic or negative, the drug effects were much smaller. The way to *avoid* this source of error is to use a double-blind design, that is, the administration of the drug, and placebos of identical appearance, in a sequence unknown to both the patient and the doctor.

Although the double-blind technique has been widely cited as a panacea for problems of experimenter bias in drug research, it has a number of limitations. For example, in many cases drugs produce side effects that are easily noticed by the experimenters. These side effects eliminate the blind condition and presumably enable the experimenters' expectations to affect their judgments. Since differential side effects are an almost universal concomitant of any therapeutically useful drug, it is practically impossible to keep an observant investigator really blind to the medication being used.

In addition, there are certain research situations where the double-blind cannot be used. For example, if a standard treatment such as electroconvulsive (shock) therapy is being compared with a new antidepressant drug, it is impossible to keep this information blind to either the patient or the experimenter.

Finally, it should be noted that even when the double-blind approach is ideally used, it does not guarantee unequivocal results. Cromie (1963) has shown clearly that there are many ways in which research can be in error or misleading even when the double-blind is used. For example, the use of fixed drug doses rather than individual adjustment of dosage for each patient may underrate the value of the drug and cause no differences to appear between the effects of the drug and those of the placebo.

Similarly, if drugs with different time-courses of effect are compared at a fixed point in time, the differences between the two drugs may be overgeneralized in favor of one of them. In other words, the optimum effect for one drug might occur earlier than that of the other but be less in overall magnitude. Another example given by Cromie concerns the period over which the drug effect is assessed. Patients who were required to evaluate retrospectively the degree of relief of arthritic pain over a two-week period reported no difference between the drug and the placebo. However, when assessments were made of brief periods associated with the time of action of single doses, the drug was found to be superior to the placebo.

These examples have been presented to illustrate research problems that the double-blind does not eliminate. In fact, Beck (1967) showed that different reviews of double-blind studies of antidepressants indicated substantial disagreements. These disagreements were apparently related to such factors as level of significance used for evaluation of results, drug dosages used, size of groups, and type of populations.

When the double-blind technique cannot be reasonably used for a particular research project, there are several alternatives that are available to deal with potential sources of error. One alternative is to distribute the bias, a second is to measure it, and a third is to exaggerate it. Details about the application of these procedures to drug research may be found in Plutchik et al. (1969).

In learning experiments it is often necessary to *distribute* errors that occur in the experiment over two or more conditions. To illustrate this, let us suppose an experimenter wishes to investigate the ability of an observer to learn nonsense syllables in lists of different lengths. The experimenter will usually present the subject with several conditions, each of which is identical except for the length of the lists. Since the ability to learn this kind of task is affected by practice and experience, the conditions that come later in the experiment would be more affected by practice than those that come earlier. The way this variable is usually controlled is to present the conditions in random or counterbalanced order; while this does not eliminate the practice variable, it does distribute any practice effects equally over all conditions.

The problem of the measurement of amount of error is particularly evident when various types of equipment are used as part of the research. If, for example, a timer is utilized, the manufacturer will usually indicate how precise the timer is by specifying a tolerance range. It might be stated that the timer measures to the nearest $\frac{1}{10}$ of a second plus or minus one $\frac{1}{50}$ of a second. This tolerance range represents the possible error associated with any recorded time value. Frequently the error is stated as plus or minus 3% or some other specified value. This kind of error cannot be avoided; in such a case it is sufficient to *measure* it and include it in the reported findings. Such an estimate should be made, as far as possible, whenever any equipment is being used, whether it be electronic, mechanical, or optical.

Summary

This chapter has attempted to show that sources of error operate in many different ways in experimental work. It has illustrated how errors may arise in the analysis of data, or by overlooking relevant variables, or through inadequate sampling, for example.

The concept of control was explored and shown to have several meanings as used in contemporary psychological research. Illustrations were given of how sources of error may be avoided, distributed, or measured. An important notion that was considered is that the development of adequate controls depends to a large degree on the state of knowledge that the experimenter has acquired in relation to a given problem.

11

Experimental Design Methods

Owing to the historical accident that the theory of errors, by which quantitative data are to be interpreted, was developed without reference to experimental methods, the vital principle has often been overlooked that the actual and physical conduct of an experiment must govern the statistical procedure of its interpretation.

—Ronald A. Fisher

The expression *experimental design* may be defined in several ways. On the one hand, experimental designs are thought of as ways of arranging the conditions of an experiment in order to answer the questions we are concerned with. These questions generally deal with the identification of relevant variables, the determination of causes of events, and the evaluation of conditions in order to produce an optimum result. These aims, however, are statements of ideals or goals, and it is not always easy to achieve them in practice. On the other hand, experimental design methods have the purpose of eliminating or minimizing sources of error or bias so that unequivocal causal connections can be established.

This chapter will describe some of the more commonly used design methods and will indicate the kinds of difficulties that may attend their use. The methods to be described are not simple rote formulas into which experimental groups can be neatly plugged and answers run off by computer. On the contrary, there are often difficult decisions to be made concerning which of a number of alternate designs should be used. Since only a minimal amount of statistical background is presupposed of the reader, the analyses will be largely qualitative.

The Random Groups Design

This design method is basically the same as Mill's *method of difference* described earlier. Ideally, in this design two large groups are selected randomly from some defined population, and one of the groups is subjected to the experimental treatment (e.g., reinforcements, drugs, teaching methods, shock, and so on). Both groups are then tested on one or more measures to see if there are any differences. Symbolically, the procedure is as follows:

Random group 1   Experimental treatment   Test
Random group 2   No treatment   Test

The group given no treatment is usually called the control group; it represents a reference level for deciding if the experimental treatment had any effect.

The basic assumption of the random groups design is that the random selection procedure will produce groups which are alike initially and which do not differ, on the average, on any variables which are likely to affect the behavior which is to be measured. This is a reasonable assumption to make theoretically, but from a practical point of view, it rarely happens that all its prerequisites are met.

For this method to enable us to make generalizations to a large population, a basic population must be defined and two random samples taken from it. If the population of interest is all the schizophrenics in a mental hospital, then the samples should be selected randomly from the entire hospital and should not be simply a group of convenient or tractable patients. If the population of interest is all the students in one college, then a couple of classes is not a random sample. These considerations are even more relevant if the population of interest is all the schizophrenics in the United States in 1980, or all college students.

Even if the assumptions are met initially, difficulties often arise because subjects are lost during the course of the experiment and/or because experimental or control groups, if small, are not always equivalent. This problem of loss of subjects sometimes arises in certain types of educational research. In recent years the problem of the "underachiever" has prompted a number of experiments which have tried to show the effect of some educational procedure on underachievers. The basic design is simple. Two groups of underachievers are chosen on some criteria, and one is exposed to a special educational environment for a period of time. Both groups are then tested on various measures to see if any significant differences have appeared.

Thorndike (1963) has pointed out that the simplicity of the design is deceptive and may cause investigators to overlook some important possible sources of error. For one thing, the special attention given to the experimental group is likely to increase the motivation of those students relative to the ones in the control group. Second, it is quite likely that a certain number of students will drop out of the program so that the ones who complete it are a biased sample of the initial group.

Sometimes the random groups method has been interpreted to mean that several large intact groups are selected to represent the experimental and control groups. For example, one class of students might be exposed to a massed learning condition while another class would be exposed to a distributed condition. Although the results might show that the groups did not differ initially on the learning task, the method of choosing the groups is still questionable. This is because the classes might differ on other relevant factors, such as motivation or age, which could modify the rate of improvement even though they did not affect initial level of performance. As an alternative, the random placement of subjects into the various groups presumably distributes all relevant factors equally.

This problem connected with the use of intact groups can be illustrated by reference to a clinical study (Brockway et al., 1954) concerned with EEG differences in several groups. In this study, 40 patients whose dominant symptom was anxiety were compared on a variety of EEG and personality measures with several groups of normal subjects. However, instead of simply using a single control group of subjects who were convenient, they obtained data on four different normal groups. Group 1 was a miscellaneous collection of young men, mostly from a local National Guard unit ($N = 59$); Group 2 consisted of Army officers ($N = 30$); Group 3 was university students ($N = 38$); and Group 4 consisted of seminary students ($N = 39$). The officers and patients had a median age around 29 years, while the median age for the other 3 groups was about 21 years. The four nonpatient groups were paid volunteers with no history of psychiatric illness.

Analyses of variance of results for the four normal control groups showed they differed significantly on Rorschach anxiety and maladjustment ratings, on figure drawing maladjustment ratings, on vocabulary mental age, and on several other measures. Some of the control groups were not significantly different from the patients on some of the measures. The distribution of overall EEG patterns was about the same in all the groups, but the amount of alpha (10 cps) activity was greater in the controls. The authors of the study drew two general conclusions: (1) "controls from different occupational, social, and economic sources may vary greatly in their psychiatric and psychological characteristics and thus a single source cannot be considered a random sample of the normal population"; (2) the fact that certain responses frequently occur in an abnormal population does not necessarily mean they are pathological since certain normal control groups will also show these same responses to the same degree.

Although this study is not an experimental one in the sense that the different groups were not exposed to various new conditions and their responses measured, it does suggest an important point. If the aim of an experiment is to enable generalizations to populations larger than the actual one used in the experiment, then some sort of random selection or random assignment of subjects is necessary.

The examples given have been chosen to suggest that the random groups design method as it is actually used in practice is no certain method for identifying variables or establishing causal relations. In summary, the main reasons for this are (1) groups used in research are not often random samples; (2) some studies lose a certain number of subjects during the course of the experiment; and (3) when the random groups design is used in a bivalent study, it shares in the various difficulties already described in Chapter 4.

These are practical difficulties which do not necessarily imply that the design method is at fault. On the contrary, when randomization is carefully used for the selection and assignment of subjects, and relatively large numbers are used, it is one of the best methods for enabling generalizations to be made.

In order to deal with the problems connected with bivalent experiments, the basic solution is to expand the number of randomly selected groups used and to expose each to a different value of the independent variable, in some such fashion as follows:

Random group 1	No treatment	Test
Random group 2	X amount of treatment	Test
Random group 3	$2X$ amount of treatment	Test
Random group 4	$3X$ amount of treatment	Test
Random group 5	$4X$ amount of treatment	Test

The different amounts of treatment refer to different levels of the independent variable, although obviously the amounts need not be exactly those listed as X, $2X$, $3X$, etc. Any increasing set of values could be used.

In analyzing the data of an expanded random group (multivalent) design, two general approaches are used. One is the analysis of variance which has been described in Chapter 7. The other involves plotting the data on a graph and finding the type of curve which best fits the points. This latter method has been outlined in Chapter 8. In general, the expanded random groups design is much to be preferred over the simple two group design, but in any case, generalizations should depend upon the congruence of results from many experiments.

Matched Groups Design

A design often used in psychological research is one based upon matched groups rather than random groups. This design eliminates some of the sampling problems mentioned previously, but it creates other problems instead. As an example, experiments concerned with transfer of training may be considered. Although there are a number of different approaches, one frequently seen uses a matched groups design somewhat as follows:

	Pretest on	Training on	Retest on
Control group	A	—	A
Experimental group	A	B	A

Assume that task A is mirror tracing with the right hand (i.e., tracing a complex pattern by means of a mirror image) and that task B is training on the same pattern with the left hand.

Equating on the pretest *A* is usually done by giving a group of subjects one trial on the *A* task and recording the amount of time it took each subject to trace the complete pattern. The subjects are then ranked and two groups are created such that the mean performance time and standard deviation of the performance times are as close as possible.

Once this is done (and it may sometimes take days or weeks to get the initial trial on a large number of subjects), the subjects in the experimental group return to the laboratory for the training trials on *B*. Then both groups are retested on the original *A* task. The amount and direction of transfer depends on the difference in performance between the experimental and control groups on the retest.

In actual practice, matching of groups may be done in four other ways.

Matching on Correlated Variables. Sometimes the matching is done not on the task being studied, but on some other task or variable believed to be related to the one under investigation. Thus, in the example given for transfer of training, the subjects might be matched on some pattern other than the one finally tested, although a task would be chosen which produced performance scores correlated with those on task A. Sometimes the subjects are matched on several other variables (age, sex, education, etc.) believed to be correlated with the task performance to be measured.

Matching by Pairs. In some studies matching is effected by selecting out pairs of subjects with similar characteristics. For example, in twin studies one member of each pair of twins might be assigned randomly to the experimental group, the other to the control group. In educational research, in order to take into account variations among teachers, two students (or some multiple of two) might be selected from each of a number of classes, with the students from each class matched on age, sex, or achievement level. This kind of matching will always produce groups of equal size. When matching on mean and standard deviation, it is not necessary that the experimental and control groups be of equal size.

Matching by Yoked Control. A number of studies have been reported in recent years which have used a special type of matching procedure called the yoked control. One such study was an attempt to solve a problem created by a prior experiment in which rats who were hungry and thirsty were given an electric shock whenever they tried to eat or drink. Under these conditions, they developed more ulcers than rats in an unshocked control group (Sawrey and Weisz, 1956). The problem raised by this experiment is that the ulcers might have been due to the electric shock per se, or they might have been due to the severe conflict set up between the desire for food and the desire to avoid the shock. What was needed was a control group of rats that experienced the same magnitude and temporal sequence of shocks, but which had little or no conflict.

Such a study was reported by Brady (1958) using a yoked control design. In this experiment monkeys were trained to press a lever to avoid an electric shock which was automatically delivered to the animals' feet every 20 seconds. The shock could be avoided if the monkey pressed the lever at least once in each 20-second interval. This technique is usually learned quickly by monkeys, and they continue to press the lever at a fairly regular rate; only occasionally do they miss a 20-second period and thus get a shock.

Monkeys who did this on a schedule of 6 hours "on" and 6 hours "off" (i.e., rest) developed ulcers. Therefore, to check on the possibility that the ulcers resulted from the shock rather than from the frustration associated with having to avoid it, another monkey was "yoked" to the first. It sat in a restraining chair which was exactly the same as that of the other monkey, but only the experimental subject could control the onset or frequency of shocks. Any shocks that did occur were delivered to both animals simultaneously. Thus the control animal had the same number of shocks and in the same sequence as the experimental animal, but it was not involved in the conflict. The yoked animal did not develop ulcers. Although these results have not been replicated, the study illustrates the yoked control design.

Matching on a Performance Criterion. The first method of matching described, which was in terms of mean and standard deviation, has at least one obvious limitation. If only one trial is given on the matching task, it is quite likely that large individual differences will be found. If all subjects are used, then it may turn out that large variabilities occur, which in turn increase the unreliability of the data and make the matches less adequate on subsequent trials. For this reason many experimenters will use two or three trials as a basis for matching and may even eliminate subjects whose initial performance is too different from that of the rest of the group.

There is, however, an alternative method for matching that has been used occasionally (Lewis et al., 1952). This involves testing the subjects until they reach a predetermined performance level within a predetermined number of trials. For example, on the basis of a pilot run it might be decided that the performance level for matching on the mirror tracing task is to be 60 seconds ± 5 seconds, and that this criterion is to be reached within three trials. If a subject reaches the criterion (55–65 seconds) on the first, second, or third trial, he stops and then goes on to the next task (the *B* task if he is in the experimental group). As subjects reach the criterion, they are randomly distributed to the two groups. If any subject does not reach the criterion performance in the three trials, or if he exceeds the tolerance limits on any of the three trials, he is simply not used in the experiment.

This method has three advantages: (1) The groups are equated both in terms of the number of trials to reach a criterion as well as in terms of the criterion level reached; therefore, implicitly, their learning curves are matched; (2) Equating at a fixed performance level ensures that the variability of the data is very small and increases the chances that the equality of groups will continue on subsequent trials; (3) Since the performance criteria are selected in advance, it is unnecessary with this approach to postpone the experiment while means and standard deviations are being computed after a certain trial. If the experimenter wishes, each subject can be run through the entire experiment without waiting for the results of other subjects to come in.

Advantages and Limitations of the Matched Groups Design

One of the principal advantages of the matched groups design is that it tends to eliminate any ambiguity about whether the groups are equal or not at the start of an experiment. Whereas the random groups design usually requires large numbers of subjects to ensure equality, matching can often produce reliable differences between control and experimental groups with Ns as small as 5 or 10. Generally speaking, matching on a pretest reduces variability because it creates a correlation between the groups on the measures which are later compared; experimental effects can therefore be identified more readily. Tests of significance based on matched groups have a smaller standard error due to the existence of this correlation. The formula for the standard error of the difference between means for correlated data depends upon the type of matching procedure that has been used. But in all cases the larger the correlation r due to matching, the smaller the number of cases needed to show a significant difference; or alternately, the larger the r, the smaller a difference in means necessary for the detection of significance.

Despite these advantages of the method, there are also some limitations. One minor disadvantage is that in most cases the procedure usually requires a lapse of time between the actual matching, ranking, and establishment of groups, and the conduct of the rest of the experiment. The longer the wait, the less adequate the matching is likely to be simply because of the possible unreliability of any test score.

A second problem with matching is that it sometimes creates inequalities of which the experimenter is unaware. For example, suppose we wanted to compare a group of schizophrenic patients with a group of normal individuals on a memory test, and we matched the two groups on an IQ test. If, however, schizophrenics in fact have lower IQs on the average than do normal individuals, then the matching procedure will be implicitly selecting the relatively brighter schizophrenics and matching them with the relatively less bright normals. This will mean that neither group will then be particularly representative of its larger population.

A third problem concerns the yoked control design. Church (1964) has criticized the method on the grounds that it does not control for the effects of individual differences. To illustrate his point, we may take the experiment mentioned earlier on the production of ulcers in monkeys. In any given pair of monkeys, it is quite possible that either the control animal or the experimental animal is much more sensitive to the effects of shock than is his yoked mate. If such is the case, then it is possible that one of the monkeys will develop ulcers before the other and that this will not be due to the conflict in the situation, but simply to the shock. However, if large numbers of pairs are used, and assignment to each pair is random, then consistent results in favor of one group probably indicates a real effect.

Another problem with the yoked control design is that the procedure in many cases does not allow control over the number and distribution of stimulus events. It is quite possible for one experimental monkey to allow many shocks to be given to its yoked control and for another experimental monkey to allow very few shocks to be given. If only a few pairs of animals are used, there is no way of knowing how much the absolute frequency of occurrence of the stimulus event determines the results. Here again, only by using large numbers of pairs of animals will this variable be distributed more or less equally over a range of values.

Of much greater importance as a limitation of the matched groups design is the fact that the more careful and circumscribed the matching of groups, the less general are the results of the experiment. This is related to two points. The first is that careful matching generally produces a loss of subjects. This may vary from the loss of three or four individuals with extreme scores in a college group being tested for bilateral transfer, to the loss of hundreds of subjects in studies of hospital patients. An example of the latter situation is found in a study by Kellerman (1964) where an attempt was made to obtain 2 matched groups of mental hospital patients with 20 subjects in each group. In order to approximately match the patients on age, sex, IQ, and education, over 300 hospital records had to be examined and rejected. Although this procedure produces closely matched groups, it is evident that the characteristics of the rejected subjects are not represented in the experiment. The conclusions may be valid for the matched subjects and others like them but not for the type of subjects not tested. The ideal random groups design, in contrast, because of its sampling of an entire population, produces results which have a potentially wider range of generalization.

However, and this is the other point, whether or not subjects are rejected, the matching process necessarily produces a loss in generality, since matching is always done on one specific value of a variable out of a large range of possible values. If college students are matched in the transfer of training experiment on a 60-second performance, then it is simply indeterminate how much the results apply to other classes of subjects or to different equating levels. Thus, although the matched groups design is more sensitive to small effects, it is less capable of providing data which permit broad generalizations to be made.

The best way of dealing with this problem is to do a series of experiments of a parametric type in which each of the major variables of interest is explored systematically. This means, as was noted in connection with the random groups method, that studies using this design method should not be limited to two conditions of a variable but should use many matched groups, each of which is exposed to different levels of some independent variable. In the context of a transfer design, it might look something like this (where the Bs refer to different levels of practice):

	Pretest on	Training on	Retest on
Control group	A	—	A
Experimental group 1	A	B_1	A
Experimental group 2	A	B_2	A
Experimental group 3	A	B_3	A
Experimental group 4	A	B_4	A

Data of the sort obtained here are then handled by means of analysis of variance or by means of curve fitting techniques.

Retrospective Research

There is a type of research design called *retrospective* or *ex post facto,* which has certain similarities to the matched group design and is frequently used in clinical investigations. This kind of research usually begins with an observation which suggests that people with one kind of illness or symptom are different from other people without the illness in terms of some previous life history experience. For example, it might be noticed that people who develop lung cancer smoke a great deal; this suggests an hypothesis about *cause;* namely, that smoking produces lung cancer. Or, it might be observed that many delinquents who are caught and brought before the court come from homes where the parents are either separated or divorced. This suggests the hypothesis: broken homes cause delinquency. As a final example, a psychotherapist might notice that several of his patients have ulcers and form the hypothesis that ulcers are caused by conflicts between feelings of dependency and feelings of aggression.

In each of these cases, an observation of a patient group suggests an hypothesis about possible causes. How can these hypotheses be tested? This is obviously not a simple problem since the hypothesized cause has occurred in the past and the experimenter has no direct control over it. The best he can do is to try to evaluate its presence in some way.

Notice that the problem is the inverse of what is usually the case in a matched groups experiment. In that situation, two (or more) groups are matched on some variable, one is exposed to a possible causal factor, and then both groups are measured on some variable believed to be affected by the independent variable. The statistical tests we use are designed to tell us whether a "real" difference is now apparent.

The retrospective design starts by assuming that a real difference does exist between two groups: one has lung cancer, the other does not; or one is delinquent and the other is not; or one has ulcers and the other does not. The problem is to justify the idea that some situation (or variable) in the past life of these individuals or some personality characteristic has caused this present difference.

It should be obvious that such an inference is not an easy one to make with any certainty. Suppose, for example, that an investigator was able to find 20 patients in psychotherapy who had ulcers. He or she then obtains 20 college students as normal controls. Both groups are then interviewed extensively and life history data relating to feelings of dependency and aggression are obtained. Suppose that some index of conflict between dependency and aggression is found to be very high in 15 of the 20 ulcer patients and in only 3 of the normal controls, and that a test of significance shows that the difference is significant. What conclusions can be drawn?

One is tempted to say that conflict produces ulcers, but before reaching this conclusion several problems must be solved. For example, to what extent are the ulcer patients in therapy a good sample of ulcer patients in general? We know that people who go into therapy are mostly of middle- and upper-class status and that disease rates generally vary with social class level. Therefore, many ulcer patients are not represented in this group. The college students, likewise, are not a representative sample of the total population and most likely would not even be a good sample of college students since they are willing to allow detailed personal questions to be asked about their past life.

Another factor to be considered is age, since ulcer rates are highest in the decade between 40 and 50 years. This suggests that the ulcer patients are probably older than the college sample with which they are being compared. In addition, there may be differences between the two groups on dozens or even hundreds of life history factors, any one of which might have much greater relevance to the production of ulcers; to cite just a few: marital state, diet, general health, normal level of gastric acid secretion, feelings of inadequacy, and hospitalization per se.

Theoretically, it would be necessary to rule out every one of these factors as possible causative agents before deciding that conflicts alone produce ulcers. To some extent this is done; in actual research practice, groups that are compared are usually matched on such variables as age, sex, IQ, and education. Sometimes, they are matched on a variable such as hospitalization experience or presence of a different type of illness.

Now, although the matching of a few broad social or personal variables may make a case seem more plausible, it still does not deal with the multitude of possible causes that could produce the illness being studied, and therefore any statement about cause and effect solely on the basis of a retrospective study is highly questionable. This is particularly true when one considers that the statistics that are typically used (e.g., t-tests) are not validly applied in situations where the samples compared are not randomly selected.

In summary, retrospective studies attempt to argue backwards, so to speak, from effect to possible cause. Basic problems concern decisions about what the control group or groups should be, and about what should be matched or held constant. But even under the best conditions, many possible factors are left uncontrolled so that conclusions are always tenuous. However, the method is sometimes useful when only a limited number of important causes are believed to exist and when these can be evaluated in some way. Those who would like a more detailed analysis of the usefulness of this method when employed under these restricted conditions might find rewarding a paper by Hammond (1958) concerning research on smoking and death rates.

Counterbalanced Designs

This type of approach has sometimes been called a crossover, randomized-block, or Latin Square design. The details of the method vary somewhat, but the basic idea is that one subject or group is tested in one sequence of conditions while another subject or group is tested in a different sequence. In all cases, the subjects must be assigned at random to the different sequences.

This may be illustrated by two studies. One was concerned with the comparability of mean scores on two different IQ tests, the Revised Stanford-Binet (S-B) and the Wechsler Intelligence Scale for Children (WISC). It is evident that if one test were given first to all the children, there might be a practice effect that enabled each child to do better than he might ordinarily do on the second test. To deal with this possible sequence effect, the children were all divided into two groups at random so that one group received the S-B first followed by the WISC, and the other received the WISC first followed by the S-B, as shown in the following Latin Square:

	Test	
Group 1	S-B	WISC
Group 2	WISC	S-B

In analyzing the results, the major interest is in comparing the mean score on the S-B with the mean score on the WISC, regardless of sequence; in other words, the data for the two groups on comparable tests are combined. This means that if there is a practice effect of some kind, it is not eliminated but simply averaged out. This design method assumes that the practice effects in the different sequences used are approximately the same. The improvement in the WISC score due to taking the S-B first is assumed to be about equal to the improvement in the S-B score due to taking the WISC first. If analysis of variance is applied to the data, then it becomes possible to actually test whether this assumption is appropriate.

The second illustration is taken from the field of psychosomatic medicine. A number of investigators had reported that hospitalized patients who showed high anxiety had larger secretions of hydrocortisone (one of the hormones secreted by the adrenal cortex) than matched normal subjects. In light of these reports, an experiment by Weiner et al. (1963) was designed to see if injections of this hormone into volunteer medical students would produce increases in subjective feelings of anxiety.

Sixteen subjects were injected with one dose level of the hormone and immediately tested with the Rorschach, as well as with tests designed to measure both immediate feelings of anxiety and persistent levels of anxiety. Three months later the same subjects returned to the laboratory, were injected with a placebo, and retested with the same tests presented in a different order.

Another 16 subjects were handled in the same general way, except for the fact that they were injected with the placebo first and then with the hormone 3 months later. Analysis of variance was used to compare the test results obtained after hormone injection with the results obtained after placebo injection, regardless of order of testing. One of the interesting things that was found was that there was a definite difference in results due to the order of testing. When the hormone was given first, test scores associated with the drug were higher than when it was given second. All the differences found were dependent entirely on this order of testing.

Advantages and Limitations of Counterbalanced Designs

One of the advantages of the counterbalanced design is that each subject serves as his or her own control. Since the performance of an individual on two different tasks, or on the same task repeated, tends to be highly correlated, the size of standard errors in tests of significance is reduced and thus it is easier to detect small effects. From this point of view, the design is more sensitive than a random groups design, or even a matched groups design. No pretest is necessary to equate groups since the basic comparison is of each individual with him or herself. In addition, statistical analysis enables the effects of order as well as those of the major variable to be evaluated.

The extent of the limitations of the method depend on how much the order of testing affects the results, and how much one position in the sequence affects, or interacts with, later positions in the sequence. If, for example, there is a large effect related to the order of testing (e.g., going from the drug to the placebo condition), then this tends to greatly increase the variability of the results and decreases the sensitivity of any tests of significance used. This loss in sensitivity may offset any advantage gained by using each subject as his or her own control.

There are, of course, definite limits on the ability to generalize if only two conditions are compared in a bivalent experiment, but this is not a necessary fault of the method. The Latin Square can be used with any number of conditions. If, in addition to the placebo, there were two dose levels of hydrocortisone used in the experiment mentioned in the previous section, the Latin Square might look like this:

Dose Level

Group 1	Placebo	Low dose	High dose
Group 2	High dose	Placebo	Low dose
Group 3	Low dose	High dose	Placebo

From such data it would be possible to plot a dose-response curve so as to establish functional relations between the dose level and the subjects' responses.

A problem remains, however. It is obviously possible to arrange the sequence of tests in a different way and still meet the general requirements of the Latin Square—that is, that each condition appear once and only once in each row and each column. Thus we might have the following sequences:

Dose Level

Group 1	Placebo	High dose	Low dose
Group 2	Low dose	Placebo	High dose
Group 3	High dose	Low dose	Placebo

If there were four conditions being tested, there would be many more possible orders that could be used. Yet, in any experiment only one particular set of sequences is actually used. Thus in cases where several conditions are being compared, the sequence is a sample from a population of sequences, and it is not known how good a sample it is. The effect of using one particular sample rather than another is probably small, but there is no certainty about this.

Finally, it should be remembered that the Latin Square was first used in agricultural research for reducing the effects of variations in soil in different parts of a test field. The field was laid out in blocks within rows and columns, and each block was given a different kind of experimental treatment. In this setting there is no necessary relationship between what is done in one block and what is done in adjacent ones. Mathematically, this statement means that there is no interaction effect between blocks. In psychological research, however, the blocks (the different conditions tested) are not independent of one another since ordinarily they are treated in sequence. This would mean that there is an interaction between them, and if there is reason to believe that this interaction is appreciable in any given case, then some other design method, such as random or matched groups, would probably be more suitable.

An example of this problem has been reported in connection with the study of one of the variables influencing conditioning—namely, the intensity of the conditioned stimulus (CS). Although several studies with human subjects have shown that the intensity of the CS has little effect on conditioning, a few experiments have indicated large effects (Grice and Hunter, 1964). A close examination of these studies and some follow-up research has shown that the probable reason for the discrepancies is the type of design method employed. When several independent groups are used so that each subject is exposed to only one intensity level, the effect of intensity is minimal. However, when each subject is exposed to all intensities in some counterbalanced sequence, the effect of CS intensity is much greater. Thus, it appears that there is a substantial interaction effect with this variable. It would be interesting to study other problems by comparing different design methods as was done in this case.

Counterbalancing with a Single Group

There are certain areas of psychological research where order effects are relatively negligible. This is true, for example, in studies of visual or auditory discrimination. In such situations the tradition that has developed over a century of research is to use very few subjects, but to study them intensively; sometimes thousands of judgments are required from a single observer. The data are therefore obtained from highly practiced subjects.

One result of this approach is essentially to eliminate any practice effects. It is possible to expose such subjects to the experimental conditions in any order and to expect that different results that are obtained will be due largely to the differences in the experimental variable and not to the effect of practice.

To take a concrete example, suppose two highly practiced observers were to be used in an experiment to study the keenness of hearing at different frequencies, and suppose that two frequencies were to be used: 1,000 Hz, and 10,000 Hz. If the observers are highly practiced, it will make no difference if the 1,000 Hz condition is given first or last. However, sometimes, if a long series of judgments are required, fatigue effects gradually become apparent and these effects, though usually small, can be balanced out by repeating the conditions in reverse sequence. Thus, in this example, the subjects would be exposed to the 1,000 Hz condition first, then the 10,000 Hz condition, followed by the 10,000 Hz condition and the 1,000 Hz condition. If we let the letters *A* and *B* stand for the two different conditions, the sequence then is *ABBA*. In analyzing the results, the two *A* conditions are combined and the two *B* conditions are combined. It is assumed that fatigue or practice effects, if they exist, are linearly related to trials or exposures.

Sometimes this *ABBA* sequence of testing is used in studies where a definite practice effect is known to exist; where, for example, it is known that the second time the *A* condition is presented the subject will perform much better than the first time. In such cases, if this design method is used at all, the *A* and *B* conditions are usually broken down into small units so that the sequence can be repeated many times over. Thus instead of giving 100 trials in the first *A* condition and 100 in the second, these 200 trials may be broken down into groups of only 10 trials each, and the whole sequence is repeated somewhat as follows:

Sequence of trials *A B B A   B A A B   B A A B   A B B A* *etc.*
Number of trials   10 10 10 10   10 10 10 10   10 10 10 10   10 10 10 10

All the *A*s are eventually combined and the mean value is compared with the mean for the combined *B*s.

One example of the use of an *ABBA* design will be briefly described. Stanley and Schlosberg (1953) were interested in finding the influence of tea on a variety of tests. As subjects they obtained 22 housewives who were habitual tea drinkers.

On the first of five days of testing, the subjects (in pairs of two) were given an opportunity to gain experience with each of the tasks to be used (e.g., hand steadiness, reaction time, strength of grip, attention, long division, and subjective ratings of fatigue and tension). The first day was simply for practice.

On the second and fifth day 14 of the women were exposed to the same tasks after a cup of tea, while on the third and fourth days the same tests were given, but without the cup of tea. For the remaining women the order was reversed (third and fourth days, tea; second and fifth days, no tea). Analysis of data was concerned with gains or losses between tea and no-tea days. It is interesting to note that the experimenters reported that practice effects appeared absent during the last two experimental periods. The only effect found in the experiment was an improvement in reaction time which lasted about an hour after drinking the tea.

Advantages and Limitations

The "*ABBA* method" as it is sometimes called is useful in situations where it is desirable to use a single subject and to compare two conditions. Since each subject is his or her own control, it reduces variability of the type due to differences between subjects and makes it somewhat easier to detect significant differences than when the random groups method is used.

However, it is not at all evident how much generalization is possible from the results of one or just a few subjects. This issue does not usually arise in most psychophysical research because the aim of such research is not to study the characteristics of the "average" person, but rather the characteristics of the eye or ear of the highly trained observer. It is this difference in aim that usually enables these investigators to ignore issues connected with subject sampling.

A second problem involved in the use of this design method relates to the assumption that practice or fatigue effects are small and linearly related to trials or exposures. If this assumption is not true, then it is necessary to break up the sequence into smaller units and repeat them many times. But how small is each small unit to be? This depends on prior knowledge of what the practice curve looks like, and such data are often not available. That is why most studies using this method give the subjects a good deal of practice before collecting any data. In essence, this makes negligible any further effects due to practice.

The use of highly practiced subjects, however, creates a problem in certain situations. The difficulty is that the subject's performance is likely to be close to his or her maximum possible performance, and any variable that is introduced is unlikely to improve it any further. The design method may thus reveal variables that produce decrements in performance but is less likely to show the effect of incremental factors.

A fourth issue related to this design method concerns the question of how to adapt it so that more than two values of some independent variable can be used. Suppose we wanted to test for keenness of hearing not only at 1,000 Hz and

10,000 Hz, but at 500, 2,000, and 5,000 Hz as well. If we were to have a single group exposed to all conditions, there are several ways this could be done. Following the plan of calling the different conditions by different letters, we could arrange the sequence in ascending and descending order:

$$A \quad B \quad C \quad D \quad E \quad E \quad D \quad C \quad B \quad A$$

Here again the two *A*s would be combined to provide a single mean, the two *B*s, etc. If there was evidence of large practice or fatigue effects, the units of testing might be made smaller and the whole sequence repeated. The other alternative is to randomize the trials of *A B C* . . . etc., using a table of random numbers. If there are enough repeated trials, then any sequence effect will be balanced out. This is an approach which is generally recommended.

The Concept of Baseline Behavior

The previous discussion of counterbalancing with a single group of subjects has brought up some points which are very similar to those made by Sidman (1960) in his book on the tactics of research. One of the fundamental ideas he presents is that there are many experimental situations where elaborate group designs and statistics are irrelevant or misleading in connection with the basic purposes of research, namely, to identify the variables affecting behavior and to show what effects they have.

The kind of behavioral measures Sidman has been mostly concerned with are rates of response (usually bar pressing in a Skinner-type box or setting). In such cases it is often possible to find some schedule of reinforcement (positive or negative) that produces a highly constant rate of response from the animal for hours or even days. As one example, he presents a shock to an animal once every 20 seconds. If the animal presses on a bar during the 20-second interval, it postpones the shock for the next 20 seconds. By responding at a constant and fairly high rate, the animal can postpone the shock indefinitely. This method establishes a steady baseline rate of response. If the experimenter now introduces some variable such as a drug or a loud noise, and the rate of response changes, it seems fairly certain that the manipulation caused the change. If the effect is reversible, and removal of the imposed stimulus is followed by a return to the same baseline in the animal's rate of response, then the experimenter can continue to introduce other conditions (more of the drug or other drugs, louder noise, etc.) to determine their effects on the response rate. In such a case the sequence of testing is irrelevant and any order can be used.

One of the difficulties with this general approach is that it is not always possible to establish constant baseline rates of response, especially if the research is being done with humans. Even when animals are used as the subjects, it may require extremely long periods before constant baseline rates are established. Sidman gives an illustration of a study using rats in which seven 6-hour sessions were run with each animal. The results for the first 18 hours were discarded because the behavior was not stable enough, and only the average rates for the last 24 hours were used.

A second difficulty is that a good deal of behavior is not reversible, which means, in essence, that there are baseline shifts for reasons that are related to the life history of the particular individual. A third problem is that many investigators are not interested in rates of bar-pressing response as measures but are concerned with other classes of behavior. The general approach, however, is worth examining since it has produced some important insights into the nature of learning.

Additive and Subtractive Designs

In many research projects, the independent variable is not a single clearly manipulated condition, but is actually a conglomerate of variables. For example, psychotherapy is believed to have many potential causal elements in the complex interactions between patients and therapists. These elements include therapist warmth and empathy; modeling behavior by the therapist; use of suggestions, questions, and interpretations; and use of specific reinforcement schedules, among others.

In such situations, the investigator may attempt to compare several groups of patients who have been exposed to different components of the complex condition. One group may be exposed to the traditional form of therapy. A second may be exposed to a modified form of the therapy in which one of the presumed active ingredients has been removed. A third group of patients may be given therapy in which two of the active ingredients have been removed, and so on.

Random assignment of patients to the different conditions must be carried out. Differences among groups on the dependent variable will reveal the extent to which the subtracted elements contributed to the overall outcome. This type of design has been referred to as "systematic dismantling" by Gottman and Markman (1978), and is here described as a *subtractive* design.

There is another side to this coin. One may create a complex treatment package by gradually adding components to a basic treatment. In the field of psychosomatic research, attempts have sometimes been made to add psychotherapeutic components to the general medical treatment of a given disorder. As an illustration, one group of patients with coronary heart disease could be treated by means of well-established medical regimens. A second group of randomly selected patients might be given the usual medical regimen plus individual psychotherapy over a limited period of time. A third group of randomly selected patients might be given the medical regimen plus individual psychotherapy plus group psychotherapy. Differences in outcome among the groups would reflect the additive contributions of the various components.

Such designs are frequently used in psychopharmacological research where the investigator is interested in determining the effects of a particular drug with or without the addition of other drugs or psychotherapy. This type of design has been called a "constructive strategy" by Kazdin and Wilson (1978).

It is important to note, however, that the interaction of components is not always additive. There are, in fact, four possible types of interactions among the components. One type of interaction is additive, in which the effect of two or more interventions combined is equal to the sum of their individual effects. A second type of interaction is called potentiation, in which the effect of two combined interventions is greater than the sum of their individual effects. A third interaction is inhibition, in which the combined effect of two interventions is less than the sum of their separate effects. The fourth type of interaction might be called reciprocation, in which the effect of two combined interventions is equal to the magnitude of the more potent intervention (Uhlenhuth et al., 1969). Since these additive and subtractive designs are often complex and difficult to carry out in practice, it is important to have a good empirical or theoretical basis for selecting the components of the additive or subtractive designs.

The Problem of Sample Size

A major decision that experimenters must make concerns the number of subjects to use. This problem has no simple or general answer, and each solution depends upon a variety of factors that usually cannot be specified in advance. However, it is clear from the research literature that, depending on the kind of problem studied, anything from one to 1,000 subjects is appropriate. What are some factors that must be considered?

In general there are three types of considerations: (1) the traditions that have developed in an area of research; (2) the kind of variability in results which is expected on the basis of previous experience; and (3) the kind of statistical analysis that is planned. Let us take these in reverse order.

If the investigator is planning a bivalent experiment, he or she will usually expect to use a t-test to determine the significance of any difference obtained. It is obvious that the larger the difference found, the easier it is to get a significant t-value; and since t is proportional to N, the larger the N, the larger the t (other things held constant). This means that if an investigator decides on a value of t for significance in advance (and almost everyone takes the 5 or 1% level), and if he or she can specify in advance a difference in means thought to be important as well as the amount of variability to be anticipated, then the value of N is determined. Note that three prior decisions must be made in order to fix the value of N. One is the significance level to be used, a second is the size of a difference between the means that is to be considered important, and the third is the variability to be expected. But this also has a large element of arbitrariness about it. It looks almost as if we are substituting three arbitrary decisions for one. It is certainly evident that decisions about the *importance* of a finding are not statistical decisions at all but relate to judgments about the implications of certain findings. Thus it is apparent that some very subtle factors enter into the choice of N in the context of testing for significance of differences.

There are three other important points to be made in relation to statistical considerations. First, Dixon and Massey (1951) point out that if groups are equal in size, it is relatively easier to find a significant difference than if they are unequal in size. Thus an experimenter who has 100 subjects available will have a more sensitive significance test if the group is divided into two equal halves rather than if 90 are placed into one group and 10 into the other. This observation is simply a consequence of the definition of a t-test.

Second, in an illuminating discussion of experiments in which two groups are compared, Ryan (1959) poses the following hypothetical situation:

> An experimenter is convinced that a certain factor should produce a difference in learning rate. He tries it once and fails to get a significant difference. He is so sure that the experiment should have worked that he reconsiders his experimental technique for possible errors. He decides that some actually irrelevant feature of the experiment is responsible, changes it, and tries again. Finally after many different revisions of the conditions, all actually irrelevant, he obtains a "significant" difference and publishes the result. We assume that, as an honest scientist, he will mention in his report that several other trials failed, but this will not usually affect his test of significance, and he will usually explain away the earlier, unsuccessful trials as due to errors in technique. Clearly, all his data should be tested as a single experiment, otherwise obtaining a "significant" difference will depend only upon the experimenter's stubbornness and patience, or upon the number of his research assistants.

An important implication of this example is that experiments do not exist in isolation but are part of a more or less continuous sequence of interrelated observations. If one considers an experiment in this way, the question of the number of subjects to be used in any one study becomes relatively less important.

The third point to be made is that if the experimenter's only concern is achieving a significant t, then he or she need only use large Ns, since any difference between two groups, no matter how small, will be significant if enough subjects are used. This would suggest that we need additional criteria for judging the meaningfulness of a finding besides the criteria of statistical significance.

Such criteria have already been discussed in Chapter 6, where we considered ways to estimate the magnitude of an experimental effect. It was suggested that the d-statistic (percent overlap of two distributions) and ω^2 (proportion of variance accounted for) could be used to provide an index of the size of an experimental effect. It was also suggested that such measures should be used routinely, along with traditional tests of significance.

Traditions and Variability

We shall now examine the other two criteria for deciding on the number of subjects, that is, experience with the amount of variability to be expected with a given type of subject or problem, and the traditions that have developed in the field.

It should be obvious that these two criteria are not unrelated since traditions develop because of certain kinds of experiences. If we look at the research done in psychophysics concerned with the measurement of sensory acuity and sensitivity, we discover that most of the published research is based on only two or three subjects per experiment. If we examine the studies concerned with the effects of different schedules of reinforcement, we discover that many of the reports are based on two or four animals per group. If we peruse the journals where social psychological research is published, we find that much larger groups are typically used with Ns ranging from 20 to many hundreds.

In order to get some data on what these traditions are, the present author examined three journals for the year 1960 and simply recorded the number of subjects used in each of the different experiments published in that year. Of the 169 experiments published in the *Journal of Experimental Psychology,* 5 experiments used only 2 subjects, 1 experiment used only 1 subject and 26 used 10 or fewer subjects. The median number of subjects per experiment was about 45. In the *Journal of Comparative and Physiological Psychology* for that year, there were 38 experiments out of 145 that used 10 or fewer subjects. The median for this journal was about 20 subjects. The *Journal of Clinical Psychology* for that year published 125 experiments; 8 used 10 or less subjects, and the median was about 90. (The medians given here are only approximate since 4 experiments in the *Journal of Comparative and Physiological Psychology* did not list the number of subjects used and 11 experiments in the *Journal of Clinical Psychology* did not.) These figures, approximate as they are, certainly suggest a range of policies in regard to choice of sample size, even though some overall trends are apparent.

The role of experience may be illustrated by two concrete examples. Sidman (1960) reported that "it had been the usual experience in this laboratory that when as many as four animals (usually less) yielded the same data, subsequent experimentation rarely failed to achieve replication." Chapanis (1956) who has had considerable experience with human engineering studies writes: "As a general rule, psychophysical experiments on simple sensory functions . . . generally require fewer subjects than most other kinds. Learning experiments, experiments involving motor performance, and so on, may give erratic results unless a minimum of about 20 or 30 subjects is used."

These quotations imply that the investigator actually uses as the criterion for choice of N the consistency and reliability of his or her results from subject to subject and experiment to experiment. In some areas of research variability is inherently much greater than in other areas, and larger numbers of subjects must therefore be used. But implicit in this criterion of consistency is the idea that each experiment is part of a sequence of related experiments and not an entity unto itself. Replication of results is a more convincing sign of reliability of data than significant ts obtained in a single experiment. In fact, a number of statisticians have begun to develop so-called sequential designs in which the number of subjects to be used is not stated in advance, but depends on the nature of the data as they are collected.

Can $N=1$?

One final point. Are experiments using a single subject meaningful? The answer given by Dukes (1965) in an interesting paper on this question is definitely "yes." He points out that experiments on single subjects have played a very significant role in the history of psychology, and that there are several general situations where they do occur.

The basic studies of memory by Ebbinghaus around 1885 were done with one subject, himself, and his methods and findings have influenced the course of research in this area up to the present time. Watson's famous study of conditioned fear (1920) was done on a single child and prompted hundreds of subsequent experiments. In the early 1930s the Kelloggs raised a chimpanzee with their son as if the chimp were their own child; this provided some important insights into the relationship between nature and nurture.

Occasionally, a phenomenon occurs so rarely that a single example of it is of great significance. This is true, for example, of the very few people who are apparently born with a total insensitivity to pain, or the rare person who is color blind in one eye but not in the other. Careful study of such single cases sometimes reveals facts of fundamental importance.

In a survey of 11 journals of psychology, which are *not* clinical journals, during the years 1939 to 1963, Dukes found that a total of 246 reported studies used only a single subject, thus suggesting that such experiments were considered meaningful at that time. These were of four main types: (1) psychophysical, where intersubject variability is usually found to be low; (2) the study of rare events such as a person with congenital insensitivity to pain; (3) the study of "negative" cases showing that an assumed universal relationship does not hold (e.g., feeblemindedness does not necessarily occur as a result of prolonged congenital hydrocephaly); and (4) the development of new approaches to a problem, such as the stabilizing of images on the retina. Studies of the single case are thus important aspects of contemporary research.

To illustrate the importance of studies using a single subject, we may consider the following example (Leuba, Birch, and Appleton, 1968). A long-standing controversy exists in psychology over the issue of whether thinking must involve subvocal talking and/or other kinds of movements of the skeletal muscles. A 21-year-old student of psychology became intrigued with the idea of testing the necessity for peripheral muscular involvement in thinking. He offered himself as a subject and agreed to take a curare-derivative, under hospital conditions, to determine if he could solve mental problems after complete paralysis of his speech and other voluntary muscles.

Various problems involving arithmetic, puzzles, and physics were given to the S in the normal state. Later, the S was given d-tubocurarine intravenously until he was completely motionless, and artificial respiration was administered by the anesthesiologist. At that point similar problems were verbally presented to the S. Finally, an anticurare drug was administered and S returned to normal. The S then immediately gave the correct answers to all but one of the problems. Here is part of the S's report after the experiment: "The testing period began. At this point I was uncomfortable due to my inability to swallow. The problems were given slowly, and with quite adequate space between for solving them. I was trying very hard to move something, particularly my bottom lip, because the breathing mask was pinching it against my teeth; I did not succeed. All during the testing period and into the end of the experiment, I tried to move (but) action was not possible. . . . I noted no change in my ability to think. I heard, comprehended and completed all of the problems given me."

Two months later the experiment was repeated on this same S with essentially similar results. It thus appeared that this S could remain alert, solve complex problems presented orally, and remember the answers under conditions of total or near total paralysis of the external skeletal muscles. This study involving a single subject would thus appear to be support for a centralist interpretation of thinking.

Summary

The examples and discussions that have been presented in this chapter have been meant to highlight two important implications. One is that there is no simple formula for handling all experimental design problems. Each method has advantages and disadvantages and each is best used in certain contexts. The second is that there are many issues to be considered in making a choice of design method, and that the issues are not all statistical. The world around us sometimes presents us with problems that the statistician does not have models for, but they are real problems nevertheless.

12

Quasi-Experimental Designs

Multiple experimentation is more typical of science than once-and-for-all definitive experiments.

—Donald T. Campbell and Julian C. Stanley

In the preceding two chapters we have considered sources of error in experimentation, the nature of controls, and a variety of experimental design methods. It should be evident from the discussions of these issues that no design method will automatically guarantee "true" results, and that sources of error or bias may operate to challenge the validity of any conclusion. In addition, there are a number of situations that occur in which subjects cannot be assigned randomly to experimental conditions, for example, when different classes of students or different schools are compared. These designs, in which subjects are assigned to treatments in nonrandom ways, are called quasi-experimental, and such designs are considered less satisfactory on various grounds than are those in which subjects are assigned to experimental conditions on a random basis. Since there has been considerable interest in recent years in quasi-experimental designs, particularly in social and clinical research, a description and evaluation of some of the more common ones is justified.

Discussions of quasi-experiments are usually presented in terms of the ideas of internal and external validity of experiments. A "good" experiment is obviously one in which a causal connection is demonstrated between the independent and dependent variables, and alternative explanations of the results can be ruled out. When these conditions occur, the experiment is said to have internal validity. If the results of an experiment can be generalized to other subjects and other settings, then it is said to have external validity (Campbell and Stanley, 1963; Cook and Campbell, 1976).

The assessment of external validity is based largely on the extent to which random sampling has been successfully carried out. Issues connected with sampling of subjects, experimenters, stimulus conditions, and responses have been discussed in Chapter 5. Internal validity is based largely on the extent to which alternative explanations of the findings can be eliminated.

Threats to Internal Validity

In their discussion of internal validity, Cook and Campbell (1976) describe 13 "threats" to internal validity. By this they mean general factors or types of explanations that are not the independent variable being manipulated but that can possibly account for the results of an experiment. These factors are briefly described below.

1. *History.* This refers to the possibility of an event occurring between the pretest and the posttest that is not the experimental variable, but is one which may have some effect on the results. To deal with this possibility the intervening history of the various groups involved in the research should be kept as similar as possible.

2. *Maturation.* Sometimes an observed effect in an experiment may be due to the fact that some of the subjects change by growing older, hungrier, more tired, or the like. When these are not the variables of interest, efforts should be made to prevent such changes from occurring in any systematic way.

3. *Testing.* It is well known that taking a test once may exert an influence on the scores obtained if the same test is taken a second time. This possible source of unwanted variability may be dealt with by using tests of high reliability and by making sure that all subjects are tested in the same way after a comparable period of time.

4. *Instrumentation.* Sometimes a measuring instrument changes in its accuracy or sensitivity between the pretest and posttest. To deal with this possible threat to internal validity, calibration procedures should be introduced on a regular basis. This issue is discussed in detail in Chapter 15, "The Role of Instruments in Research."

5. *Statistical Regression.* Sometimes, groups of subjects are selected for an experiment because they score unusually high or unusually low on a pretest. When this is done, then the high scorers on the pretest will tend to score lower on the posttest, and the low scorers on the pretest will tend to score higher on the posttest. Such changes are called "statistical regression toward the mean" and cannot be attributed to the operation of the experimental variable. To deal with this problem it is generally desirable to utilize subjects whose test scores cover the entire range of possible scores and not to rely on extreme groups.

6. *Selection.* This is a threat to validity if the subjects in the different groups are not randomly assigned or matched. In such cases, the results of an experiment may be due to such selection rather than to the operation of the independent variable.

7. *Mortality.* In many experiments, a certain number of subjects drop out for a variety of reasons. If the loss of subjects is different in the different groups, then a selection-type of artifact may result, and the outcome of the experiment may be due to the differential loss of subjects rather than to the operation of the variable of interest.

8. *Interactions with Selection.* A number of the factors listed above as threats to internal validity can interact. For example, in educational research comparing middle- and lower-class children, groups are sometimes composed of students who may be maturing or learning at different speeds. If the groups are tested at different points in time, differences may appear that are due to the interaction between maturation and selection rather than to the educational programs that are being evaluated.

9. *Diffusion of Treatment.* In the effort to create equal groups for an experiment, it sometimes happens that members of the control groups learn about the nature of the experiment, or the nature of the experimental manipulations. This may produce reactions on the part of the control group subjects that act to decrease the differences between the different conditions.

10. *Compensatory Equalization of Treatments.* In certain large-scale experiments, particularly in the field of education, special programs such as Head Start or Follow Through are provided to randomly selected schools. Because administrators or school boards often consider these programs desirable, some special efforts are made on behalf of those schools that are randomly chosen as controls; for example, more money is appropriated. The effect of such procedures is to tend to equalize the different schools and to decrease differences that might be attributable to the experimental procedures.

11. *Compensatory Rivalry.* In certain experimental settings such as industrial organizations, the nature of the experimental and control conditions must often be made public. When this happens, social competition or rivalry may be generated between members of the experimental and control groups. Such rivalry has been reported in studies of performance contracting of public school teachers where the results of the experiment may threaten the job security of some of the teachers. Rivalry may increase the performance of the control group members and thus decrease the apparent effects of the independent variable.

12. *Demoralization Effects.* An effect that is the opposite of compensatory rivalry may also occur. If the members of the control group are aware of the treatments and if they believe that their treatment is socially less desirable, they may work less hard than normal. If this happens, it may appear that the effect of the experimental variable is large, whereas it may be mostly the result of poor performance of control group members due to their "resentment" or "demoralization."

13. *Local History.* If all subjects in the experimental group are tested at the same time and place, and all members of the control group are tested at a different time and place, there is always the possibility that some special local event affects one group more than the other. The possibility of environmental (e.g., temperature or humidity) or experimenter effects cannot be ignored. One way of dealing with this possibility is to administer the independent variable to individuals or to small groups so that such extraneous "local history" factors will tend to be distributed.

These 13 classes of variables that can affect the validity of an experimental conclusion are not common to all experimental settings. In fact, the use of random selection procedures and the standardization of conditions will effectively deal with most of them. However, the possibility of their existence should always be considered. "Estimating the internal validity of a relationship is a deductive process in which the investigator has to be his own most trenchant critic and has to systematically think through how each of the above factors may have influenced his data. Then, he has to examine the data to test which relevant threats can be ruled out" (Cook and Campbell, 1976).

Quasi-Experimental Designs

Quasi-experimental designs refer to situations in which the experimental and control groups are not selected by random procedures; the groups, therefore, differ by unknown amounts, and the effects of the independent variable cannot be unequivocally determined. Such situations occur when existing, intact groups are selected to be compared. Examples of this kind of situation occur when two intact classes are selected as control and experimental groups respectively, or when two groups of patients are compared.

Despite the unknown degree of comparability of the subject samples and other conditions of the experiment, it is sometimes possible to arrange conditions so that some degree of confidence can be placed in causal statements made about the operation of the independent variable. This implies that the "goodness" of the experiment is not an all-or-nothing matter, but can vary as a function of the degree to which rival hypotheses can be ruled out. Quasi-experiments allow some, but not all, alternative hypotheses to be ruled out, so that the conclusions of the experiment about causal connections may be plausible but not definitive. To illustrate these ideas, three quasi-experimental designs will be described and evaluated.

Selection Cohort Designs

In certain settings such as schools or training programs there is a regular turnover of students from semester to semester or year to year. It is possible to use all of the students in a given year as the experimental group and all of the students in the next year as the control group (or vice versa).

A variation on this design was used by Minton (1975) in her study of the effects of *Sesame Street* on kindergarten children. At the end of *Sesame Street's* first season, data were collected on the Metropolitan Readiness Test (a test of reading readiness) from a group of children who had been watching the program regularly. As a control the investigator used the scores on the reading readiness test of the older siblings of the kindergarten children, scores that had been obtained when they were the same age as their younger siblings. She was therefore able to compare the postkindergarten scores of children who were *Sesame Street* viewers with the postkindergarten scores of their siblings who could not have watched the show because it was not yet being broadcast.

This is a quasi-experimental design because there is no assurance that the two groups, older and younger siblings, were in fact comparable at the times the test data were collected. For example, since the older siblings are more likely to be first-born children, this difference in birth order might account for any observed differences. This hypothesis could be checked by analyzing the data separately for second-born older children and their third-born siblings, for third-born children and their fourth-born siblings, etc.

Another problem with this design is that the older siblings have experienced a history different from the younger ones and there is no way to evaluate the possible impact of such differences directly. However, one can carry out an internal analysis to try to deal with this hypothesis. It is possible to separate the children into light viewers and heavy viewers of the program, and each group can be separately compared with its own older siblings. Since both the heavy and light viewers have experienced the same general history, any differences between heavy viewers and their siblings that contrast appreciably with the differences between light viewers and their siblings could probably be attributed to the effect of the educational television program. It is thus evident that various internal analyses may be carried out in a quasi-experimental design setting to reduce the number of alternative explanations and to strengthen the internal validity of the results.

Interrupted Time-Series Designs

These designs involve the repeated measurement of an effect both before and after the introduction of an experimental stimulus, or before and after the introduction of a new experimental program. If we designate a series of measurements at different times by the letters O_1, O_2, O_3, etc., and the introduction of an experimental variable by the letter X, then a variety of different outcomes of a series of tests can occur as illustrated in Figure 12–1. This figure represents a number of different kinds of outcomes resulting from the introduction of the experimental condition X into a time series of measurements O_1 to O_8. The different time-series have been drawn in such a way as to make the gain from O_4 to O_5 the same. Despite this, it is evident that the likelihood of a real effect of X is greatest for the top three series A, B, and C, and is lowest for the three bottom series D, E, and F. This judgment is based largely on the abruptness of the change that occurs at the point in time when the experimental condition is introduced.

A possible weakness of the interrupted time-series design is that there is no control of history; that is, one may propose the rival hypothesis that not X but

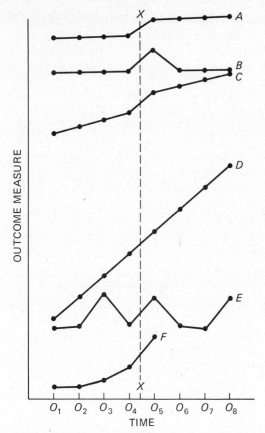

Figure 12–1. Some possible outcome patterns that could result from the introduction of an experimental variable at point X into a time-series of measurements, O_1–O_8. The O_4–O_5 gain is the same for all time-series, while the legitimacy of inferring an effect varies, being strongest in A and B and unjustified in D, E, and F. (From Campbell, D. T., and Stanley, J. C. Experimental and quasi-experimental designs for research. American Educational Research Association, Washington, D.C., 1963. By permission.)

some other event that occurred at the same time produced the abrupt change in the time-series. For example, suppose a group of students were shown a film designed to change their attitudes about Russia. It is possible that day-to-day changes in current events may produce a larger impact on the students' attitudes than the experimental film does. However, the longer the time-series continues without an abrupt change, the less likely are current events to be appropriate interpretations of the discontinuity in the time-series at the particular time the experimental condition was introduced. Although changes in weather, season, and maturation may be proposed as rival hypotheses to account for an abrupt change in a time-series, they do not generally represent strong hypotheses. Cook and Campbell (1976) conclude that "Interrupted time-series are among the most powerful quasi-experimental designs. Their use is rapidly increasing."

Regression-Discontinuity Designs

In certain situations in education or industry, a bonus or award is given for output that is greater than a designated level. The assumption is usually made that the award affects subsequent performance. One way in which this hypothesis can be tested is to plot a graph of posttest values against pretest values for a group of persons, some of whom have received the award and some of whom have not. If the award is effective, there should be an abrupt change in the curve at the value which determines whether the award is to be given. This design is called regression-discontinuity analysis and may be illustrated by a study of the effect of assignment to Dean's List on subsequent performance (Seaver and Quarton, 1973).

These investigators collected grades from the Registrar's office for over 1,000 students, some of whom made Dean's List and some of whom did not. They then plotted grade point average in one term against grade point average in the following term and drew best best fitting lines through the points as shown in Figure 12–2.

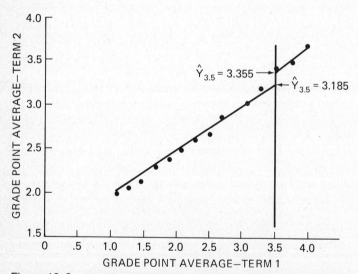

Figure 12–2.   Best fitting lines showing the relation between grade point average during Term 1 and Term 2 for students who made Dean's List and for those who did not. (From Cook, T. D., and Campbell, D. T. The design and conduct of quasi-experimental and true experiments in field settings. *Handbook of industrial and organizational psychology,* ed. M. D. Dunnette. Chicago: Rand McNally, 1976. By permission.)

Their data showed that there was a difference in the Y-intercept ($\hat{Y}$) for the regression line of those students who did not make Dean's List as compared to those students who did. This shift in the Y-intercept occurred at a grade point average of 3.5, which is the cut-off point for assigning someone to Dean's List. On the basis of the best fitting curve, we would estimate that a person who just made Dean's List in Term 1 should make a grade point average in Term 2 of 3.185. In reality such people obtain an average grade of 3.355. This difference implies that students who made Dean's List did better than those who did not by a factor over and above what would be expected on the basis of their generally superior performance.

One problem with regression-discontinuity designs is that awards are often given to the especially gifted or especially needy. This results in a restricted range of scores for the regression analysis and limits the possibility of obtaining clear-cut evidence of a discontinuity if it exists. Another problem that may occur with these types of quasi-experimental designs results from vague, ambiguous, or "fuzzy" cut-off points for assignment of an award. In such cases evidence for a discontinuity in regression lines will also be less clear.

Summary

Quasi-experiments involve the use of nonequivalent groups or settings in which there is no explicit control group. This usually means that groups have not been formed on the basis of random procedures. Among the most important of these designs are selection cohort designs, interrupted time-series designs, and regression-discontinuity designs. The internal validity of these types of experiments can be compromised because of the possibility of rival hypotheses to account for observed changes. Such rival hypotheses may be based on factors related to history, maturation, testing, instrumentation, statistical regression, selection, mortality, and other variables. However, internal or supplementary analyses may often refute some of the alternative hypotheses so that probable conclusions can be drawn concerning the influence of the independent variable. Another possibility is that multiple-control groups can be used to rule out various alternative hypotheses. A point worth emphasizing is that single studies usually cannot deal with all alternative hypotheses resulting from quasi-experiments. But this can be said of "true" experiments as well.

13

An Introduction to Psychophysics

By psychophysics . . . *I mean a theory which, although ancient as a problem, is new here insofar as its formulation and treatment are concerned; in short, it is an exact theory of the relation of body and mind.*

—Gustav Fechner

Classical psychophysics—the psychophysics of the last century—was primarily concerned with the study of sensory thresholds. These thresholds were of two general types: *absolute* and *differential.* The absolute threshold refers to the minimum energy needed to elicit a response; the differential threshold refers to the minimum energy needed before a difference is noticed relative to some fixed level. The determination of the dimmest light the eye can see would be an example of an absolute threshold, while the smallest pitch difference the ear can detect would illustrate the differential threshold. In order to determine these various kinds of thresholds with minimum possibilities of error, several standard procedures were developed, called psychophysical methods. Although these methods were first proposed in the context of the study of the threshold, they have been adapted to many other kinds of problems including the construction of intelligence and attitude tests. In this chapter some of the basic psychophysical methods and concepts will be introduced.

The Basic Issues

Modern psychophysics has considerably expanded the range of questions to be studied. Galanter (1962) suggests that there are four basic problems implicit in the analysis of sensory function: (1) the detection problem ("Is anything there?"); (2) the recognition problem ("What is it?"); (3) the discrimination problem ("Is this different from that?"); and (4) the scaling problem ("How much of X is there?"). Another way of describing the modern task of psychophysics is by comparing a person's sensory system with that of a complex machine such as a television camera. We might then ask such questions as: (1) How sensitive is the system? (2) How accurate is it? (3) How reliable is it? (4) How small a change can it detect? (5) What is its speed of response? (6) What is its range of response? (Granit, 1955).

Perhaps the simplest way of describing the basic issues of concern to psychophysics is in terms of the following three problems: (1) the matching problem (when are two things equal?); (2) the discrimination problem (how small a difference is detectable?); and (3) the scaling problem (how much of the stimulus is judged to be present?). We will use these three questions as a basis for an introduction to some psychophysical methods and concepts.

The Matching Problem

Suppose a piano tuner is called to your home. One way he might go about his job of tuning would be by matching the tones produced by the piano to the tones produced by a standard set of tuning forks. Similarly, in order for a physicist or psychologist to calibrate the intensity or luminance of a light source, he or she tries to match it against a standard known illumination. When an artist paints the colors of the sunset, he or she is usually dealing with the problem of matching.

All of these situations have several elements in common. First, there is a reference or *standard stimulus* (e.g., frequency, luminance, or wavelength). Second, a *variable stimulus* is matched as closely as possible to the standard. The value of the variable at the point where the observer considers that the two quantities are matched is called the *point of subjective equality* (PSE). For example, if the tuning fork produces a tone with a frequency of 256 cycles per second (Hz), and the piano tuner sets the piano key at 258 Hz, this latter value is his point of subjective equality.

Once the PSE is determined it will usually be found that it differs from the standard by some small value. This difference between the PSE and the standard represents an error of judgment in matching and is called the *constant error* or CE. In symbolic terms, by definition, CE = PSE − Standard.

If, as is usually the case, a series of matching settings are made, then the PSE will vary somewhat from trial to trial and the constant error is then defined as the average value of the different PSEs minus the standard. The different matching settings (i.e., the different PSEs from trial to trial) can be used to determine a measure of how consistent the subject's judgments are. Such a measure of variability is called the *variable error* or VE and is usually measured by a standard deviation or by the interquartile range of the subject's series of settings.

To summarize: when making matching judgments we have a standard stimulus and a variable stimulus that is compared with it. The value judged equal to the standard is called the point of subjective equality. The difference between the mean point of subjective equality and the actual value of the standard stimulus is called the constant error. The standard deviation of a series of judgments

(PSEs) is called the variable error. All these measures can be obtained when a variable stimulus is matched against a standard stimulus.

The Method of Adjustment

The usual procedure followed when matching is called the method of adjustment. This simply requires the observer to manipulate the variable stimulus, changing it gradually (like tuning in a radio station), until it is considered to be matched to the standard. Sometimes a bracketing procedure will be used with the observer making the variable alternately larger and smaller than the standard until it appears exactly equal.

Let us take a simple example. Suppose subjects (*S*s) are presented with a standard line exactly 10 inches long. They are requested to draw a series of lines on several separate sheets of paper which they judge to be equal to the standard in length. Assume the results of four trials for a single *S* are as follows: 9¼ inches, 10⅛ inches, 9¾ inches, and 9⅞ inches. These judgments are actually points of subjective equality, and the mean of them is 9¾ inches. Since the constant error is defined as PSE — Standard, it is therefore 9¾ inches — 10 inches = — ¼ inch. This S thus shows a slight tendency to underestimate the length of the standard line or to overestimate the length of the drawn line. The variable error is defined by the standard deviation (or any other measure of variability), and thus the PSE, the CE, and the VE are all easily determined.

Although the method of adjustment is a simple and obvious procedure for making matching settings, it has sometimes been criticized on several grounds. First, since it requires the *S* to physically manipulate some object, we are inadvertently studying not only perceptual characteristics of the *S,* but also motor skills. It would seem desirable to find a method that would separate these two factors. Second, different *S*s will manipulate the variable stimulus at different rates (like tuning a radio quickly or slowly) and this has been found to influence judgments. It was because of problems of this sort that other standard psychophysical methods were developed.

It should be kept in mind that the method of adjustment can be used not only for matching studies, but for studies of discrimination as well. This will become obvious after a discussion of the discrimination problem.

The Discrimination Problem

Several new concepts are introduced when we go from the matching problem to the discrimination problem. As an illustration we might consider the musical aptitude test developed a number of years ago by Seashore. Although there are many aspects to it, we shall consider only the pitch discrimination subtest.

In it, the *S* is presented with a randomized series of paired tones, and is asked to judge whether the two tones of each pair are the "same" or "different." Sometimes the tones differ by a relatively large frequency and sometimes by a relatively small one. The *S*'s keenness of discrimination is measured by the smallness of the frequency differences in tones which can be consistently detected.

This kind of testing procedure is essentially an example of a well-known psychophysical method called the *method of constant stimuli* which we shall now examine.

The Method of Constant Stimuli

This method is often used to determine an *S*'s differential threshold. In order to do this the *S* must be presented with a standard stimulus, which is to be the fixed reference point, and a series of other stimuli which are slightly different in magnitude from the standard. The smaller the difference that can be consistently detected, the smaller is the differential threshold.

Since an *S*'s threshold is never absolutely constant, but varies slightly from time to time, we cannot expect the *S*'s responses to be entirely consistent. In other words, if two stimuli which differ slightly are presented to an *S* many times, it is perfectly reasonable to expect that judgments concerning them will vary. Sometimes, one stimulus will be judged larger, sometimes the other. Such inconsistency of judgment usually occurs only over a small range of values. This range is called the *interval of uncertainty,* and outside of this interval, the *S* is always correct in comparative judgments of the two stimuli. The method of constant stimuli is only concerned with stimuli in this interval of uncertainty.

The method has several general characteristics: (1) two stimuli are compared at a time, either simultaneously or successively; (2) the stimuli used are all selected from the interval of uncertainty; (3) the paired stimuli are presented in random order; (4) the pairs are presented many times; and (5) the *S*'s responses are usually limited to two categories of judgment such as "larger" and "smaller," or "higher" and "lower."

This may be illustrated with the following hypothetical example. Suppose we wish to determine a person's keenness of hearing (or differential threshold) at a frequency of 1,000 cycles per second (now defined as hertz or Hz). Our procedure might be as follows. We would first do a pilot study to quickly and roughly estimate the *S*'s interval of uncertainty. We might discover that when the tone was at 1,010 Hz the *S* seemed to consistently recognize it as higher in pitch than the standard of 1,000 Hz, and when it was at 990 Hz, consistently recognized it as lower in pitch. When the second tone was placed somewhere between 990 and 1,010 Hz the *S* had difficulty in making a judgment and sometimes was incorrect. This then roughly determines the *S*'s interval of uncertainty.

Our second step would be to select at least five stimuli within the *S*'s interval of uncertainty to be used as comparison stimuli. For example, we might choose 992 Hz, 996 Hz, 1,000 Hz, 1,004 Hz, and 1,008 Hz as our comparison stimuli, with 1,000 Hz as the standard. Notice that it is perfectly possible and valid to use a 1,000 Hz tone as a comparison stimulus.

We would then arrange all these pairs in random order and would present each pair to the subject many times. Reports in the literature suggest that 100 repetitions of each pair are sufficient in most cases for reliable results, although reliable data have been obtained with as few as 40 or 50 repetitions of each pair. This means that if 5 comparison stimuli are used and 50 repetitions of each pair are given, the S must make 250 judgments.

The type of judgment the S makes is limited to two categories; in this case S would be asked to simply state whether the comparison tone was "higher" or "lower" in pitch than the standard tone. When such data are compiled they tend to look somewhat as represented in Table 13–1. It is typically found that the percent of "higher" judgments increases as the frequency of the comparison tone becomes higher. Similarly, as the comparison tone becomes lower, the percent of "higher" judgments becomes lower. If these data are plotted on a graph, they produce an S-shaped curve which is called the *psychophysical function.* The curve approximates an ogive and is illustrated in Figure 13–1.

From the figure it is evident that the ogive is relatively linear in its middle portion and sharply curved near both ends. This means that the most accurate estimates and interpolations can be made from the middle portion of the curve.

Based on the ogive it is possible to estimate the PSE, the CE, and the VE as well as one additional measure called the *just noticeable difference* (JND), or *difference limen* (DL). The PSE is interpolated from the 50% point of judgments of "higher" and turns out in this example to be approximately 999.6 Hz. This means that the constant error is 999.6 − 1,000 = −0.4 Hz, indicating that the S has a slight tendency to underestimate the 1,000 Hz tone when judging. The variable error is usually estimated from the ogive by the interquartile range; that is, the difference between the 75th percentile point and the 25th percentile point. In this case it turns out to be 1,001.7 Hz − 997.7 Hz = 4.0 Hz. In general, the smaller the VE the more consistent are the judgments of the S. Sometimes, the

TABLE 13–1 THE DISTRIBUTION OF "HIGHER" (H) AND "LOWER" (L) JUDGMENTS IN A PITCH DISCRIMINATION EXPERIMENT USING THE METHOD OF CONSTANT STIMULI (THE STANDARD TONE IS 1,000 Hz)

Trials	Comparison Tones (Hz)				
	992	996	1,000	1,004	1,008
1	L	L	H	L	H
2	L	L	L	H	H
3	L	H	H	H	H
4	H	H	L	L	H
5	L	L	H	L	H
.	.	.	.	.	.
.	.	.	.	.	.
.	.	.	.	.	.
49	L	H	H	L	H
50	L	L	H	H	H
Number of Hs	2	6	28	46	50
Percent of Hs	4	12	56	92	100

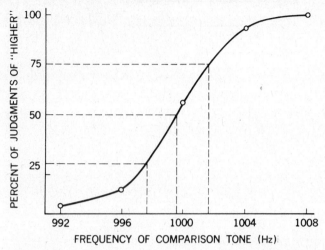

Figure 13–1.   Hypothetical ogive obtained in a differential threshold experiment.

standard deviation can be estimated from the ogive by taking the distance between the 84th percentile point and the 16th percentile point and dividing by 2. This is based on the assumption that the ogive is actually a cumulated normal distribution, and in a normal distribution, ± 1 standard deviation on either side of the median, includes 68% of the cases.

The concept of a just noticeable difference is a little more complex. What is the smallest increment in frequency that is just detectable? A little reflection will convince you that no one answer is possible, simply because there is always some probability that any increment in frequency, however small, will be correctly identified. This means that the value we choose for the JND is somewhat arbitrary. As a result, it has become fairly conventional to take as the JND the stimulus value between the PSE and the 75th percentile point. This distance, however, is actually the semi-interquartile range and is simply a measure of variability. Therefore, any one of the variability measures can be used as a measure of the JND.

This notion can perhaps be made clearer another way. Figure 13–2 shows two hypothetical ogives obtained from two Ss, A and B. Ogive A is steep and ogive B is relatively flatter.

It should be evident that subject A is more accurate in judgments than subject B. A has better pitch discrimination than B since A is far less likely to make errors in comparisons. A thus has a smaller JND than B. One way to measure the slope of the ogive is to find the difference in frequency that corresponds to the difference between the 75th and 25th percentile points, and this value, of course, is the interquartile range. In general, any measure of variability could be used as an index of the relative slope of different ogives, and thus could be used as an index of the JND. It is important, however, that investigators be consistent in their choice.

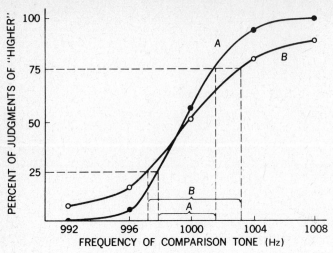

Figure 13–2.   Hypothetical ogives from two *S*s differing in relative sensitivity.

There is one further point that should be commented on and that concerns the use of only two categories of judgment in this method. In the past, there have been reports published in which investigators allowed *S*s three categories of judgment, such as "larger," "equal," "smaller," or "higher," "equal," "lower," etc. This would seem perfectly natural since there are undoubtedly many situations that arise where the *S*s believe the comparison stimulus to be equal to the standard one. In such cases, why force them to choose either "higher" or "lower"?

There are two main reasons. The first is that *S*s usually turn out to be better judges than they realize when forced to guess. Their guesses are always better than chance. The other reason for a two-category system is that the "equal" judgment has been found to be very sensitive to attitude and personality factors. Because of the method used for computing the JND, sometimes an observer uses the equal category when he or she has even the slightest doubt, while another observer might use it only rarely. It turns out that the first observer will have a large JND and the second a small one. The size of the JND in this case will reflect the *S*s attitudes about the task, or their criteria of judgment, more than it will reflect the sensitivity of their auditory system. The two-category procedure seems to be less affected by such variations in criteria of judgment and is therefore used more frequently by experimenters.

The Method of Limits

Another of the classical psychophysical methods used in studies of discrimination is called the method of limits. It can be illustrated by describing its use in determining a person's absolute threshold of hearing, that is, the softest tone one can hear.

The basic procedure involves the presentation of a given tone to an S at lesser and lesser discrete intensities until the subject can no longer hear it. The intensity of the tone at the point where the response changes from "Yes" (I hear it) to "No" (I do not hear it) is approximately the S's absolute threshold. Once this is determined, the tone is presented in reverse order, that is, starting at intensities well below what the S can hear, the intensity is increased in a series of steps until he or she just hears it. The series of alternating descending and ascending intensity are continued so as to get several estimates of the absolute threshold.

If an audiometer test were being run on an S to get the absolute threshold the procedure would be somewhat as follows: (1) A particular frequency would be selected, e.g., 1,000 Hz. (2) Series of tones of this frequency would be presented at decreasing intensity levels until the S could no longer hear the tone. (3) A fixed time for each exposure of the tone would be used. (4) Series of tones would be presented alternately in ascending and descending order, starting in each case well above or well below the estimated intensity threshold. (5) In order to avoid errors due to the Ss expectations about the length of the series, each sequence of intensities would be started at a different value. Another way to avoid expectation errors is to occasionally repeat a given step. Sometimes "check" trials are used; that is, no tone is given at a time the S expects one, to see if he or she reports a "false positive." (6) The S is requested to simply state whether the tone is present or absent, using "Yes" or "No" as responses (or the S may be requested to hold a key down for as long as he or she hears each tone). Each sequence is discontinued when the response changes from "Yes" to "No" or vice versa. The threshold is defined at the midpoint of the change from one response to the other.

Table 13–2 gives an illustration of the kind of data that might be obtained from an S during such threshold determinations. On the first trial the response

TABLE 13–2   HYPOTHETICAL DATA SHOWING HOW THE METHOD OF LIMITS MIGHT BE USED TO DETERMINE THE ABSOLUTE THRESHOLD. DESCENDING AND ASCENDING SERIES ARE ALTERNATED (Y STANDS FOR "YES" AND N FOR "NO")

Intensity of Tone in Decibels	Series					
	1	2	3	4	5	6
40	Y				Y	
35	Y				Y	
30	Y		Y		Y	
25	Y	Y	Y		N	Y
20	N	N	Y	Y		N
15		N	N	N		N
10		N		N		N
5		N				N
Estimated thresholds	22.5	22.5	17.5	17.5	27.5	22.5

changed in going from 25 decibels (db) to 20 decibels and we therefore estimate the threshold on that series as 22.5 decibels. (Decibels are a measure of sound intensity.) The absolute threshold is simply defined as the mean based on a number of determinations. A measure of variability can be obtained which is usually the standard deviation of the individual estimated thresholds.

One word of caution about the method. Several studies have shown that the actual threshold which is obtained depends upon both the step-interval size and the rate at which trials are given. Brackmann and Collier (1958) have reported that the brightness threshold based on a series of increasing light intensities is lower than that based on decreasing intensities, and that this difference increases as the step interval increases. In addition, the variability of the data was directly proportional to the size of the step interval. Day (1956) has reported that successive responses to a repeated near-threshold stimulus tend to be serially correlated if the time interval between them is less than about three seconds. If intervals longer than this are used, the responses tend to be more nearly independent. These studies indicate that such factors should be carefully controlled if these sources of variability are to be avoided.

Although the example which has been given is concerned with the absolute threshold, it is important to recognize that the method could be used to determine a differential threshold as well. In the latter case there would be a fixed reference stimulus, and the variable stimulus would be increased and decreased in a series of steps. The S would be required to indicate whether each value of the variable stimulus was larger or smaller than the standard one. As a matter of fact, the point cannot be too strongly emphasized that each of the psychophysical methods described can be used for matching studies, for absolute threshold determinations, or for the measurement of differential thresholds. The basic measures that are obtained are one or more of the following: PSE, CE, VE, and JND. Over the years variations in these methods have been reported (e.g., the use of the method of limits with only ascending series), but the basic concepts are those described above.

The Scaling Problem

People constantly make subjective estimations of the magnitude of things or events. We estimate heights, weights, personality traits, and degrees of conservatism, as well as the brightness of lights, the loudness of sounds, and the softness of textures. Ever since the middle of the last century a controversy has existed on the nature of the relationship between the magnitude of physical quantities and the magnitude of the corresponding subjective sensations. It is known, for example, that doubling the physical intensity of a light does not make the light appear twice as bright and that, in general, there is no linear relation between physical magnitudes and the corresponding subjective sensations.

Early in the nineteenth century, E. H. Weber made a number of observations on the relative sensitivity of our sense modalities under different conditions.

He tried to measure the differential threshold, or JND, at different frequencies of sound, different intensities of light, different weights of objects, and so on. An interesting generalization seemed to emerge. As the initial frequency, intensity, or weight increased, the JND also increased, roughly in proportion. This meant that the ratio of the JND to the standard was approximately constant for different-sized standards. The actual value of the constant varied from one modality to another.

In 1860, Fechner published his book on psychophysics in which he named this generalization Weber's law, and then went on to use it as the basis for a statement about the relation between subjective sensations and physical stimuli. Fechner proposed that the subjective sensation was proportional to the logarithm of the physical intensity and was defined mathematically as given in Chapter 8.

Over the past century, considerable debate has existed over the question of whether Fechner's logarithmic relation was the "true" one, and a number of alternatives have been proposed. The alternative which has achieved the greatest prominence is Stevens' *power law* (1957), which states that the magnitude of the subjective sensation depends on the intensity of the physical stimulus raised to some power.

Is there any way of determining empirically which of these two laws—the logarithmic law or the power law—is more consistent with empirical data? To do this we need to be able to measure subjective sensation in quantitative terms; that is, we need to be able to apply numbers reliably to our sensations. There are a number of different ways of doing this, but, unfortunately, when they are compared, they do not provide us with equivalent answers. The issues involved in this problem are deep and subtle and only some of them will be mentioned here. First, however, we will examine one of the methods used in establishing subjective scales.

The Method of Magnitude Estimation

In this method, the S is presented with a standard stimulus to which a number is arbitrarily assigned. For example, S might be given a tone at 90 decibels and told that this was to be called "100." The S is then given a series of tones and is asked to numerically judge their intensity relative to the standard. If the variable tone sounds one-half as loud as the standard, S is to call it "50," if it sounds one-tenth as loud, he or she is to call it "10," etc.

In one experiment using this method (Stevens, 1958) the Ss were asked to estimate each variable against a 90-db standard arbitrarily called "100," and then asked to estimate each variable against a 45-db standard arbitrarily called "1." The results were like those shown in Figure 13–3, where the logarithm of the magnitude estimations is plotted against the sound intensity in decibels (which is a logarithmic scale). Two parallel curves were obtained with identical slopes, implying that a power function fits the data nicely. As a matter of fact, the method

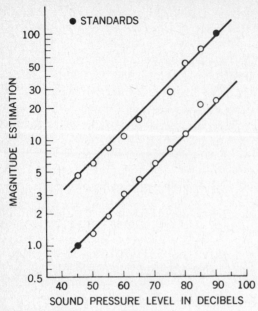

Figure 13–3. Loudness estimations based upon two different standards. In upper curve 90 decibels equals "100." In lower curve 45 decibels equals "1." (Adapted from J. C. Stevens, 1958.)

of magnitude estimation has become a preferred method for demonstrating that the data on many of the senses show a power function.

In using this method, there are a number of "rules" that should be followed if the data are to be of maximum consistency. These rules have been summarized by Stevens, Herrnstein, and Reynolds (1965) and are paraphrased here.

1. Do not require too many judgments from each S; two or three per stimulus is usually sufficient.

2. Each S should be presented the stimuli in a different and irregular order.

3. The S is asked to choose a number to stand for the subjective intensity of the first stimulus. He or she assigns numbers to the other stimuli in proportion to the first one. Sometimes, the first stimulus is assigned a number by the experimenter, but this is not a necessary aspect of the method.

4. It is not necessary to present a "standard" before each stimulus.

5. Since the distribution of judgments of a number of Ss is usually skewed, either the median or the geometric mean is used as a measure of central tendency. (The geometric mean is the nth root of the product of n numbers.)

This method basically assumes that an S is capable of arranging his or her subjective sensations in accord with knowledge of the real number system. Many studies have been done using this method and the results generally support a power law concept.

A number of other scaling methods have been proposed, however, that do not produce equivalent results. Some of these are called the method of equal appearing intervals, the method of fractionation, the constant-sum method, the method of multiple stimuli, and the method of successive categories. These all represent attempts to establish a numerical connection between subjective sensations and physical stimuli, but the assumptions they make are different and the results also differ.

A Recent Development: Signal Detection Theory

In a study using college students, naive with respect to the purposes of the experiment, subjects were asked to taste some samples of water and to report if each was salty or not. Unknown to the students, the samples in each case consisted only of distilled water. The results showed that 82% of the Ss made at least one "salt" response, and that the median "salt" response was 24% (Juhasz and Sarbin, 1966).

This study simply illustrates the existence of so-called "false alarms" in perception, that is, an erroneous statement that a stimulus exists, when in reality it does not. Such false alarms are well known in psychophysical studies and are more likely to occur when the limits of a person's sensitivity are being explored. If a person is intently listening for a very faint tone, he or she may occasionally report a tone present when none exists. Some Ss are more likely to do this than others. This fact raises a very important issue for psychophysics. It suggests the possibility that the actual threshold which is measured for a given S will depend partly upon the sensitivity of his or her sensory processes *and* partly on the response criterion. The response criterion is simply the basis an S uses for deciding whether or not to report having heard a faint tone or seen a dim light.

As an illustration of this point we may consider the testing procedure for visual threshold. The S is usually presented with brief, circular flashes of light that are very dim. S is to report whether the light is seen or not. Some Ss will report the light as present only if they see a complete circle of light. Other Ss will report the light as present even if they see a faint flash with no definite contours. The sensitivity of the two Ss might be equal, but one has a more liberal response criterion for reporting when the light is present, and that S will show up as apparently having a lower threshold. Therefore, the usual methods for testing thresholds confuse, to some degree, the Ss response criterion and his or her actual sensitivity.

One way in which this problem has been handled in the past is by inserting "catch" trials into the testing series, that is, random trials in which a stimulus is not presented. If the S reports the stimulus as present, he or she is usually warned by the experimenter to be more careful, or, if the S persists, his or her data may simply be disregarded.

The result of this procedure is that a good deal of the psychophysical data of the past have been obtained from a small number of highly trained observers, who have established consistent but high response criteria.

During the past two decades, a new approach to this problem has been developed called *signal detection theory*. Although the details are complex and depend upon the mathematics of statistical decision theory, a few general ideas may be presented here.

A basic aim of detection theory is to separate, by experimental procedures, the response criterion of the S from the S's actual sensitivity. One of the ways this can be done is by presenting the observer with a large number of "catch" trials so an independent estimate can be made of his or her response criterion (i.e., the S's probability of saying "yes" when no signal is given). Another approach to this problem is to use a different kind of psychophysical method—what Swets (1961) has called the *second-choice experiment*. In this procedure, the S is told that a signal will be presented during one, and only one, of four time intervals during each trial. The task is to judge in which of the time intervals the stimulus is present. S is also asked to make a second choice. This kind of data can be analyzed in such a way as to minimize the effects of response criterion and maximize the effects of sensitivity alone. The analysis of "false alarms" in this approach—which were usually considered simply as errors—has led to some interesting ideas concerning sensory function.

Let us consider a few examples. Suppose that an auditory stimulus is chosen that is close to the limits of hearing and that this tone is presented 100 times along with 100 randomly interspersed trials in which no tone is given. The S is asked to report on the presence or absence of the tone. The results of this series of observations can be summarized in a simple 2×2 table in which the number or proportion of "Yes" and "No" are indicated for the condition when the tone is presented and for the condition when the tone is not presented. This is shown in Table 13–3.

These results would indicate that 60% of the time the S said "Yes" when the tone was presented (i.e., showed a "hit") and 40% of the time S missed the stimulus. These values reflect the S's sensitivity under these particular conditions. When the tone was not presented, S correctly said "No" 75% of the time, but showed a "false alarm" 25% of the time. The number of "false alarms" reflects the S's expectations. Thus it is possible to find separate measures of the S's sensitivity and expectations.

TABLE 13–3 PROPORTION OF RESPONSES OF "YES" AND "NO"

		"Yes"	"No"
Stimulus	On	0.60 (Hit)	0.40 (Miss)
	Off	0.25 (False alarm)	0.75 (Correct rejection)

The results presented here, however, were obtained under conditions in which the stimulus was given on 50% of the trials. If the tone is presented on (say) 80% of the trials, a different set of proportions would be obtained for the table. In order to carry through a signal detection experiment using this approach, four or five different stimulus probabilities would be used at several intensity levels. From these data separate estimates may be made of the Ss perceptual sensitivity and response criterion (Corso, 1967). An alternative method requires the S to make a rating of his or her confidence that the stimulus is present on each trial. This is described by Price (1966).

What are some implications of this general approach for the study of sensory function? One observation that has been made is that the use of the PSE did not discriminate between schizophrenic patients and normals on a size-constancy task, although the use of a separate measure of perceptual sensitivity, unaffected by the Ss response criterion did discriminate between some of the groups (Price and Erickson, 1966). This approach helped to clarify some of the inconsistencies reported in this area of research.

Another important implication relates to studies of motivation and perception. It has been noted that many such studies have confounded the Ss sensitivity with his or her response criterion. For example, if an S shows a higher threshold to certain kinds of words (e.g., sexual) it does not follow that the Ss needs or values influence perception. The difference may be due to a change in sensitivity or to a change in criterion for reporting a perception or to a change in both. An S may be unwilling to report a particular type of word until quite confident that he or she knows what it is. This means that the false-alarm rate would decrease even though sensitivity might remain constant. Since the usual threshold measure does not enable us to obtain an independent estimate of these two factors, the interpretation of a difference obtained between two thresholds is unclear. The theory of signal detection has thus provided important new insights into some of the traditional problems of psychophysics.

Some Applications of Psychophysics

Almost all the examples thus far given have utilized situations where an observer is presented with a simple, usually discrete stimulus and required to make some kind of judgment about it. However, psychophysical methods have also been applied to much more complex situations where there is no simple relationship between the stimulus as physically measured and the observer's judgment.

One of the important uses of such methods is in the construction of attitude scales. For example, Ss may be presented with pairs of nationalities and asked to state their preferences. This method of paired comparisons enables a systematic scaling of preferences for each S for all nationalities tested. Such scales have been used for evaluating the effects of propaganda on attitudes. The method of paired comparisons has also been used to establish scales for the judgment of the relative seriousness of crimes.

Other psychophysical methods have been used to measure the emotional meanings of words in contrast to their cognitive meanings, the relative similarity of different types of packaging in retail stores, the optimum inventory for mail order houses in certain items in order to please the majority of customers, the most desirable menus to use in certain types of restaurants, the esthetic value of paintings, and the effects of running certain kinds of candidates in political elections. In fact, it should be evident by now that psychophysics deals with the general nature of human discrimination.

14

The Nature of Measurement

Science is an art. There are no ab initio *principles to tell us how to be clever in devising procedures of measurement. The way to empirical discovery lies not through mathematics, even, but through the exercise of uncommon experimental sense and ingenuity. We invent mathematical models, but we discover measures in the laboratory.*

—S. S. Stevens

Why Measure?

Most of the events or objects that scientists are concerned with vary in magnitude. The basic dimensions of physics—length, mass, and time (from which most other dimensions are derived)—can vary from zero magnitude to indefinitely large ones, and although dichotomies are sometimes used for convenience, they are recognized as crude approximations.

Many of the variables studied in psychology are also continuous. People are not extroverted *or* introverted any more than minerals are hard *or* soft. Although practice is often described as massed *or* distributed, and reinforcements are categorized as continuous *or* partial, it is recognized that such dichotomies are simply convenient names representing the extremes of continuous variables.

In their effort to represent the fact that events or objects vary in magnitude, scientists utilize numbers, partly because numbers are a well understood system of concepts that involve magnitude. To say this another way, numbers (plus the operations associated with them) can be considered to be a general analogue or model of the relationships existing among many events that occur naturally. If people vary in intelligence from low to high, we can represent this idea with numbers that also vary from low to high. If some people are slightly prejudiced and others highly prejudiced, we can also represent this idea by numbers that vary from low to high. Generality obtains because the very same numbers are used to represent the magnitudes of very different kinds of events. In fact, one of the purposes of assigning numbers to events is to provide a common and universal language for describing the magnitudes of many different kinds of things.

There is another reason for assigning numbers to events. When this is done, it becomes possible to make fine distinctions in situations where only broad or vague verbal distinctions were previously possible. The assignment of numbers enables us to distinguish between "dull normal" intellects and "normal" ones, as well as between "normal" and "bright."

Thus, if we define measurement as *the assignment of numbers to objects or events according to certain rules,* it appears that there are at least two good reasons for doing this. One is that numbers represent a universal language for describing many different kinds of things; the other is that numbers enable us to make finer magnitude distinctions than would otherwise be possible.

Do Events Match Numbers?

Once the value of measurement is recognized several other important questions may be raised. Since numbers are considered to be similar to many events that occur in the "real" world we may ask whether the events and the numbers correspond in all respects. For example, the real number system includes not only the property of magnitude, but also of additivity. In the number system 40 plus 40 is always equal to 80. But the question arises as to whether events also operate in this way, or to put the matter differently, whether events have the property of additivity as defined in the number system.

If two 1-foot rulers are placed end to end, their combined length is 2 feet; if two 100-ohm resistors are placed in series, their combined resistance is 200 ohms. These findings are thus in accord with our number system analogy.

But suppose the two 100-ohm resistors are added in parallel instead of in series; then their combined resistance is 50 ohms rather than 200 ohms. If water is boiling at 100°C, and more boiling water is added at 100°C, the temperature of the combined water is still 100°C.

One point being made here is that many events occur in nature which can be described with the use of numbers, but which do *not* show all the properties of the number system. Another point that is implicit is that the word *addition* must be defined anew each time we deal with a new physical or psychological system.

Let us examine a problem from the field of audition. Suppose we produce a pure tone of 1,000 Hz whose intensity is 40 decibels. Assume we then play a second 40-decibel pure tone of 1,000 Hz from a loudspeaker adjacent to the first. Do the two sounds add arithmetically from the point of view of a listener? It turns out that they do not add arithmetically although there is some increase in apparent loudness. The problem is much more complicated for the addition of frequencies. Two 1,000 Hz tones played at the same time do not sound like a 2,000 Hz tone, but only a 1,000 Hz tone. If a 1,000 Hz tone is played at the same time as a 2,000 Hz tone, the result is a complex mixture of tones and harmonics. Two people, each with an IQ of 100, and working together on a given problem, do not function equally as well as one person with an IQ of 200.

It should thus be evident that some of the ways events may be added in the real world do not always match the addition of numbers in our theoretical model, the real number system.

Scales of Measurement

The preceding observations lead to an important concept, the concept of scales of measurement. Although the properties of numbers and the properties of events do not always match exactly, it is often possible to indicate the *degree* to which they agree or disagree. For example, sometimes numbers can be used simply to designate different events or objects without regard to the magnitude of the object or event. This is done when numbers are used to indicate different football players or when numbers are used to indicate items in a catalog. In such cases order is of no significance; numbers are used only as labels. It is debatable whether this use of numbers should be considered measurement, but Stevens (1958b) has called this a *nominal* scale.

Situations of greater significance to the psychologist are those in which it is possible to rank-order a group of objects or events. When an expert rates beef as "prime," "choice," or "good" this represents a rank ordering on estimated fat content, but no attempt is made to indicate that "prime" has twice as much fat as "choice" or five times as much as "good" beef. The numbers 1, 2, and 3 could be given to these three grades, but any other set of increasing numbers could just as well be applied, for example, 2, 7, and 10 or 4, 15, and 25. Since the relative differences between rankings are not specified, any set of numbers of increasing rank could be used. Such a scale is called an *ordinal* scale, and it is evident that adding or multiplying such arbitrary ranks could lead to misleading results. In psychology, ratings of personality traits, ratings of sales ability, ratings of creativity and the like are usually rank-order or ordinal scales.

There are certain events which match the number system more closely; not only do they show increasing order of magnitude, but they imply that equal differences in the magnitude of the events are associated with equal intervals between numbers applied to the events. The difference between 10°F and 20°F is the same difference of temperature as that between 40°F and 50°F, or 80°F and 90°F. If we convert scores on an intelligence test for a group of students into percentiles, then we have equal numbers of students between the 10th and 20th percentile, the 40th and 50th percentile, or the 80th and 90th percentile. But this does not mean that intelligence as theoretically conceived is equally distributed among these percentiles. The difference in intelligence between students in the 40th and 50th percentile (the middle portion of the normal distribution) is not as great as the difference in intelligence between students in the 80th and 90th percentiles (the upper tail of the normal distribution). If intelligence test data are converted to standard scores, the *assumption* is usually made that equal standard scores represent equal differences in intelligence. This is, however, an assumption and not directly verifiable. Scales of this type are called *interval* scales.

Finally, certain events occur which match the number system not only in terms of increasing order of magnitude and equal intervals, but also in terms of the existence of a meaningful zero point. In the Centigrade temperature scale the freezing point of water is arbitrarily called zero degrees. This same physical occurrence is 32 degrees on the Fahrenheit scale. Since the zero point is arbitrary it is not correct to speak of 40°F indicating twice as much heat as 20°F (since 40°F is equal to 4.4°C and 20°F is equal to −6.7°C). The actual numerical ratio between any two numbers will depend on the choice of a zero point.

If, however, a meaningful and unique zero point exists, then all ratios between numbers are meaningful and unique, and most mathematical operations appropriate to the number system can be performed. Such scales are called *ratio* scales.

The concept of scales of measurement described above has been presented most fully by Stevens in several papers (1946; 1958b; 1959). There are, however, several problems relating to the generality of this viewpoint about the nature of measurement.

The first problem concerns the fact that in practice it is extremely difficult to know whether or not we have an equal unit, interval scale. The examples of equal unit scales given by Stevens are taken mostly from physics; he lists temperature, time, and potential energy; he then adds "intelligence test standard scores (?)." Stevens gives no other psychological examples and no formal rules for determining whether we have obtained such a scale or not.

Guilford (1954), in discussing this same problem, points out that one way of determining whether or not an equal unit scale exists is by demonstrating additivity. If 10 units of intelligence plus 20 units of intelligence are equal to 30 units of intelligence then additivity is shown. However, Guilford notes that

> The property of additivity is rarely experimentally demonstrable, even in the physical sciences. . . . On the ordinary temperature scales there is no operation for the summation of two temperature levels. Even in the realm of length or distance there are very serious limitations to the proof of addition by experimental operations. No one has ever placed light-years end to end, nor has anyone demonstrated the addition of atomic distances. . . . In all the sciences, then, the assumption of applicability of number properties rests on very limited empirical proof.

Despite the limited proof of additivity of measures there is no doubt that physics and technology in general have made remarkable progress in the last century. This at least raises the question of whether additivity and equal unit scales must be proven at all. To anticipate a point to be made in the next section, physicists seem to be far less concerned about the existence of equal unit scales than are psychologists.

A second problem that has been mentioned in discussions of scaling concerns the question of "context" effects. In an effort to obtain ratio scales in psychology, Stevens has used a method called *fractionation*. This requires the subject or observer to adjust one light until it is one-half as bright as another light, or to adjust one tone until it is one-third as high in pitch as another. Any fraction can be used and the technique can be applied to any sense modality. The essential requirement is that the subject make direct ratio estimates of the numerical relationships between subjective magnitudes.

Although this technique has been widely used, a number of criticisms have been raised against it. For example, Garner (1954) reported a study in which three different groups of subjects were given the same standard reference auditory intensity, but varying ranges of comparison stimuli. The results showed that the mean half-loudness judgment for each group was approximately at the middle of the range of comparison intensities that were used, thus indicating that the stimulus context had a marked effect upon the subjective scales obtained from subjects by the fractionation method. As a result of a subsequent experiment, Garner (1959) concluded that half-loudness judgments mainly reflect individual response sets typical of ambiguous situations and are therefore of doubtful validity.

Poulton and Simmonds (1963) have also shown in connection with the visual modality that fractional (or multiple) estimates of sensory magnitude are considerably modified by the ranges of stimuli used and by the ranges of numbers available to the subjects. They also conclude that numerical estimates of sensory magnitude are of doubtful validity. Since Stevens has described the fractionation methods as the major technique for obtaining ratio scales for psychological dimensions, these criticisms raise the question of whether ratio scales can be constructed in psychology at all.

How Physicists Measure Things

In England in A.D. 965 a law was passed stating that the standard of length was to be kept at London and a series of copies were to be used throughout the kingdom. This standard yard was defined to be 36 inches. The yard that had been used until then was 39.6 inches and this standard was eventually prohibited by law.

In 1760 a new standard was made consisting of a brass bar a little over a yard in length with gold studs near the ends. The yard was then defined as the distance between the center of two dots, one punched in each of the gold studs, when the temperature of the bar was 62°F.

In the middle of the nineteenth century, five bronze bars were made as nearly alike as possible and used as the new standards. Every 10 years these 5 standards are compared with one another, and it has been observed that one of them showed a gradual decrease in length over the first 40 years amounting to 228 millionths of an inch.

In France, a standard meter was made in 1801 and replaced in 1889. It is made of a platinum-iridium alloy with two engraved lines near the ends defining the length of the meter. This is true, however, only when the temperature of the bar is that of melting ice and the bar is supported in a certain standard way.

This bit of history has been given to emphasize the fact that what we take to be the unit of measurement of any quantity is essentially an arbitrary convention. Another important point to be made is that stable units, in a practical sense, require considerable knowledge of the nature of the world, in this case, of the nature of physical properties of bodies. A physicist puts the matter this way: "Much of this knowledge depends upon observations which involve measurements of length based on an earlier and less satisfactory standard. In general, science advances through stages of successive refinement" (Feather, 1959).

There is one other point of fundamental significance for an understanding of the nature of measurement, and this concerns the question of addition of units. When a person wants to measure the length of something, he or she lays a ruler or yardstick down end over end until some subdivision of the ruler is lined up with the end of the object. In doing this, two assumptions are made: (1) that the length of the ruler remains the same no matter where it is moved, and (2) that the mathematical operation of addition is to be represented by the process of placing rulers end to end.

Now the fact is that neither of these assumptions can be proven to be logically necessary. Euclid recognized this first point in relation to geometry and simply made the assumption that figures may be moved freely in space without change of shape or size. The second assumption is not necessary either since it is perfectly possible to imagine measuring the length of objects in other ways. For example, in a treatise on measurement Ellis (1966) suggests that we imagine measuring lengths by placing the measuring rods at right angles to one another. In such a case, the length of an object is the diagonal of the triangle formed by this "right-angled addition," and it turns out to satisfy all the logical requirements of length measurement.

The basic reason this method of addition or any one of the other logically possible ones is not used is that the results of such measurements would make the laws of science more complicated than they are now. This means that the problem of how best to add units is at least partly a question of convenience.

The same sort of considerations apply also to the measurement of time. Because every process occurring in nature involves duration, any recurrent process can be used as a clock. The rising and setting of the sun, the movement of a pendulum, the vibrations of a tuning fork, and the speed of radioactive decay have all been used to measure the passage of time. But one fundamental *assumption* must be made—that the unit of time tomorrow is the same length as the unit of time today. In short, equality of units is assumed and not proven.

The Physical Measurement of Roughness

Let us look at another example of measurement in an area which is less clear-cut. How might a physicist develop a technique for measuring the roughness of surfaces?

According to Wilson (1952), four basic steps are necessary for developing a measurement scale. The first requires some kind of *intuitive feeling* for the quality to be measured. The second requires the development of a method for *comparing* two samples so that it can be said that one has more of the quality than the other. The third involves setting up *standards,* and the fourth requires the development of a set of *rules* for relating the standards.

When we apply these criteria to roughness, it is evident that we can usually make subjective judgments about the roughness of surfaces on the basis of touch. Alternately, it would be possible to move a phonograph needle and pickup across the surface and record the magnitude of the electrical signals produced by the vibration of the needle. The magnitude of the signal could be used to compare two surfaces.

As a third step, a set of standard plates could be prepared having different degrees of roughness as measured by the phonograph needle system. Copies of the plates could then be prepared and used in different places.

Finally, a scale of roughness might be defined in terms of the voltage outputs produced by drawing the needle over different surfaces under standard conditions.

The physicist does not generally concern him or herself with the question of whether a scale has equal units. However, physicists are very concerned about the *consistency* and *reliability* of the data resulting from their methods. They are also concerned with their relations to other kinds of data, for example, with measurements of coefficient of friction. The physicist may also try some practical tests. An attempt may be made to determine whether surfaces with higher roughness indices actually wear out faster than those with lower measures. In general, simple linear relations between the roughness measure and wearability or coefficient of friction are not expected. But, so long as the relationship is a consistent one, it can be dealt with. If, however, some other method of measuring roughness, (e.g., a reflected light technique), shows mathematically simpler relations to other types of measures, the physicist will be inclined to drop the phonograph needle technique and adopt the mathematically simpler one.

The preceding description is obviously an oversimplified account of the development of a measurement scale. It does suggest, however, that the physicist is not generally concerned with whether the scale dealt with is an ordinal, interval, or ratio scale. The physicist does not measure equality of units in any direct way, but on the contrary, simply assumes it. The major concerns are with the consistency of the data and their relations to other kinds of measures. These same considerations can meaningfully apply to the psychologist as well.

Some Implications

There are some interesting implications of the views that have been presented. If we examine the physicist's apparently successful approach to the problem of measurement, we find that the basic requirements are the establishing of standards and specification of rules for comparing the things to be measured with the standards so that numbers may be assigned. It has not been shown that addition of scale values is either a necessary or a sufficient condition to ensure meaningful measurement. In fact, many fundamental physical quantities do not show additivity of the sort implied by the arithmetic number system (e.g., temperature, density, hardness). What is essential is that the results obtained by applying a particular measurement procedure be consistent and related in an orderly fashion to other kinds of measures.

These considerations apply also to the measurement of quantities of concern to psychologists. This includes measures used in the study of learning, intelligence, motivation, stress, and even psychophysics. No one has seriously tried to show that rate of response, number of errors, trials to reach a criterion, probability of a response, or proportion of animals responding (to name a few) are based on an equal unit scale or show the property of additivity. Some of these measures of learning may turn out to be more useful than others, but the grounds for this assertion have nothing to do with whether or not the measures are additive. On the contrary, the criteria refer to such matters as ease of making the measurement, generality of the measurement approach to many situations, consistency of the data obtained by it, and responsivity of the measure to important experimental variables. In relation to this issue Ehrenberg (1955) has commented that, "no reasons seem ever to have been suggested, let alone shown to be cogent, why an empirical correspondence with arithmetical addition, which is only one out of all the many mathematical operations which have been defined and studied, should be *the* criterion of 'measurability.' " In other words, the key questions of research concern the issue of whether measures are *valid,* rather than whether they are permissible. Scientists seek generality and invariance of concepts, but such generality has little to do with the type of scale one uses in research or the kinds of statistics one applies to data. It is perfectly possible and practicable for psychologists to attempt measurement using whatever measures are available or whatever measures can be invented, without concern in advance as to whether or not an equal unit scale is implied. Consistency of data obtained, relation to other variables and other considerations will eventually indicate whether the measure is useful or not.

Let us briefly examine one final illustration. If an investigator was interested in measuring the strength of hunger motivation, a variety of measurement approaches would be available. One approach is to record some event designed to produce the state being measured, for example, the time the animal is deprived of food. A second approach would be to use some measure of the animals' behavior as an index of the degree of hunger, for example, the speed of running a maze to get food might be one such index. Another might be the rate of bar pressing for pellets. Still a third approach would be a measure based on the degree of noxious stimulation needed to prevent a response; thus, we might measure the strength of hunger by the magnitude of shock just needed to stop the animal from crossing an electrified grid to food, or we might find the amount of quinine that must be added to the food to prevent the animal from eating. These examples are

What Instruments Do

Although some aspects of science will always rely relatively more on careful observation alone, the tendency is toward increasing use of instruments. There are several reasons for this.

The first is that instruments help acquire data under known conditions. Observing the behavior of fish in their natural environment has provided many interesting kinds of information about such things as schooling behavior, migrations, social interaction, and predation. However, most of this information suffers from one defect; it is often difficult, if not impossible, to determine the causes of the observed behavior. If, however, the fish are raised in a large tank and such conditions as illumination, temperature, and salinity are varied systematically, it becomes possible to determine what factors produce changes in the events that are observed. The instruments enable us to know the conditions under which the observations are made.

When an animal is placed in a maze or a Skinner box, or when a human subject is placed in an iron lung in a sensory deprivation experiment, the instrument is designed to limit the environment so that whatever data are collected are obtained under known conditions.

This fact suggests a second purpose of instruments; they can be used to standardize data acquisition procedures from experiment to experiment. Once an instrument has been designed to limit the environment in a certain way, it sometimes becomes apparent that it can be used in the acquisition of data in a large variety of situations. This is true, for example, of the Skinner box which is used routinely in all sorts of learning studies, in drug research, and in physiological research. This is also true, to a lesser degree, of the Wisconsin General Test Apparatus, developed by Harlow and his associates for use with all types of animals in the study of learning. In Russia, the Pavlovian conditioning techniques have become standardized to a considerable degree and many kinds of experiments have been done in the same basic setting. This standardization due to the use of instruments enables a large body of information to be built up within a common framework, simply because different investigators are using the same equipment.

The third major reason for the increasing use of instruments is that they enable the permanent recording of events. This is done with cameras and tape recorders, as well as ink-writing polygraphs. In clinical research, for example, there is an increasing reliance on tape recordings of interviews and therapy sessions, on motion picture records of psychotherapy interactions, and on physiological recording of such variables as heart rate and respiration rate. These instruments provide permanent records so that repeated observations may be made of any and every aspect of the events by the original observer as well as others. Needless to say, there are often things discovered about the interactions that were not immediately obvious to an observer. Through these methods, detailed analyses have been made of the facial expressions and postures of patients, and of their idiosyncratic uses of language, including such things as inflections, pauses, interruptions, and other aspects of the speech pattern.

There is one other and probably most significant purpose of instruments—to enable us to measure and record things not available to our unaided senses. In any living organism there are literally thousands of chemical, electrical, and thermal events that occur at all times, and yet they are not directly perceptible. Only by interposing special instruments does it become possible to record or measure them.

Brain waves can only be recorded with special, highly sensitive amplifiers. Skin resistance changes (or the GSRs) require electrical measuring devices. Blood pressure can be measured in an animal by probes placed directly into arteries, or indirectly in man in a variety of ways. Reaction time in man is measured in tenths of a second, while nerve action potentials are measured in thousandths of a second. The loudness of sounds is measured by pressure changes in the atmosphere, while psychophysical research on color vision requires the accurate specification of colors. Microscopes and telescopes extend the range of action of our sense organs, just as the various measuring instruments mentioned above make all kinds of events potentially available to our senses. It is thus obvious that many areas of science would be largely inaccessible without special measuring instruments.

The points that have been made may now be summarized. Instruments are important to science because: (1) they enable data to be obtained under known conditions; (2) they standardize data acquisition procedures from experiment to experiment; (3) they enable information to be permanently recorded for future analysis; and (4) they enable measurement of events which are not directly observable by the senses.

It is obvious that these are important values, but as is so often the case, the blessings are not unmixed. There are many problems created by instruments that require considerable caution and thought concerning their use.

Problems Created by Instruments

The very fact that instruments allow the collection of information under standard conditions means that a sampling process has been utilized. This is true simply because the conditions that are standardized by the instrument are only a few out of a potentially large number of conditions that could have been used.

The first maze used in this country was designed in 1900 by Willard Small. It was designed for rats and was 6 by 8 feet in size with wire netting for walls. Several years later, J. B. Watson reduced the size of the maze to 5 by 7 feet and made his alleys of wood. Since that time a large number of modifications have been introduced in the details of the construction of the maze (Lyons, 1965). Now, although this meant that the conditions of an experiment were probably constant for any one experimenter, they were not constant for all researchers in a given field. Differences in results obtained by different investigators could then be attributed at least partly to differences of procedure and equipment. To take a simple example, no one knew the influence of the width of the alley in the maze on learning ability in rats.

In light of these problems it would seem at first glance that one solution to the problem would be to standardize equipment so that all investigators in a field used the same instruments. This solution creates a difficulty too, namely, that it may artificially limit the direction of research and prevent creative innovations. For example, by the middle 1920s, multiple T-mazes and multiple U-mazes had become fairly standard devices used in studies of learning, but it often took hundreds of trials for the rat to learn to discriminate between simple visual patterns. Around 1930, Karl Lashley developed an alternate method for studying discrimination, a device which he called a "jumping stand." In this device, the rat was placed upon a small stand, a foot or two off the floor, and was forced to jump toward one of two doors, each marked with a different visual pattern. If the rat hit the "correct" pattern, the door opened and a food pellet became available; if it hit the "wrong" pattern, the door remained shut and the rat fell into a net. With this equipment, a rat could often learn the same discrimination in 20 or 30 trials. Thus the study of learning became much more efficient.

The same considerations also apply to the invention of the Skinner box. This was, in some ways, a simplified version of Thorndike's 1898 "puzzle box" in which an animal had to open a latch in order to escape from a small cage. The Skinner box is simply a small closed chamber in which the animal must press a lever or peck a key in order to receive some kind of reward such as food, water, or escape from electric shock. One of the major values of the instrument is that all of the procedures used with it can be made automatic so that rewards can be given in any kind of sequence and responses may be recorded on moving strips of paper. Large numbers of animals can be run simultaneously and the response records can be examined at the convenience of the experimenter. This instrument has therefore made many kinds of studies possible which would have been almost inconceivable a few decades ago.

However, standardization is not necessarily a desirable thing. This is even true of the Skinner box. Because of the discrete (on-off) characteristics of the response measure, problems related to use of continuous responses, such as the degree of force with which an animal presses the bar, were relatively ignored. Another difficulty created by the Skinner box is that it limits the kinds of problems that can be studied. For example, Harlow (1953) has criticized the use of the Skinner box partly on the grounds that such phenomena as "curiosity," "exploratory drive," and "affection" are not readily observable in that setting.

The picture that emerges from all this is that although standardization is often desirable, it should never limit or prevent innovation. Researchers constantly strive to develop instruments which are simple, adaptable to many kinds of problems, and which allow information to be gathered reliably and in permanent form. The danger in all this is that the results of the experiment may reflect certain arbitrary properties of the apparatus, such things as size, lighting conditions, types of responses that are required, etc.

The physicists have also faced this problem and they have arrived at two general approaches to a solution. One approach is to conceive of instruments as ways of measuring theoretically important variables whose properties are inferred from the instrumental results, but are not equivalent to them. In other words, they are concerned with instruments as measures of hypothetical constructs (see Chapter 3). Physicists who tried to measure the charge on the electron could do this in half a dozen different ways using as many different kinds of instruments. But in every case, there were theoretical links between the readings obtained on dials and the concept "charge on an electron." Similarly, it is possible to measure breathing characteristics in a person by means of a pneumatic system, a strain gauge, a variable resistance device, and a variable impedance device, all of which are based on different physical principles, but all of which (under proper conditions) can produce identical answers.

The other approach to the problem of equating different instruments is through *calibration*—a set of procedures of fundamental importance in all research. Calibration refers to the process of exposing the instrument to precisely known inputs or standard conditions, so that its readings under those conditions can be determined. This enables different instruments to be set or adjusted to produce equivalent results. For example, whenever an EEG machine is used to record brain waves, a calibration check is usually made at the beginning. This means that a carefully controlled 50-microvolt electrical signal is fed into the device and the size of the output on the record is noted. This is then used as a reference for evaluating the magnitude of the EEG changes during the experiment itself. Variations in the accuracy of the instrument over time may be compensated for by knowledge of the calibration values.

The various standards used for calibration of electrical, mechanical, thermal, and other instruments are kept at the National Bureau of Standards in Washington, D.C. Copies of these standards are made available to scientists and instrument manufacturers for calibration of their instruments. In addition, scientists meet periodically to discuss the establishment of standards for all nations as well as to consider new and more refined ways of defining the fundamental standards. These facts give some idea of the importance researchers attach to the problem of accurately calibrating their instruments. It is a good rule to periodically check the calibration on all instruments in use.

How to Specify the Properties of Instruments

When an instrument is used as a measuring device there are many requirements which it must fulfill. For example, it should provide a faithful reproduction of the event measured without introducing any distortion. It should also be sensitive enough to record events which are either very rapid or very small. These criteria (among others) are not always easily satisfied, so that it becomes necessary to have ways of describing, in quantitative terms, how close an instrument comes to providing satisfactory measurement. Some of these ways will now be outlined. Many of the concepts used will be taken from the language of electronics simply because electrical instruments are being used more and more for all types of recording. It should also be noted that it is now generally possible to change the energy in any given system into an electrical signal which can then be easily measured.

Sensitivity. This refers to the minimum energy, signal, or input which the instrument can reliably distinguish. If the device is an electrocardiograph, the sensitivity is usually measured in terms of a few millivolts that it can record. If the device is an electroencephalograph, its sensitivity is measured in microvolts or millionths of a volt. If the device is designed to measure skin resistance, its sensitivity might be given in terms of the smallest change in resistance (ohms) that it can reliably record.

When investigators consider the purchase of some measuring equipment it is important for them to have some idea of the approximate size of the input signal they want to measure so that they can check it against the manufacturer's sensitivity specifications.

Range. All measuring instruments have a range within which they are designed to normally operate. This range includes an upper maximum value of the input energy or signal as well as a lower maximum sensitivity value. For example, a sound level meter used for measuring the intensity of sounds might be designed to operate within the range of 40 to 110 decibels, which roughly covers the range of sounds normally encountered in the environment. However, for special purposes, a sound level meter might be used to record sounds up to 130 decibels, which is approximately the auditory pain threshold.

Similarly, light meters are designed to work in different ranges. If investigators are concerned with measuring the absolute threshold, they might use a very sensitive meter with a small range of action. If they were studying differential thresholds at higher intensities they would use a light meter with a larger range of response.

Linearity. Another characteristic of a good measuring instrument is called linearity, which means that there is a simple and direct relationship between the size of the signal entering the instrument and the size of the response or output of the instrument.

Most recorders used in psychophysiological research have three major elements. There is first an electrode or a transducer, which either picks up small electrical signals coming from the body (e.g., the electrocardiogram) or transforms another form of energy into an electrical signal (e.g., blood pressure into an electrical change, or a volume displacement, as in breathing, into an electrical change). These small electrical signals are then fed through an amplifier which is simply designed to increase greatly the size of the signal so that it can operate a recording device of some sort. For example, the 10 to 100 microvolt signals picked up as the EEG of the human brain are amplified until they may be as large as several volts, which is an increase of about 50,000 times. Finally, the output of the amplifier is sent to a recording device which usually consists of a galvanometer with an ink-writing pen attached to it. When current flows through the galvanometer, it causes the pen to be deflected by an amount which is proportional to the amount of current flowing. If the pen deflection in millimeters (or any unit of distance) is directly proportional to the amount of current flow (in milliamperes or other appropriate unit), the recorder is said to be linear.

Similarly, if a strain gauge produces an electrical output which is directly proportional to the volume displacement of the chest during breathing we describe it as linear. If the resistance change of a thermistor (a small bead of semiconducting material used for temperature measurement) is directly proportional to the temperature change, it is operating as a linear device. Linear devices are desirable because they are easier to calibrate and work with.

However, in practice most pens on ink-writing recorders are not linear and this is due partly to the fact that the pen is fixed at one point of the galvanometer and swings in an arc when current flows. This has two undesirable effects: (1) the tip of the pen becomes slightly displaced from the true time axis, and (2) the speed of rise of the pen gets slower, the further up it gets. These facts introduce some errors and the errors get larger as the deflection of the pen increases. Figure 15–1 shows what happens to a square wave or a sine wave as a result of the arcing of the pen in a recorder. It indicates that the shape of any signal will be distorted to some degree by this kind of recording.

How can this problem be dealt with? There are several approaches to a solution. (1) Some recorders do not use an ink-writing pen, but use an electron beam instead, as in cathode ray oscilloscopes. The electron beam deflection is usually fairly linear with respect to the input. To get permanent records, however, a photograph must be taken of the pattern shown on the face of the oscilloscope. (2) Certain special pens have been built which do not swing in an arc. If the input is a sharp rise, ideally the pen will show a sharp rise. The major difficulty with this method is that it adds considerable expense to the recorder, and it also slows the speed of the pen. If the event to be described is a rapid one, this kind of pen might not record it accurately. (3) The most common solution is to use a pen with a relatively long arm so that the arc described by the point is a reasonable approximation to a straight line. In other words, if we have a circle with a 5-inch radius, then an arc of 2 inches on the circumference will be almost straight. Most manufacturers will specify how much of a deflection is tolerable in order for the record to remain approximately linear. In addition, the degree of linearity *within that range* is specified by a percent figure such as 1% or 5%. Obviously, once that range is exceeded, these linearity specifications no longer apply.

Accuracy. Every measuring instrument has a certain accuracy which can be specified. For example, if a timer is used to measure the speed of an event such as a reaction time, the result is usually expressed in terms of fractions of a second, (e.g., 0.24 seconds). However, such an answer implicitly assumes that the instrument is absolutely accurate whereas, in reality, *all* instruments are in error to some degree.

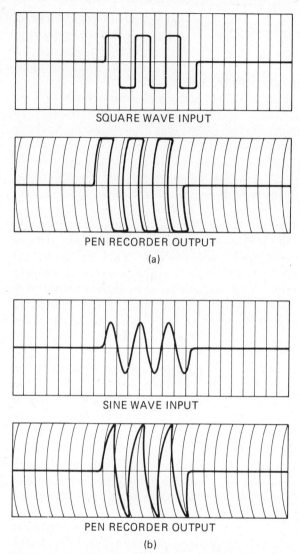

SQUARE WAVE INPUT

PEN RECORDER OUTPUT

(a)

SINE WAVE INPUT

PEN RECORDER OUTPUT

(b)

Figure 15–1.   An illustration of how a typical pen recorder tends to distort certain signal inputs because of the arcing of the pen.

The degree of error is determined by a calibration procedure which uses some other instruments believed to be more accurate than the one being tested. In order to calibrate a timer, some highly reliable time signal of known duration would be fed into the timer on a large number of trials, say 100. This signal, let us say, is almost exactly 0.20 seconds and is known not to vary from this by more than one millisecond in either direction. Therefore we can specify the input duration as varying between 199 and 201 milliseconds, or, as the engineers would put it, the input signal is 0.20 ± 0.001 seconds (read "plus or minus").

With such an input we would find that the timer did not produce exactly the same reading on every one of the 100 trials. On most trials it might read 0.20 seconds, but on some it might read as low as 0.19 seconds or as high as 0.21 seconds. We might then specify the accuracy of the timer as accurate within plus or minus 1/100 of a second or $\pm$ 0.01 seconds.

Such a calibration check would have to be made for other parts of the range of action of the timer, since accuracy often depends on the part of the scale we measure with. Because of such variation, accuracy is usually stated in terms of percent. Thus, you might buy a timer with a 1% accuracy. This would mean that the "true" value of the time being measured is within 1% of the reading on the instrument at the maximum value the instrument reads. This is usually called "full-scale deflection" and is the typical way in which accuracy is specified. It means that accuracy is much less at other parts of the scale. When instruments are bought, accuracy specifications should always be requested and examined.

Frequency Response. Many of the events that psychologists try to measure are periodic events, for example, heart rate, brain waves, and sound waves. All such periodic events are said to have a certain frequency, usually measured in terms of cycles per second (Hz). Sound waves that are audible can vary from about 20 Hz to 20,000 Hz. Brain waves vary from around 2 or 3 Hz to about 40 Hz, and heart rates are around 1 Hz, with certain parts of the complex much faster than that. The galvanic skin response is a relatively slow acting event, with one cycle taking as long as several seconds.

Measuring instruments vary greatly in their ability to record events that are periodic. Many commercial EEG machines have a frequency response from 2 Hz to about 60 Hz. Some manufacturers have tried to make their machines more versatile by extending the range at both ends with the lower limit designated as "DC" and the upper limit about 120 Hz. "DC" refers to direct current which means a frequency of zero Hz. Paradoxical as it may sound, the amplification of a steady, direct current signal is actually one of the most difficult things to amplify without distortion or drift, and psychologists had to wait until the engineers had developed reliable methods for doing this (since about 1950) before they could study certain kinds of problems. For example, there are certain kinds of eye movements that are very slow so that the electrical changes associated with them may be considered almost DC. These changes could not be recorded with conventional amplifiers but required the special "DC" amplifiers.

At the other end of the frequency spectrum, a recorder which has a good high frequency response can record events which are very rapid, such as a spike potential generated by a nerve. As another illustration, we know that blood pressure changes are relatively slow, but there is one very brief event, called the dicrotic notch, which is associated with closure of one of the heart valves. This transient spike can only be measured with a recorder that has a high frequency response. Otherwise it is simply absent from the record.

The instrument specifications which have been described are not the only ones which should be considered, but they are undoubtedly among the more important. Anyone interested in the use of equipment should certainly be aware of such factors and should examine any company brochure carefully in the light of these considerations. The potential buyer of equipment should be wary of any company that does not supply specifications on all these and other points. In addition, one should consider such things as the reputation for reliability of the instrument, the type of warranty given, and the availability of repair services. It may be taken as an axiom that the more complex the equipment to be used, the greater the likelihood that repair and maintenance services will be necessary.

One other useful word on equipment purchasing. Companies that market devices have usually spent a good deal of time and effort designing them, testing them, and getting the "bugs" out. Rarely does an individual investigator have the opportunity to check out a piece of homemade equipment to the same extent. Therefore, even though it may seem that a financial saving will occur if you build a complex piece of equipment yourself, this often turns out to be an illusion. In general, if you can afford to buy it, don't make it!

An Instrument Can Change the Event Measured

One of the dangers in the use of equipment that is sometimes unrecognized by the user is that the instrument may change the event being measured, and thus distort its nature. The electrical engineers have recognized this phenomenon for a long time and have called it *loading the circuit.* Psychologists have sometimes called this *backward action* (Wendt, 1938). It can be illustrated in a number of ways.

Ever since the beginning of the century psychologists have been interested in the Féré effect, or what is now usually called the galvanic skin response. If a small current is passed through the skin of a person and the resistance of the body is measured, it will be found that many conditions (e.g., noise, lights, mental arithmetic, emotions) will cause changes in the apparent resistance of the body. This effect seemed to be a valuable tool for studying psychological phenomena.

It was gradually discovered, however, that many factors, including those of no interest per se to psychologists, could cause changes in the apparent resistance of the body. These included the size of the electrodes used, their pressure, the type of electrode paste used, its concentration of salt, and the actual level of current sent into the skin. In fact, if the current used was high enough (although still below the threshold of sensation), it could cause the skin to generate a potential at the point of contact with the electrode, so that, in essence, a small battery was formed. This battery then produced a counter electromotive force, or voltage, which resulted in an apparent decrease in skin resistance. Therefore the application of a current to the skin produced a back action which changed the apparent property of the skin being measured. Recent research has therefore suggested that current levels used be below 10 microamperes per square centimeter of electrode area (Edelberg and Burch, 1962).

Another example of back action relates to the problem of measuring blood pressure in the human. The usual manual procedure employed by a physician is to use a pressure cuff on the upper arm inflated until the pulse in the lower arm is no longer heard with a stethoscope. At the point at which the lower pulse is just cut off, the pressure in the cuff is approximately equal to the maximum pressure in the artery (i.e., systolic blood pressure).

A second method, used in "lie detectors," is to inflate the cuff about midway between diastolic and systolic blood pressure and keep it there. Fluctuations in pressure around this point presumably relate to various psychological conditions. This method limits blood flow to various tissues and can have a detrimental effect if prolonged too long.

Another method that has been developed is one which uses sophisticated equipment to automatically inflate and deflate the cuff mounted on the upper arm. A device which measures the pulse in the wrist or finger, or a microphone which listens for the pulse, sends signals periodically which determine when the cuff is to inflate or deflate.

What is common to all these methods is the production of effects on both the blood pressure itself and organ systems which have something to do with the maintenance of blood pressure. Davis (1957) has shown that the sudden application of pressure to the cuff produced large increases in the finger volume of the hand opposite to the side where the cuff was placed. In some subjects, contralateral decreases in pulse volume were found. Temperature changes of the skin were also noted. Davis concluded: "The application of pressure seems to arouse widespread circulatory reflexes, changing the very thing the occlusion method is intended to measure." Thus a back action is again evident. One of the solutions to this problem is to use the artery in the wrist and measure its amplitude displacement; another is to place the pressure cuff on the finger instead of the upper arm and thus reduce the magnitude of the reflex reactions.

Backward action may appear in many different guises. If motivation of students is being measured and they are put into a frustrating problem-solving situation, they might redouble their efforts as a result of the frustration so that it is not at all typical of how they would usually behave. Some people seem to improve their performance over normal in competitive situations and some deteriorate. From all the examples given it is evident that the possibility of backward action exists in almost any measurement situation and should always be considered by the experimenter.

Summary

Certain areas of psychology are primarily descriptive and do not depend to any important extent on the use of instruments. In many other areas of psychology instruments are being used to an increasing degree. This is because they standardize the conditions of an experiment, they make different experiments more comparable, they record data in a permanent form, and they measure events not accessible to man's senses. These values are partly offset by the fact that experimental findings sometimes reflect the arbitrary properties of the equipment used and sometimes innovation is stifled in the interests of comparability of results.

When measuring instruments are used intelligently, many specifications have to be considered, such as: sensitivity, range, linearity, accuracy, and frequency response. Sometimes the very act of measurement creates a condition which modifies the event measured. This "backward action" has to be carefully watched for.

Finally, we should always remember that instruments are always sampling devices, and that only part of a process is usually explored. It is important to be cautious about overgeneralizing on the basis of limited situations or limited measures.

Computers in Research

Information is information; it is neither matter nor energy.

—Norbert Wiener

The widespread use of machines to augment the power available to human beings led to the Industrial Revolution. The introduction of computers after the Second World War has also had a tremendous impact, not only on the daily operations of science, technology, and commerce, but also on the way people think. Just as machines increased the physical power available to humans, computers have increased the intellectual powers that are available. And, during the last two decades, computers have had an increasing impact on psychology as a science. This chapter will describe the nature of computers and some of their contributions to research.

A Brief History

People have always recognized the need for assistance in doing arithmetic calculations. Over 2,000 years ago the Chinese invented the abacus, which is simply a device for representing numbers by means of beads on wires arranged in different spatial locations. One wire represents the "units" location, another the "tens" location, etc. Arithmetic operations are carried out by moving the beads to new locations.

In the seventeenth century several mathematicians invented calculating machines that were based on the principle of wheel and gear counters. The wires and beads used on the abacus were replaced by a circle with different-size teeth. When the "units" wheel revolved one full turn, it produced an advance of one tooth of the "tens" wheel. Similarly, one complete rotation of the "tens" wheel produced an advance of one unit of the "hundreds" wheel.

By the beginning of the twentieth century electrical power was added to these calculating machines to speed up the arithmetic processes. In addition, an important development had been made by a statistician who worked for the U.S. Census Bureau. He prepared a card for each person who was interviewed and arranged columns of numbers on the card. The various columns were then defined as representing characteristics of the person such as sex, age, or size of family. Holes were then punched through the appropriate numbers in each column. An electrical counter made a count for each hole in each card, and then provided a total for all persons in the census.

In addition to the use of punched cards to represent the characteristics of persons, it was also possible to use paper strips with holes punched in them to determine a sequence of operations, such as add, subtract, or divide. This is somewhat like a player-piano roll, in which the holes determine the sequence of tones that are played automatically by the piano. Similarly, the sequence of holes in the paper tape determined the sequence of arithmetic operations or, in other words, determined the program by which the calculator operated. This same principle is sometimes used today.

By 1946 the first electronic computer was built and put into operation. This machine contained over 18,000 vacuum tubes, weighed 30 tons, and was capable of carrying out long chains of mathematical operations by means of programs that had to be manually changed for each new problem. A number of large computers of this type were built in the next 10 years mainly for large-scale scientific or census data computations. The programs were determined by punched paper tapes or by punched cards, and the numbers were recorded on magnetic tapes and drums.

A so-called second generation of computers was introduced in 1958 as a result of use of transistors instead of vacuum tubes, which increased the speed and reliability of the computer and decreased its heat production and physical size. Not only were punched cards used for programs, but magnetic tapes and other special magnetic devices were used to store data. This greatly increased the complexity of the problems that could be handled.

The third generation of computers was based upon the development of integrated circuits on tiny silicon chips only 29-thousandths of an inch square. These tiny chips perform the same basic functions as did the vacuum tubes and transistors, but do them much faster. In 1944, the speed of internal operations of a calculator was 3/10 of a second per addition; by 1970 it was about one 10-millionth of a second. In addition, the ability of the computer to store numbers in its "memory" has grown from a few dozen locations of memory to hundreds of thousands. These developments allowed many mathematical and logical problems to be handled simultaneously by a computer, a process called time-sharing.

The reduction in size of computers and the increase in the speed of processing of data led to the development of minicomputers that were inexpensive enough to be purchased by individual departments of a university. In 1975, a survey reported that of 800 psychology departments contacted, 450 had individuals who were using minicomputers in the teaching of psychology (Sidowski, 1975). These minicomputers were capable of carrying out many of the same operations as the larger computers of the previous decade.

In the early 1970s the fourth generation of computers was introduced by the development of the "computer on a chip," in which one single chip takes the place of many integrated circuits. As a basis of comparison, one single chip would have replaced all 18,000 tubes in the first electronic computer. This technological development has created the microcomputer, which is a computer often not much larger than an ordinary typewriter that can duplicate many of the functions of the larger minicomputers at a small fraction of their cost. These new computers allow research tasks to be performed in a large variety of settings and in ways that would have been impossible only a short time ago.

The Computer as a Model of a Human Being

Many people have pointed out that the sophisticated computers that are currently available have many functional similarities to a human being. Humans take in information about the world through the senses. This information is related to information which is already stored in our brains in short- or long-term memory, and it is then evaluated. The evaluations often lead to decisions and to actions.

Figure 16–1 shows how some of these same functions apply to the modern computer. Table 16–1 lists the actual elements that function in these various capacities.

One interesting point that may be seen is that many of the same devices can act as input and output. For example, punched cards provide data to the computer and also store data that has been produced by the computer. In addition, there are a variety of memory devices that differ in their size (that is, the amount of information they can hold) and in the access time (the speed with which information can be retrieved or moved around). In actual usage, there are usually at least three and often more separate physical components to any computer system. These components such as teletypes, tapes, and processors are called the system *hardware.*

The Languages of Computers

There are several different kinds of languages that are involved in a computer system. The memory core of the digital computer uses the binary system for coding of all information. In this number system there are only two numbers, 1

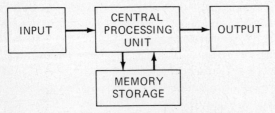

Figure 16–1.   Basic functional units of a computer system.

TABLE 16-1   ELEMENTS THAT FUNCTION IN VARIOUS COMPUTER CAPACITIES

Input Devices	**Output Devices**
Punched Cards	Punched Cards
Paper Tape	Paper Tape
Magnetic Tape	Magnetic Tape
Mark Sense Cards	Electric Teletypes
Optical Scanning Devices	Line Printers
Electric Teletypes	Cathode Ray Screen
Light Pens	X-Y Plotter

Central Processing Unit (CPU)
Permanent Memory Program Instructions (ROM = Read Only Memory)
Temporary Random Access Memory (RAM)
Operating, Programming, and Debugging Software

Mass Memory Storage (outside the CPU)
Paper Tape
Magnetic Tape
Floppy Disc
Hard Disc
Drum

and 0. This is called the *machine language.* It is based on the simple idea that all numbers and letters can be represented by means of a binary code, just as dots and dashes are used in Morse code to represent all letters and numbers. It is, therefore, obvious that all words and sentences can be represented by long strings of dots and dashes or sequences of 1s and 0s. Inside the computer this usually means that a tiny element is either magnetized or it is not; symbolically this is represented as either a 1 or a 0. Binary numbers are also used to represent *operations* such as addition or multiplication. Therefore, a machine language solution to a problem is written entirely in terms of 0s and 1s.

Although computers can perform millions of binary operations in a second, humans cannot, and it is necessary to have a different kind of language available in order to communicate with a computer. Such languages have been developed and are called "problem-oriented" or "program" languages. These languages are general codes that programmers use and are closer to natural language. For example, tables of codes are prepared in advance where certain letters (e.g., ADD) correspond to certain binary machine language instructions. It is quite possible that a single word such as ADD or STORE may correspond to hundreds or even thousands of machine language events. Various problem-oriented languages have been developed for different applications. Some are designed for use in business, others in engineering and still others for automated natural language translation. For engineering, and statistical work FORTRAN is most often used, while for most other applications BASIC is now the language of choice. A great advantage of BASIC is that it provides quick access to the Control Processing Unit without the need for punched cards. These various languages and the programs written in these languages are the *software* of the computer.

Measuring Information

One of the ways in which a computer may be described is in terms of its memory capacity, which reflects, in turn, its ability to handle large amounts of information. The unit of information is based on the idea, taken from cybernetics, that information indicates choices made between alternatives. When a person says "yes" instead of "no," or sends a dash instead of a dot in Morse code, then a single unit of information has been conveyed. This unit, since it clearly is based on a binary decision, is called a "binary digit" or *bit*. In the computer, one bit of information refers to a decision between a 1 and a 0.

However, memory capacity is defined in terms of larger units. In order to represent a number or a letter in the binary machine language, many bits are needed. It is now typical to define each letter of the alphabet in terms of a seven bit code. For example, A = 1000001, B = 1000010, etc. This seven bit code, plus an additional bit which functions to help identify errors in the rest of the seven bit code (making a total of eight bits), defines a computer "word" or *byte*. Memory storage is usually defined by how many bytes of a given length are available. In many of the larger computers, the length of a "word" may be 16 bits or even 32 bits, so that a complete specification of memory capacity should also specify "word" length as well as number of bytes. Some of the large computers have a memory capacity of one million or more "words" while the mini- or microcomputers usually have a 16,000 to 64,000 byte capacity. (These numbers are often written 16K or 64K.)

Uses of Computers

At one time computers were used almost exclusively as high-speed automatic calculators. They made it possible to do statistical computations of great complexity in a very brief period, and this use of computers remains an important one. Standard statistical packages have been developed that provide the software programs for frequently used statistics such as correlations, *t*-tests, analysis of variance, regression analysis, and factor analysis. The better known statistical programs are labeled Statistical Package For The Social Sciences (SPSS), Statistical Analysis System (SAS), and Biomedical Data Processing (BMDP). However, over the years many additional functions have been added to the repertoire of the computer. These include such things as natural language translation, pattern recognition, medical and psychiatric diagnoses, content analyses of verbal interactions, stimulus programming, monitoring of biofeedback data, and interactive teaching, among others. Some of these uses may be illustrated in the following examples.

Psychophysiology

Biofeedback has been shown to enable an individual to learn to control, to some degree, certain physiological processes. For example, a man who receives detailed information about his heart rate may gradually learn to increase or decrease its average rate. What is needed is the establishment of a criterion; for example, an increase of five beats per minute, and the provision of continuous information to the subject about how close he is to the criterion (by auditory tones, for example).

The actual procedure may be illustrated by the following example of biofeedback training to promote deep muscle relaxation (Pope and Gersten, 1977). An electromyograph (EMG) is used to measure the amount of activity in a particular muscle. The size of the EMG signal is used to determine the pitch of a tone that is provided to the subject. The task of the subject is to relax the muscle being monitored in order to bring the tone to a low pitch and to keep it there. As the subject gradually gets better at relaxing, the computer automatically makes the task more difficult by requiring increasingly more relaxation to produce the same steady, low-pitched tone. If, however, the subject is having difficulty keeping the pitch of the tone low, the computer automatically makes the task easier, so that less relaxation can produce a sense of success. The process of automatic adjustment of difficulty of the task goes on continuously under the control of the program of instructions set in the computer. The basic idea is that the task be kept challenging but not frustrating.

Simulation

Another major and increasing use of computers is in the field of *simulation*. The basic idea of simulation is simple; that is, a model is made to represent a device, an environment, or a process. Model airplanes are simulations of real airplanes, just as wind tunnels are simulations of the environment of high velocity, high altitude flights. The process that a physician uses when making a diagnosis can also be simulated by a complex program in a computer.

The combination of device, environment, and process can be illustrated in aeronautical flight simulation. Flight simulators of varying degrees of complexity have been built almost from the beginning of aviation. A major function of simulators is to provide safe and efficient training for pilots. However, research simulators have been built whose purpose is to discover more about the characteristics of humans engaged in complex, dangerous, and highly unusual activities (e.g., responses to very high accelerations).

Figure 16–2 shows the major elements of an ideal flight simulation system (Huff and Nagel, 1975). The arrows indicate the kinds of information (feedback) that are provided to the pilot. The feedback includes information about the environment of the aircraft including obstacles and air traffic; the instruments used in the plane itself; the qualities of motion involved in various maneuvers; the position of the plane relative to various landmarks; and the purpose of the

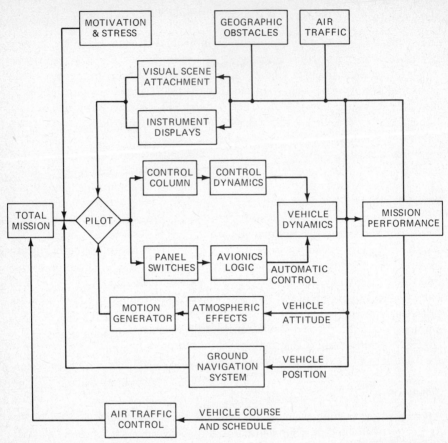

Figure 16–2. The major elements of an ideal flight-simulation system showing progressively wider feedback loops to the pilot, including aircraft attitude, position, and course feedback information. The total environment contains ground control stations, navigation aids, other aircraft, and atmospheric disturbance. Motivation and stress factors also influence the pilot. (From Huff, E. M., and Nagel, D. C. Psychological aspects of aeronautical flight simulation. *American Psychologist,* 1975, 30, 426–439. Reprinted by permission.)

mission. Motivation and stress factors also influence the pilot, and may be included in the feedback loops in the form of biofeedback of physiological reactions. A simulation system must also contain the instruments needed to measure pilot reactions.

Computers are used to produce the graphic displays that the pilot sees (e.g., cockpit panels, terrains, landing lights, etc), and such displays are related to the control manipulations carried out by the pilot. Special simulation systems have been developed for air-to-air combat, air-to-ground weapons delivery, and more peaceful uses such as the navigation of ships out of hazardous harbors. Computer color-generating techniques allow realistic investigations of visual approaches to runways, and the effects of contrast and intensity of lights on pilot performance.

Some flight simulators are placed on movable platforms which are used to provide vertical and lateral accelerations of various degrees.

From a research point of view, computerized flight simulation allows precise control over the information inputs to the pilot and crew. Conditions can be simulated that are highly unusual, or are only encountered in extreme or emergency conditions. In addition, the information-monitoring and decision-making abilities of the pilot and crew can be evaluated in a systematic way for all levels of training and all levels of simulation fidelity. The simulations, therefore, provide not only practical benefits related to more efficient training, but may provide new basic insights as well.

Computer Models

Another important aspect of simulation is the use of computers to provide a model of a theoretical process. For example, computers have been programmed to solve problems in ways that are comparable to the way a human being solves problems. Chess-playing computers have reached the point where they rank among the top 300 players in the United States. Computer models have also been built to simulate rote learning, medical diagnosis, long-term memory, concept attainment, and language acquisition, among others (Simon, 1979). Also of great interest are the models of personality that have been developed. Let us examine one of these models in more detail.

Loehlin (1968) has presented information on four different computer models of personality. The simplest is called "Aldous" in honor of Aldous Huxley, author of *Brave New World*. Its program consists of 750 machine language instructions. It requires a permanent memory storage of about 1,300 memory locations or "addresses" an immediately accessible memory of about 30 "addresses," and several auxiliary programs designed for special procedures such as assessing "his" attitudes from time to time.

Aldous has three emotions—attraction, anger, and fear—and corresponding behaviors of approach, attack, and withdrawal. Stimulus information is provided by an electric teletype, and Aldous' reactions are also printed out. If several emotions are aroused by an object or event, then conflict may occur. The general sequence of events in the computer model is presented in Figure 16–3.

The operation of this model begins by having someone enter *(input)* an initial description of a person into the computer, for example, girlfriend. The *recognition* subprogram determines what information is stored in permanent memory about a girlfriend, stores an indication of this search in immediate memory, and then passes the information to the next subprogram, *emotional reaction.*

This part of the program then calculates a weighted sum of the various emotional attitudes (attraction, anger, fear) that exist in both permanent and immediate memory. The program is set so that more intense emotions weaken less intense emotions. The emotions are stored in immediate memory (displacing those from the previous trial), and the *action* subroutine is activated. If the

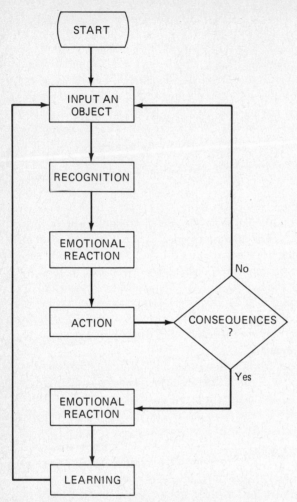

Figure 16–3.   Flow chart of the program for Aldous.

strength of the emotion is 0–2 on a 9-point scale, no action is taken. If it is 3–5, mild action is taken, and if it is 6–8, strong action. An emotion at level 9 leads to paralysis (no action). The actions taken correspond to the dominant emotion present, approach for attraction, attack for anger, and withdrawal for fear.

The *consequences* subprogram is based on the idea that the people in Aldous' environment have certain degrees of power relative to Aldous, and that they can react to him with satisfaction (for affection), with injury (for fear), and with frustration (for anger). Depending on the magnitude of the consequences, Aldous will have an emotional reaction to the encounter, and will store this information in immediate memory, from which it will be moved to permanent memory to influence the permanent emotions concerning "girlfriend." The program gives less weight to a particular experience as the number of prior encounters with the person increases.

The personality of Aldous can be changed by modifying certain aspects of the program; for example, the weight given to immediate experiences relative to permanent memory, or the readiness to react as a function of the intensity of the emotions evaluated by the action subroutine. Several such versions of Aldous have been tested: Decisive Aldous, who acts strongly on slight emotion; Hesitant Aldous, who acts only weakly on strong emotion; Radical Aldous, who is highly reactive to current conditions; and Conservative Aldous, who is more governed by his past. These different personalities have been exposed to different types of environments, including other models of Aldous, some benign and some hostile, and the results compared.

What implications stem from this and other computer models of personality? Loehlin (1968) suggests that there are both theoretical and practical implications.

From a theoretical point of view, it may be argued that a computer model of a process is, in fact, a theory of that process. This is particularly true if the model is based on certain explicitly defined principles and "acts" the way we usually expect human beings to act. However, although a chess-playing model must be able to play a good game of chess, it is not entirely evident what a personality model is expected to do.

Loehlin suggests at least two requirements of a personality model. First, it should have assumptions (i.e., programs or subroutines) that can be changed in systematic ways so that one can explore the consequences of such changes. Second, since personality theories are often wordy and ambiguous, and sometimes contain unstated assumptions, the computer model will bring some of these weaknesses to light. In addition, the attempt to construct an explicit model may lead to new and interesting ideas that may be worthy of study in their own right.

There are at least three practical implications of computer models. Prediction of behavior is one. However, prediction of behavior from a knowledge of personality traits has not been particularly successful. This may be a reflection of the large number of factors that enter into any given outcome in a real-life situation. Only a computer model can conceivably integrate the thousands of facts that may be necessary to make meaningful predictions. A second possible role for computer models of personality might be to train persons in interpersonal skills such as salesmanship or psychotherapy. Students can be exposed to all kinds of individuals, practice as often as they wish, and try a variety of approaches, both unsuccessful as well as successful ones. Diagnostic skill can be evaluated, and psychotherapy can be carried out with hypothetical patients. Finally, the computer itself can take the role of the therapist and carry out psychotherapy with a real patient at any time of the day or night and at any rate of speed. Time-sharing will allow many clients to engage in psychotherapy with the same computer model.

Problems of Computer Utilization

The potentials of the computer are obviously great and we may expect increasingly important results of their use. However, there are some problems that result from the use of computers and whose recognition may lead to more efficient computer utilization. Fliege (1966) has pointed out that most scientists who use computers should develop a working relationship with a computer programmer who can provide needed technical support and guidance. New programs that are developed should be carefully tested for errors; it is not unknown for programmers and computers to make mistakes. A more subtle problem is where an error in the program leads to a plausible set of correlations, for example, all of which are incorrect. Test cases should be run routinely so that the program output can be compared with an expected or known output. Since the output of a computer may sometimes be overwhelming, there is a danger that the researcher may lose some of the "feel" of the data. Therefore, as much data reduction and analysis as possible should be done within the computer, and the experimenter should try to have a very clear idea of what output is desired. Finally, since preparation of data for entry into the computer is often a tedious and lengthy process, whenever possible, data should be collected in a form that can be input directly to the computer.

One last set of recommendations may be given for the many investigators who will sooner or later be involved in research with the aid of computers. This is based on an amusing description written by Mayer (1980) of "My Many Mistakes With Microcomputers." In the article he describes his attempt to purchase an inexpensive microcomputer in the mid-1970s so that he could automate his reaction-time experiments. He bought a computer in kit form. This required his shop technician to spend a large amount of time to assemble it only to discover that the peripheral components (such as a paper tape reader) made by another manufacturer were not easily compatible with his computer. He then discovered that his computer did not have a permanent memory for BASIC as a programming language, which created the need to hire a programmer who could talk the computer's language. When the computer was finally able to carry out the experiments (after two years) Mayer discovered that occasional repairs that were needed could not be easily done since the computer company was out-of-state and had no local service people. It took Mayer 4 years to test his first group of 20 subjects using stimuli monitored by the computer, and to record their responses automatically. The experience led him to suggest eight remedies for those people who would like to use microcomputers for their own research. Briefly, they are as follows:

1. Carefully research the alternative systems you can buy for your allotted money.
2. Don't buy computers in kit form unless you are an electronics whiz and have plenty of time.

3. Buy your computer as a fully integrated system including all needed interfacing peripheral components (such as video display, tape reader, etc.), rather than part by part.

4. Be sure to find out what comes with the computer in terms of ease of start up and diagnostics (for example, does it "speak" a simple language such as BASIC?).

5. Remember that software is a great hidden expense. Try to make arrangements to share programs.

6. Make sure there is a service person or place in your area for your equipment.

7. Use the appropriate technology; for example, paper tapes should be replaced by a cassette tape system or by a floppy disc.

8. Don't give up too soon.

Summary

Computers have become an increasingly essential part of the research enterprise. This is particularly true as computers have become smaller in size and more versatile in function. Among the more important contemporary uses of computers are the following: rapid analysis of increasingly complex statistical problems; control of stimulus conditions in research laboratories; automatic recording and analysis of responses; content analyses of verbal interactions; interactive teaching; and simulation of complex tasks and environments for training purposes. One of the most important recent uses of computers is in the development of computer models to simulate a theoretical process. Examples of such usage are models of artificial intelligence designed to simulate rote learning, long-term memory, concept attainment, and language acquisition, among others. Computer models of personality and of psychotherapeutic interactions have also been developed. Some practical problems of computer utilization are also discussed.

Bibliography

Aaronson, B. S., and Welsh, G. S. The MMPI as diagnostic differentiator: a reply to Rubin. *Journal of Consulting Psychology*, 1950, *14,* 324–326.

Ad Hoc Committee on Ethical Standards in Psychological Research. *Ethical principles in the conduct of research with human participants.* Washington, D.C., American Psychological Association, 1973.

Adler, F. Operational definitions in sociology. *American Journal of Sociology,* 1947, *52,* 438–444.

Adler, H. L., and Roessler, E. B. *Introduction to probability and statistics,* (3rd ed.). San Francisco: Freeman, 1964.

Andrews, T. G. *Methods of psychology.* New York: Wiley, 1948.

Attneave, F., and Arnoult, M. D. The quantitative study of shape and pattern perception. *Psychological Bulletin,* 1956, *53,* 452–471.

Azrin, N. H., Holz, W., Ulrich, R., and Goldiamond, I. The control of the content of conversation through reinforcement. *Journal of the Experimental Analysis of Behavior,* 1961, *4,* 25–30.

Bakan, D. *On method.* San Francisco: Jossey-Bass, 1967.

Baldwin, A. L. The study of child behavior and development. In P. H. Mussen (Ed.), *Handbook of research methods in child development.* New York: Wiley, 1960.

Barber, T. X., Pitfalls in research: nine investigator and experimenter effects. In R. M. W. Travers (Ed.), *Handbook of research on teaching.* (2nd ed.) Chicago: Rand McNally, 1973.

Barber, T. X., Forgione, A., Chaves, J. F., Calverley, D. S., McPeake, J. D., and Bowen, B. Five attempts to replicate the experimenter bias effect. *Journal of Consulting and Clinical Psychology,* 1969, *33,* 1–6.

Barber, T. X., and Silver, M. J. Fact, fiction and the experimenter bias effect. *Psychological Bulletin,* 1968, *70,* 1–29.

Barker, R. G., and Wright, H. F. *Midwest and its children.* New York: Harper & Row, 1955.

Beach, F. A. Experimental investigations of species-specific behavior. *American Psychologist,* 1960, *15,* 1–18.

Beck, A. T. *Depression: clinical experimental and theoretical aspects.* New York: Harper & Row, 1967.

Becker, W. C., Madsen, C. H., Jr., Arnold, C. R., and Thomas, D. R. The contingent use of teacher attention and praise in reducing classroom behavior problems. *Journal of Special Education,* 1967, *1,* 287–307.

Bell, C. R. Personality characteristics of volunteers for psychological studies. *British Journal of Social Psychology,* 1962, *1,* 81–95.

Benjamin, A. C. *Operationism.* Springfield, Ill.: Charles C. Thomas, 1955.

Bijou, S. W., Peterson, R. F., Harris, F. R., Allen, K. E., and Johnston, M. S. Methodology for experimental studies of young children in natural settings. *The Psychological Record, 19,* 177–210.

Binder, A., McConnell, D., and Sjoholm, N. A. Verbal conditioning as a function of experimenter characteristics. *Journal of Abnormal Psychology,* 1957, *55,* 309–314.

Boneau, C. A. The effects of violations of assumptions underlying the *t*-test. *Psychological Bulletin,* 1960, *57,* 49–64.

Bozarth, J.D., and Roberts, R.R., Jr. Signifying significant significance. *American Psychologist,* 1972, *27,* 774–775.

Brackmann, J., and Collier, G. The dependence of probability of response on size of step interval in the method of limits. *Journal of Experimental Psychology,* 1958, *55,* 423–428.

Brady, J. V. Ulcers in "executive" monkeys. *Scientific American,* 1958, *199,* 95–100.

Bridgman, P. W. *The logic of modern physics.* New York: Macmillan, 1927.

Bridgman, P. W. *Reflections of a physicist.* New York: Philosophical Library, 1950.

Brockway, Ann L., Gleser, G., Winokur, G., and Ulett, G. A. The use of a control population in neuropsychiatric research (psychiatric, psychological and EEG evaluation of a heterogeneous sample). *American Journal of Psychiatry,* 1954, *111,* 248–262.

Bronson, F. H. Agonistic behaviour in woodchucks. *Animal Behaviour,* 1964, *12,* 470–478.

Bruner, J. S., Goodnow, J. J., and Austin, G. A. *A study of thinking.* New York: Wiley, 1956.

Brunswik, E. *Perception and the representative design of psychological experiments.* Berkeley: University of California Press, 1956.

Burke, C. J. A brief note on one-tailed tests. *Psychological Bulletin,* 1953, *50,* 384–387.

Campbell, D.T., and Stanley, J.C. *Experimental and quasi-experimental designs for research.* Chicago: Rand McNally, 1963.

Chapanis, A. Theory and methods for analyzing errors in man-machine systems. *Annals of the New York Academy of Sciences,* 1951, *51,* 1179–1203.

Chapanis, A. *The design and conduct of human engineering studies.* Tech. Rept. No. 14, Project NR 145-075; San Diego State College Foundation, 1956.

Chapanis, A. Engineering psychology. *Annual Review of Psychology,* 1963, *14,* 285–318.

Chapanis, A. Color names for color space. *American Scientist,* 1965, *53,* 327–346.

Church, R. M. Systematic effect of random error in the yoked control design. *Psychological Bulletin,* 1964, *62,* 122–131.

Cochran, W. G. Some consequences when the assumptions for the analysis of variance are not satisfied. *Biometrics,* 1947, *3,* 21–38.

Cohen, J. *Statistical power analysis for the behavioral sciences.* New York: Academic Press, 1969.

Collier, G.H., Hirsch, E., and Hamlin, P.H. The ecological determinants of reinforcement in the rat. *Physiology and Behavior,* 1972 *9,* 705–716.

Conant, J. B. *On understanding science.* New Haven: Yale University Press 1947.

Cook, T.D., and Campbell, D.T. The design and conduct of quasi-experiments and true experiments in field settings. In M. D. Dunnette (Ed.), *Handbook of industrial and organizational psychology.* Chicago: Rand McNally, 1976.

Corso, J. F. *The experimental psychology of sensory behavior.* New York: Holt, Rinehart and Winston, 1967.

Cromie, B. W. The feet of clay of the double-blind trial. *Lancet,* 1963, *2,* 994–997.

Davis, R. C. Continuous recording of arterial pressure: an analysis of the problem. *Journal of Comparative and Physiological Psychology,* 1957, *50,* 524–529.

Day, W. F. Randomness of threshold responses at long interstimulus intervals. *Perceptual and Motor Skills,* 1956, *6,* 205–208.

Delgado, J. M. R. Chronic radio-stimulation of the brain in monkey colonies. *Excerpta Medica International Congress,* Series No. 87, 1965, 365–371.

Dixon, W. J., and Massey, F. J., Jr. *Introduction to statistical analysis.* New York: McGraw-Hill, 1951.

Dukes, W. F. $N = 1$. *Psychological Bulletin,* 1965, *64,* 74–79.

DuShane, G., Krauskopf, K. B., Lerner, E. M., Morse, P. M., Steinbach, H. B., Straus, W. L., Jr., and Tatum, E. L. An unfortunate event. *Science,* 1961, *134,* 945–946.

Edelberg, R., and Burch, N. R. Skin resistance and the galvanic skin response. *Archives of General Psychiatry,* 1962, *7,* 163–169.

Edwards, A. K. *Experimental design in psychological research.* (3rd ed.) New York: Holt, Rinehart and Winston, 1968.

Ehrenberg, A. S. C. Measurement and mathematics in psychology. *British Journal of Psychology,* 1955, *46,* 20–29.

Ellis, B. *Basic concepts of measurement.* Cambridge: Cambridge University Press, 1966.

Eysenck, H. J. The concept of statistical significance and the controversy about one-tailed tests. *Psychological Review,* 1960, *67,* 269–271.

Feather, N. *Mass, length and time.* Baltimore: Penguin, 1959.

Feigl, H. Operationism and scientific method. *Psychological Review,* 1945, *52,* 250–259.

Fisher, R. A. *Statistical methods for research workers.* (12th ed.) London: Oliver & Boyd, 1954.

Fitts, P. M. The influence of response coding on performance in motor tasks. In *Current trends in information theory.* Pittsburgh: University of Pittsburgh Press, 1954.

Fleiss, J. L. Estimating the magnitude of experimental effects. *Psychological Bulletin,* 1969, *72,* 273–276.

Fliege, S. Digital computers. In J. B. Sidowski (Ed.), *Experimental methods and instrumentation in psychology.* New York: McGraw-Hill, 1966.

Friedman, H. Magnitude of experimental effect and a table for its rapid estimation. *Psychological Bulletin,* 1968, *70* (4), 245–251.

Friedman, N. *The social nature of psychological research.* New York: Basic Books, 1967.

Galanter, E. Contemporary psychophysics. In R. Brown (Ed), *New Directions in Psychology.* New York: Holt, Rinehart and Winston, 1962.

Garner, W. R. Context effects and the validity of loudness scales. *Journal of Experimental Psychology,* 1954, *48,* 218–224.

Ginsberg, A. Operational definitions and theories. *Journal of General Psychology,* 1955, *52,* 223–248.

Gottman, J., and Markman, H. J. Experimental designs in psychotherapy research. In S. L. Garfield and A. E. Bergin (Eds.), *Handbook of Psychotherapy and behavior change: An empirical analysis.* New York: Wiley, 1978.

Graham, C. H., and Kemp, E. H. Brightness discrimination as a function of the duration of the increment in intensity. *Journal of General Physiology,* 1938, *21,* 635–650.

Granit, R. *Receptors and sensory perception.* New Haven: Yale University Press, 1955.

Grice, G. R., and Hunter, J. J. Stimulus intensity effects depend upon the type of experimental design. *Psychological Review,* 1964, *71,* 247–256.

Guilford, J. P. *Psychometric methods.* New York: McGraw-Hill, 1954.

Hammond, E. C. Smoking and death rates—a riddle in cause and effect. *American Scientist,* 1958, *46,* 331–354.

Harlow, H. F. Mice, monkeys, men, and motives. *Psychological Review,* 1953, *60,* 23–32.

Harlow, H. F., Harlow, M. K., Rueping, R. R., and Mason, W. A. Performance of infant rhesus monkeys on discrimination learning, delayed response, and discrimination learning set. *Journal of Comparative and Physiological Psychology,* 1960, *53,* 113–121.

Hart, B. M., Allen, K. E., Buell, J. S., Harris, F. R., and Wolf, M. M. Effects of social reinforcement on operant crying. *Journal of Experimental Child Psychology,* 1964, *1,* 145–153.

Hays, W. L. *Statistics for psychologists.* New York: Holt, Rinehart and Winston, 1963.

Hodos, W., and Valenstein, E. S. An evaluation of response rate as a measure of rewarding intracranial stimulation. *Journal of Comparative and Physiological Psychology,* 1962, *55,* 80–84.

Huff, E. M., and Nagel, D. C. Psychological aspects of aeronautical flight simulation. *American Psychologist,* 1975, *30,* 426–439.

Hughes, J. An evaluation of contemporary research and methods in the field of mental disorders. In P. H. Hoch and J. Zubin (Eds.), *Current problems in psychiatric diagnosis.* New York: Grune & Stratton, 1953.

Hull, C. L. *Principles of behavior: an introduction to behavior theory.* New York: Appleton-Century-Crofts, 1943.

Hunt, J. McV. The effects of infant feeding-frustration upon adult hoarding behavior. *Journal of Abnormal Psychology,* 1941, *36,* 339–360.

Johnson, R. F. Q. The experimenter attributes effect: a methodological analysis. *The Psychological Record,* 1976, *26,* 67–78

Jones, F. N., and Marcus, M. J. The subject effect in judgments of subjective magnitude. *Journal of Experimental Psychology,* 1961, *61,* 40–44.

Juhasz, J. B., and Sarbin, T. R. On the false alarm metaphor in psychophysics. *The Psychological Record,* 1966, *16,* 323–327.

Jung, J. Current practices and problems in the use of college students for psychological research. *Canadian Psychologist,* 1969, *10,* 280–290.

Jung, J. *The experimenter's dilemma.* New York: Harper & Row, 1971.

Kazdin, A. E., and Wilson, G. T. *Evaluation of behavior therapy, issues, evidence and research strategies.* Cambridge, Mass.: Ballinger, 1978.

Kellerman, H. The development of a forced-choice personality index and its relation to degree of maladjustment. Ph.D. dissertation. New York: Yeshiva University, 1964.

Kelman, H. C. Human use of human subjects: the problem of deception in social psychological experiments. *Psychological Bulletin,* 1967, *67,* 1–11.

Kelman, H. C. The rights of the subject in social research: an analysis in terms of relative power and legitimacy. *American Psychologist,* 1972, *27,* 989–1016.

Kirchner, W. K., and Dunnette, M. D. An industrial psychologist's lament: the problem of shrinking sample size. *American Psychologist,* 1959, *14,* 299–300.

Kubany, E. S., Weiss, L. E., and Sloggett, B. B. The good behavior clock: a reinforcement/time out procedure for reducing disruptive classroom behavior. *Journal of Behavior Therapy and Experimental Psychiatry,* 1971, *2,* 173–179.

Lacey, J. I., and Lacey, B. C. Verification and extension of the principle of autonomic response-stereotypy. *American Journal of Psychology,* 1958, *71,* 50–73.

Lasagna, L., and von Felsinger, J. M. The volunteer subject in research. *Science,* 1954, *120,* 359–461.

Lashley, K. S. *Brain mechanisms and intelligence.* New York: Dover, 1963. (Original edition, 1929.)

Leuba, C., Birch, L., and Appleton, J. Human problem solving during complete paralysis of the voluntary musculature. *Psychological Reports,* 1968, *22,* 849–855.

Lewis, D., and Burke, C. J. The use and misuse of the chi-square test. *Psychological Bulletin,* 1949, *46,* 433–489.

Lewis, D., Smith, P. N., and McAllister, D. E. Retroactive facilitation and interference in performance on a modified two-hand coordinator. *Journal of Experimental Psychology,* 1952, *44,* 44–50.

Lindquist, E. F. *Design and analysis of experiments in psychology and education.* Boston: Houghton Mifflin, 1953.

Loehlin, J. C. *Computer models of personality.* New York: Random House, 1968.

Loevinger, J. Person and population as psychometric concepts. *Psychological Review,* 1965, *72,* 143–155.

Lundberg, G. A. *Foundations of sociology.* New York: Macmillan, 1939.

Lykken, D. T. Statistical significance in psychological research. *Psychological Bulletin,* 1968, *70,* 151–159.

Lyons, J. *A primer of experimental psychology.* New York: Harper & Row, 1965.

MacCorquodale, K., and Meehl, P. E. On a distinction between hypothetical constructs and intervening variables. *Psychological Review,* 1948, *55,* 95–107.

Maher, B. A. Stimulus sampling in clinical research: representative design reviewed. *Journal of Consulting and Clinical Psychology,* 1978, *46,* 643–647.

McFarland, R. A., and Moseley, A. L. *Human factors in highway transport safety.* Boston: Harvard School of Public Health, 1954.

Masden, C. H., Jr., Becker, W. C., and Thomas, D. R. Rules, praise, and ignoring: Elements of elementary classroom control. *Journal of Applied Behavior Analysis,* 1968, *1,* 139–150.

Maslow, A. H., and Sakoda, J. M. Volunteer-error in the Kinsey study. *Journal of Abnormal Psychology,* 1952, *47,* 259–262.

Mason, B., and Ammons, R. B. Note on social class and the Thematic Apperception Test. *Perceptual and Motor Skills,* 1956, *6,* 88.

Mayer, R. E. My many mistakes with microcomputers. *American Psychologist,* 1980, *35,* 117–119.

Meehl, P. E. Theory-testing in psychology and physics: a methodological paradox. *Philosophy of Science,* 1967, *34,* 103–115.

Melton, A. W. Editorial. *Journal of Experimental Psychology,* 1962, *64,* 553–557.

Miller, N. E. Analytical studies of drive and reward. *American Psychologist,* 1961, *10,* 739–754.

Miller, N. E. Objective techniques for studying motivational effects of drugs on animals. In S. Garettini and V. Ghetti (Eds.), *Psychotropic drugs.* Amsterdam: Elsevier, 1957.

Miller, N. E., Bailey, C. J., and Stevenson, J. A. F. Decreased "hunger" but increased food intake resulting from hypothalamic lesions. *Science,* 1950, *112,* 256–259.

Minton, J. H. The impact of Sesame Street on readiness of kindergarten children. *Sociology of Education,* 1975, *48,* 141–151

Mixon, D. Temporary false belief. *Personality and Social Psychology Bulletin,* 1977, *3,* 479–488.

Moran, G. Severe food deprivation: some thoughts regarding its exclusive use. *Psychological Bulletin,* 1975, *82,* 543–557.

Morison, R. S. "Gradualness, gradualness, gradualness" (I. P. Pavlov). *American Psychologist,* 1960, *15,* 187–197.

Parsons, H. M. What happened at Hawthorne? *Science,* 1974, *183,* 922–932.

Parsons, H. M. What caused the Hawthorne Effect? A scientific detective story. *Administration and Society,* 1978, *10,* 259–283.

Perlin, S., Pollin, W., and Butler, R. N. The experimental subject. *Archives of Neurology and Psychiatry,* 1958, *80,* 65–70.

Piaget, J. *The language and thought of the child.* New York: Meridian, 1955.

Plutchik, R. Further remarks on the hypothetical construct. *Journal of Psychology,* 1954, *37,* 59–64.

Plutchik, R. *The emotions: facts, theories and a new model.* New York: Random House, 1962.

Plutchik, R. Operationism as methodology. *Behavioral Science,* 1963, *8,* 234–241.

Plutchik, R., McFarland, W. L., and Robinson, B. W. Relationships between current intensity, self-stimulation rates, escape latencies, and evoked behavior in rhesus monkeys. *Journal of Comparative and Physiological Psychology,* 1966, *61,* 181– 188.

Plutchik, R. Emotions, evolution and adaptive processes. In M. Arnold (Ed.), *Feelings and Emotions: The Loyola Symposium.* New York: Academic Press, 1970.

Plutchik, R., Platman, S. R., and Fieve, R. R. Three alternatives to the double-blind. *Archives of General Psychiatry,* 1969, *20,* 428–432.

Plutchik, R. *Emotion: A psychoevolutionary synthesis.* New York: Harper & Row, 1980.

Pope, A. T., and Gersten, C. D. Computer automation of biofeedback training. *Behavior Research Methods and Instrumentation,* 1977, *9,* 164–168.

Price, R. H. Signal-detection methods in personality and perception. *Psychological Bulletin,* 1966, *66,* 55–62.

Price, R. H., and Erikson, C. W. Size constancy in schizophrenia: A reanalysis. *Journal of Clinical Psychology,* 1966, *71,* 155–160.

Reiss, B. F., Schwartz, E. K., and Cottingham, A. An experimental critique of assumptions underlying the Negro version of the TAT. *Journal of Abnormal Psychology,* 1950, *45,* 700–709.

Rheingold, H. L. The measurement of maternal care. *Child Development,* 1960, *31,* 565–575.

Robinson, E. S., and Brown, M. A. Effect of serial position on memorization. *American Journal of Psychology,* 1926, *37,* 538–552.

Rosenthal, R. How often are our numbers wrong? *American Psychologist,* 1978, *33,* 1005–1008.

Rosenthal, R. Letter. *Behavioral Science,* 1964, *9,* 66.

Rosenthal, R., and Fode, K. L. The effect of experimenter bias on the performance of the albino rat. *Behavioral Science,* 1963, *8,* 183–189.

Rosenthal, R., and Gaito, J. The interpretation of levels of significance by psychological researchers. *Journal of Psychology,* 1963, *55,* 33–38.

Rosenthal, R., and Gaito, J. Further evidence for the cliff effect in the interpretation of levels of significance. *Psychological Reports,* 1964, *15,* 570.

Ross, O. B., Jr. Use of controls in medical research. *Journal of the American Medical Association,* 1951, *145,* 72–75.

Runyon, R. P., and Haber, A. *Fundamentals of behavioral statistics.* Palo Alto, Calif.: Addison-Wesley, 1967.

Ryan, T. A. Multiple comparisons in psychological research. *Psychological Bulletin,* 1959, *56,* 26–47.

Sakoda, J. M., Cohen, B. H., and Beall, G. Test of significance for a series of statistical tests. *Psychological Bulletin,* 1954, *51,* 172–175.

Sawrey, W. L., and Weisz, J. D. An experimental method of producing gastric ulcers. *Journal of Comparative and Physiological Psychology,* 1956, *49,* 269–270.

Schachter, S., and Singer, J. E. Cognitive, social and physiological determinants of emotional state. *Psychological Review,* 1962, *69,* 379–399.

Scott, J. P. The social behavior of dogs and wolves: an illustration of sociobiological systematics. *Annals of the New York Academy of Sciences,* 1950, *51,* 1009–1021.

Seaver, W. B., and Quarton, R. J. Social reinforcement of excellence: Dean's List and academic achievement. Paper presented at the 44th annual meeting of the Eastern Psychological Association, Washington, D.C., May 1973.

Sidman, M. *Tactics of scientific research.* New York: Basic Books, 1960.

Sidowski, J. B. Instrumentation and computer technology: applications and influences in modern psychology. *American Psychologist,* 1975, *30,* 191–196.

Siegel, S. *Nonparametric statistics for the behavioral sciences.* New York: McGraw-Hill, 1956.

Simon, H. A. Information processing models of cognition. *Annual Review of Psychology,* 1979, *30,* 363–396.

Smith, M. L., and Glass, G. V. Meta-Analysis of psychotherapy outcome studies. *American Psychologist,* 1977, 752–760.

Smith, M. L., Glass, G. V., and Miller, T. I. *The benefits of psychotherapy.* Baltimore: Johns Hopkins Press, 1980.

Snedecor, G. *Statistical methods.* (5th ed.). Ames, Iowa: Iowa State College Press, 1956.

Srole, L., Langner, T. S., Michael, S. T., Opler, M. K., and Rennie, T. A. C. *Mental health in the metropolis: the midtown Manhattan study,* Vol. 1. New York: McGraw-Hill, 1962.

Stanley, W. C., and Schlosberg, H. The psychophysiological effects of tea. *Journal of Psychology,* 1953, *36,* 435–448.

Stevens, J. C. Stimulus spacing and the judgment of loudness. *Journal of Experimental Psychology,* 1958, *56,* 246–250.

Stevens, J. C., Herrnstein, R. J., and Reynolds, G. S. *Laboratory experiments in psychology.* New York: Holt, Rinehart and Winston, 1965.

Stevens, S. S. On the theory of scales of measurement. *Science,* 1946, *103,* 677–680.

Stevens, S. S. On the psychophysical law. *Psychological Review,* 1957, *64,* 153–181.

Stevens, S. S. Problems and methods of psychophysics. *Psychological Bulletin,* 1958, *55,* 177–196.

Stevens, S. S. Measurement, psychophysics, and utility. In C. W. Churchman and P. Ratoosh (Eds.), *Measurement: definitions and theories.* New York: Wiley, 1959.

Stewart, C. G. Consistency, generality, magnitude, and significance of experimenter expectancy effects in human research. *The Psychological Record,* 1971, *21,* 449–458.

Stott, L. Parental attitudes of farm, town, and city parents in relation to certain personality adjustments in their children. *Journal of Social Psychology,* 1940, *11,* 325–339.

Swets, J. A. Is there a sensory threshold? *Science,* 1961, *134,* 168–177.

Thorndike, R. L. *The concepts of over- and underachievement.* New York: Teachers College, Columbia University, 1963.

Tukey, J. W. Analyzing data: sanctification or detective work? *American Psychologist,* 1969, *24,* 83–91.

Uhlenhuth, E. H., Lipman, R. S., and Covi, L. Combined pharmacotherapy and psychotherapy. *Journal of Nervous and Mental Diseases,* 1969, *148,* 52–64.

Verplanck, W. S. Since learned behavior is innate, and vice versa, what now? *Psychological Review,* 1955, *62,* 139–144.

Warren, R. M., and Warren, R. P. A critique of S. S. Stevens' "New Psychophysics." *Perceptual and Motor Skills,* 1963, *16,* 797–810.

Weiner, S., Dorman, D., Persky, H., Stach, T. W., Norton, J., and Levitt, E. E. Effect on anxiety of increasing the plasma hydrocortisone level. *Psychosomatic Medicine,* 1963, *25,* 69–77.

Wendt, G. R. Methods of recording action. *Archives of Psychology,* 1938, Whole No. 228.

Willems, E. P. Toward an explicit rationale for naturalistic methods. *Human Development,* 1967, *10,* 138–154.

Wilson, E. B. *An introduction to scientific research.* New York: McGraw-Hill, 1952.

Winer, B. J. *Statistical principles in experimental design,* (2nd ed.). New York: McGraw-Hill, 1971.

Wolins, L. Responsibility for raw data. *American Psychologist,* 1962, *17,* 657–658.

Woodworth, R. S., and Schlosberg, H. *Experimental psychology,* (2nd ed.). New York: Holt, Rinehart and Winston, 1954.

Woolsey, T. D. Sampling methods for a small household survey. Public Health Monograph No. 40, Publication No. 480, 1956.

Wright, H. F. Observational child study. In P. H. Mussen (Ed.), *Handbook of research methods in child development.* New York: Wiley, 1960.

Appendixes

Appendix I

Writing Experimental Reports

An experiment is never really completed until its results are communicated to other scientists and it becomes part of the total body of scientific knowledge. This is sometimes done through oral reports at scientific meetings, but the basic mode of communication is publication in scientific journals. No research develops in an historical vacuum, and the permanent record made available by publication enables anyone to trace the development of ideas, instruments, and theories.

There are over three-quarters of a million articles published each year in the scientific and technical fields. In psychology alone there are many thousands. In order to deal with this huge volume of information various policies have been established on the forms that technical reports should have. For one thing, reports have become considerably shorter. The average report now is about 10 to 15 typewritten double-spaced pages. In addition, the format of presentation has become almost standardized to facilitate rapid evaluation of the contents by both editors and readers.

The clearest and most detailed description of what these expectations are may be found in the *Publication Manual* published by the American Psychological Association. Everything is discussed there from the organization and style of the writing to the correction of proof. This appendix is not to be thought of as a substitute for that manual, but is simply a summary of some of the major points covered there.

The Introduction. The first part of the report should briefly make clear to the reader why the particular problem presented is being studied. For example, the experiment may be designed to test a theory or hypothesis, or it may simply be concerned with establishing or extending a relationship between two variables. Sometimes experiments are done in an effort to determine the reliability of some previously reported findings. Occasionally, experiments are done in an attempt to clarify certain inconsistencies in previous works. In any case the reader should have a reasonably clear idea, after reading the introduction, of the contemporary or historical framework of the experiment. A carefully selected number of related experiments should be referred to in order to help provide this framework.

(It is worth mentioning in this connection that one of the best sources of information about current research in the field of psychology is the *Psychological Abstracts,* which contains brief abstracts of articles on psychology and related subjects published in most countries of the world. For problems related to physiology and medicine, the *Index Medicus* and *Biological Abstracts* are helpful. In addition, the *Annual Review of Psychology* contains surveys of current research in selected areas, with each survey written by a specialist.)

The Method Section. The method should be described in sufficient detail to permit the reader to repeat the experiment. Sometimes other articles may be referred to for descriptions of specialized pieces of equipment or of certain procedures. The number and type of subjects used should be mentioned as well as how they were assigned to groups and how treatments were imposed upon them. Any special controls or calibrations used in the experiment should be presented here as well as some indication of the accuracy of the measurements being used.

The Results Section. Presentation of results is often a difficult section to write partly because the writer tends to vacillate between presenting too much or too little. Editors of journals generally prefer only a brief summary of the major findings of a particular study; there is rarely space available for all the basic data that have been collected in the experiment.

Partly because of the highly condensed nature of the published material in most journals, the Library of Congress has established an auxiliary publication service called the American Documentation Institute (ADI). Any material that is relevant to a published work, but which is too detailed for inclusion in the original article, may be filed with the ADI and will then be available to all readers for a small charge to cover the cost of microfilm or photocopies. Data of individual subjects or trials, subgroup performance, statistical analyses, and additional tables or figures may all be deposited with the ADI. This is done through the editor of the journal that publishes the original manuscript.

In the results section the author should attempt to summarize his major findings as simply and clearly as he can. Figures are usually more revealing than tables, but they are also more expensive to prepare and print. In any case, data should not be prepared in two different ways. It is unacceptable to present a table and then show the same information in the form of a graph.

The Discussion Section. In this section the author should compare the results of his experiment with those of previous investigators. If discrepancies exist, he should try to explain them. He may also elaborate on his theoretical position and suggest further implications. Sometimes an author may point out sources of error that may have operated in the experiment as well as their possible influence on the results.

References. Some journals prefer that all references cited be included in the body of the report in the form of footnotes. Most, however, recommend that references be alphabetically arranged by surname without numbering. The exact form to be used for journal and book citations may be found in the APA *Publication Manual.*

The Abstract. At one time, most articles ended with a brief summary of the main points of the paper. Since 1963 this has been superseded by a 120-word abstract that goes at the front of the report. This abstract should contain a brief statement of the problem, the results, and the conclusions.

It should be borne in mind that the preceding suggestions represent only general guidelines and that variations exist in editorial policies in different journals. These will become evident as the student begins to read widely in the psychological literature.

Appendix II

Some Ethical Issues in Research

In 1965 the Congress of the United States conducted several investigations into the problems of the use and abuse of psychological tests, particularly personality tests. Claims had begun to increase in recent years that psychologists were "brainwatching," "brainwashing," "snooping," "spying," and violating the "rights of privacy." Some personality tests contain questions concerning a person's religious beliefs and sex life, and these were the major subjects of the attacks during the investigation. At about the same time the medical profession was made painfully aware that there had been a number of published papers in recent years describing patients or normal control subjects who, in the interests of research, had been given drugs without their consent.

These facts led the National Institutes of Health, the major research-funding agency in medicine and psychology, to reevaluate their policies governing the use of human subjects for research and to become more careful in examining this phase of any proposed new research.

Standards for the humane treatment of animals have been known and respected for a long time. It is expected, for example, that all due consideration be given the animal's bodily comfort and that adequate housing facilities be made available. Surgery should be done only under suitable anesthesia and the animal should be cared for properly at all times. If an animal must be killed, this should be done in a humane way. If animals are used by students as part of their education, this work should be supervised by an experienced teacher. Since universities or laboratories must be licensed by the state in most cases, there are certain penalties which can result from infringement of these standards.

The situation in regard to the use of humans in psychological research is quite different. In 1953 a formal statement was issued by the APA concerning the general welfare of human research subjects. In 1959 it was formalized into a code of ethical standards for psychologists and then revised and published in 1973.

The book deals with a number of important issues. These include the need for informed consent from subjects before participation in experiments; freedom from coercion to participate in research; freedom from exploitation in the research relationship; protection from physical and mental stress; guarantees of anonymity of the individual and confidentiality of data; responsibilities of research participants following completion of the research; and problems in the utilization of research results, among others. These ideas are concisely expressed in the following 10 ethical principles adopted by the American Psychological Association (Ad Hoc Committee, 1973).

1. In planning a study the investigator has the personal responsibility to make a careful evaluation of its ethical acceptability, taking into account these Principles for research with human beings. To the extent that this appraisal, weighing scientific and humane values, suggests a deviation from any Principle, the investigator incurs an increasingly serious obligation to seek ethical advice and to observe more stringent safeguards to protect the rights of the human research participant.

2. Responsibility for the establishment and maintenance of acceptable ethical practice in research always remains with the individual investigator. The investigator is also responsible for the ethical treatment of research participants by collaborators, assistants, students, and employees, all of whom, however, incur parallel obligations.

3. Ethical practice requires the investigator to inform the participant of all features of the research that reasonably might be expected to influence willingness to participate and to explain all other aspects of the research about which the participant inquires. Failure to make full disclosure gives added emphasis to the investigator's responsibility to protect the welfare and dignity of the research participant.

4. Openness and honesty are essential characteristics of the relationship between investigator and research participant. When the methodological requirements of a study necessitate concealment or deception, the investigator is required to ensure the participant's understanding of the reasons for this action and to restore the quality of the relationship with the investigator.

5. Ethical research practice requires the investigator to respect the individual's freedom to decline to participate in research or to discontinue participation at any time. The obligation to protect this freedom requires special vigilance when the investigator is in a position of power over the participant. The decision to limit this freedom increases the investigator's responsibility to protect the participant's dignity and welfare.

6. Ethically acceptable research begins with the establishment of a clear and fair agreement between the investigator and the research participant that clarifies the responsibilities of each. The investigator has the obligation to honor all promises and commitments included in that agreement.

7. The ethical investigator protects participants from physical and mental discomfort, harm, and danger. If the risk of such consequences exists, the investigator is required to inform the participant of that fact, secure consent before proceeding, and take all possible measures to minimize distress. A research procedure may not be used if it is likely to cause serious and lasting harm to participants.

8. After the data are collected, ethical practice requires the investigator to provide the participant with a full clarification of the nature of the study and to remove any misconceptions that may have arisen. Where scientific or humane values justify delaying or withholding information, the investigator acquires a special responsibility to assure that there are no damaging consequences for the participant.

9. Where research procedures may result in undesirable consequences for the participant, the investigator has the responsibility to detect and remove or correct these consequences, including, where relevant, long-term aftereffects.

10. Information obtained about the research participants during the course of an investigation is confidential. When the possibility exists that others may obtain access to such information, ethical research practice requires that this possibility, together with the plans for protecting confidentiality, be explained to the participants as a part of the procedure for obtaining informed consent.

One issue which has generated considerable discussion centers around the use of deception in some psychology experiments. For example, suppose the experimenter tells a subject that some (fictitious) test the subject took reveals that he possesses several very undesirable traits. At the end of the experiment the subject is told about the nature of the deception. (In one experiment, these debriefing statements were actually used as part of a second deception practiced on the subject.)

If such deceptions become frequent the public may develop an image of psychologists as practicers of deceptions, so that even when they tell the truth they will not be believed. These considerations suggest the ethical concept that statements about confidentiality and trust must be followed literally by the psychologist, and all debriefing statements must be true.

These considerations have led some psychologists to attempt to reevaluate the use of deception as an experimental technique and to look for alternatives. Baldwin (1960) has put the matter this way:

It is necessary on some occasions that the adult subject be unaware of the purpose or the procedure of an experiment. This circumstance is sometimes used to put adult subjects into experiments that they would never enter voluntarily, even when the knowledge would not affect their behavior in the experiment as much as it would lead them to refuse to participate. The general practice of deceiving the subjects of psychological experiments is roundly condemned by a large section of the psychological profession, perhaps the majority. They argue that in most cases the experiment can be done equally well without deception, that if necessary the subject can be told frankly that it is necessary for him to be ignorant of the purpose of the experiment and that the few experiments in which deception is absolutely required are better left undone.

This point has also been discussed in detail by Kelman (1967). He too has emphasized that the widespread use of deception in psychological experiments not only may have harmful effects on some subjects, but it undermines the quality of the relationship between the psychologist and the public. There is increasing evidence that subjects are becoming less naïve, more distrustful of psychologists, and increasingly likely to try to "figure out" or define the experimental situation in their own terms. To the extent that this is true, the experimenters themselves may be misled into thinking that they have defined the subject's interpretation of a particular experimental situation when in fact they have not.

Kelman points out in this paper and in a later one (1972) that there are several alternatives to deception that are available. One is the use of role-playing and conscious simulation of defined situations by subjects. Another is what Kelman calls "participatory research," meaning that subjects play an active role in the formulation and conduct of the research. These alternatives appear not to suffer from the ethical problems of deception. Mixon (1977) provides a review of issues in research using role-playing.

There may come a time when these ethical issues have been solved and principles appropriate to all situations are firmly codified. Until that time it would be desirable for the experimental psychologist to be careful in manipulations, conscientious in the establishment of safeguards, and sensitive to the interpersonal relations that develop during the experiment.

Appendix III

TABLE A. AREAS OF THE NORMAL CURVE IN TERMS OF z-VALUES

z	Area in Larger Portion	z	Area in Larger Portion
0.00	0.5000	1.60	0.9452
0.10	0.5398	1.70	0.9554
0.20	0.5793	1.80	0.9641
0.30	0.6179	1.90	0.9713
0.40	0.6554	2.00	0.9772
0.50	0.6915	2.10	0.9821
0.60	0.7257	2.20	0.9861
0.70	0.7580	2.30	0.9893
0.80	0.7881	2.40	0.9918
0.90	0.8159	2.50	0.9938
1.00	0.8413	2.60	0.9953
1.10	0.8643	2.70	0.9965
1.20	0.8849	2.80	0.9974
1.30	0.9032	2.90	0.9981
1.40	0.9192	3.00	0.9987
1.50	0.9332		

TABLE B. DISTRIBUTION OF t

df	.1	.05	.01	.001
1	6.314	12.706	63.657	636.619
2	2.920	4.303	9.925	31.598
3	2.353	3.182	5.841	12.941
4	2.132	2.776	4.604	8.610
5	2.015	2.571	4.032	6.859
6	1.943	2.447	3.707	5.959
7	1.895	2.365	3.499	5.405
8	1.860	2.306	3.355	5.041
9	1.833	2.262	3.250	4.781
10	1.812	2.228	3.169	4.587
11	1.796	2.201	3.106	4.437
12	1.782	2.179	3.055	4.318
13	1.771	2.160	3.012	4.221
14	1.761	2.145	2.977	4.140
15	1.753	2.131	2.947	4.073
16	1.746	2.120	2.921	4.015
17	1.740	2.110	2.898	3.965
18	1.734	2.101	2.878	3.922
19	1.729	2.093	2.861	3.883
20	1.725	2.086	2.845	3.850
21	1.721	2.080	2.831	3.819
22	1.717	2.074	2.819	3.792
23	1.714	2.069	2.807	3.767
24	1.711	2.064	2.797	3.745
25	1.708	2.060	2.787	3.725
26	1.706	2.056	2.779	3.707
27	1.703	2.052	2.771	3.690
28	1.701	2.048	2.763	3.674
29	1.699	2.045	2.756	3.659
30	1.697	2.042	2.750	3.646
40	1.684	2.021	2.704	3.551
60	1.671	2.000	2.660	3.460
120	1.658	1.980	2.617	3.373
∞	1.645	1.960	2.576	3.291

SOURCE: Table B is taken from Table III of Fisher & Yates: *Statistical Tables for Biological, Agricultural, and Medical Research,* published by Oliver & Boyd Ltd., Edinburgh, and by permission of the authors and publishers.

TABLE C. RANDOM NUMBERS

Rows									Columns											
	01	02	03	04	05	06	07	08	09	10	11	12	13	14	15	16	17	18	19	20
01	7	5	9	1	0	7	4	0	1	0	7	7	3	6	9	4	8	7	0	2
02	8	2	7	3	9	8	4	0	6	9	2	3	2	8	0	7	5	2	2	4
03	5	3	4	1	7	5	4	8	3	7	4	8	5	7	2	3	2	1	6	6
04	2	6	3	3	9	2	8	1	9	4	0	6	3	2	0	5	4	6	7	8
05	9	8	5	2	0	2	7	8	5	4	3	2	8	2	8	6	7	6	3	2
06	0	9	8	4	0	4	3	9	9	0	7	1	8	5	4	9	9	5	1	2
07	1	4	7	9	3	9	4	8	3	3	8	9	2	0	0	7	3	9	2	5
08	4	1	3	4	8	1	6	9	5	6	2	0	6	4	6	1	6	8	1	7
09	9	2	8	1	6	9	2	3	1	9	8	8	6	8	7	0	3	9	2	4
10	6	4	9	4	1	2	7	2	0	3	9	3	8	6	6	5	0	5	5	5
11	6	0	1	6	9	1	6	3	5	1	7	2	6	5	9	0	6	0	3	8
12	7	5	9	8	3	4	4	1	0	4	6	9	6	2	7	5	8	4	7	3
13	5	8	1	3	3	1	0	0	1	1	5	6	2	9	2	6	2	9	9	8
14	9	1	4	7	5	4	9	3	4	3	1	9	4	2	2	5	1	8	9	1
15	9	3	6	5	1	7	7	5	6	3	5	2	0	1	6	8	6	7	0	5
16	3	8	1	6	4	6	4	3	0	6	1	3	4	1	7	7	9	7	8	6
17	9	0	3	1	7	6	8	8	6	6	3	0	8	0	1	8	2	2	5	4
18	1	6	1	4	3	8	5	5	0	7	7	1	8	6	5	7	9	4	8	7
19	0	9	2	5	5	2	0	2	3	9	1	3	8	7	5	3	2	5	4	9
20	6	8	0	3	7	6	7	1	3	5	6	1	5	5	9	7	0	6	7	5

Here is an example of how the table of random numbers might be used. Suppose there are 90 classes in a University and you wish to select a sample of 10 classes to be tested. Number the classes from 01 to 90 and then pick any arbitrary starting point in the table, for example, column 08 and row 15. You may now proceed in any direction from this point, taking the numbers in pairs. Thus, if you proceeded sideways, you would select classes numbered 56, 35, 20, 16, 86, and 70. When you reach the end of a row you may change direction or begin at a new point. If you find a number repeated, or if you come upon a number over 90, then disregard the number and continue the process.

TABLE D. VALUES OF F NEEDED FOR SIGNIFICANCE AT THE 5% LEVEL

Degrees of Freedom for Denominator	Degrees of Freedom for Numerator									
	2	4	6	8	10	12	16	20	30	∞
2	19.00	19.25	19.33	19.37	19.39	19.41	19.43	19.44	19.46	19.50
3	9.55	9.12	8.94	8.84	8.78	8.74	8.69	8.66	8.62	8.53
4	6.94	6.39	6.16	6.04	5.96	5.91	5.84	5.80	5.74	5.63
5	5.79	5.19	4.95	4.82	4.74	4.68	4.60	4.56	4.50	4.36
6	5.14	4.53	4.28	4.15	4.06	4.00	3.92	3.87	3.81	3.67
7	4.74	4.12	3.87	3.73	3.63	3.57	3.49	3.44	3.38	3.23
8	4.46	3.84	3.58	3.44	3.34	3.28	3.20	3.15	3.08	2.93
9	4.26	3.63	3.37	3.23	3.13	3.07	2.98	2.93	2.86	2.71
10	4.10	3.48	3.22	3.07	2.97	2.91	2.82	2.77	2.70	2.54
12	3.88	3.26	3.00	2.85	2.76	2.69	2.60	2.54	2.46	2.30
15	3.68	3.06	2.79	2.64	2.55	2.48	2.39	2.33	2.25	2.07
20	3.49	2.87	2.60	2.45	2.35	2.28	2.18	2.12	2.04	1.84
30	3.32	2.69	2.42	2.27	2.16	2.09	1.99	1.93	1.84	1.62
40	3.23	2.61	2.34	2.18	2.07	2.00	1.90	1.84	1.74	1.51
∞	2.99	2.37	2.09	1.94	1.83	1.75	1.64	1.57	1.46	1.00

SOURCE: Reprinted from *Statistical Methods,* 5th edition, by George W. Snedecor. © 1956, by the Iowa State University Press, Ames, Iowa 50010.

TABLE E.   TABLE OF Q-VALUES TO BE USED WITH TUKEY-SNEDECOR METHOD FOR GROUP COMPARISONS AFTER ANALYSIS OF VARIANCE

Degrees of Freedom	Number of Groups							
	2	3	4	5	6	7	8	9
1	17.97	26.98	32.82	37.08	40.41	43.12	45.40	47.36
2	6.08	8.28	9.80	10.89	11.73	12.43	13.03	13.54
3	4.50	5.91	6.83	7.51	8.04	8.47	8.85	9.18
4	3.93	5.04	5.76	6.29	6.70	7.06	7.35	7.60
5	3.64	4.60	5.22	5.67	5.93	6.38	6.58	6.80
6	3.46	4.34	4.90	5.31	5.63	5.89	6.12	6.32
7	3.34	4.16	4.68	5.06	5.35	5.59	5.82	5.99
8	3.26	4.04	4.53	4.89	5.17	5.40	5.60	5.77
9	3.20	3.95	4.42	4.76	5.02	5.24	5.43	5.60
10	3.15	3.88	4.33	4.66	4.91	5.12	5.30	5.46
11	3.11	3.82	4.26	4.58	4.82	5.03	5.20	5.35
12	3.08	3.77	4.20	4.51	4.75	4.95	5.12	5.27
13	3.06	3.73	4.15	4.46	4.69	4.88	5.05	5.19
14	3.03	3.70	4.11	4.41	4.64	4.83	4.99	5.13
15	3.01	3.67	4.08	4.37	4.59	4.78	4.94	5.08
16	3.00	3.65	4.05	4.34	4.56	4.74	4.90	5.03
17	2.98	3.62	4.02	4.31	4.52	4.70	4.86	4.99
18	2.97	3.61	4.00	4.28	4.49	4.67	4.83	4.96
19	2.96	3.59	3.98	4.26	4.47	4.64	4.79	4.92
20	2.95	3.58	3.96	4.24	4.45	4.62	4.77	4.90
24	2.92	3.53	3.90	4.17	4.37	4.54	4.68	4.81
30	2.89	3.48	3.84	4.11	4.30	4.46	4.60	4.72
40	2.86	3.44	3.79	4.04	4.23	4.39	4.52	4.63
60	2.83	3.40	3.74	3.98	4.16	4.31	4.44	4.55
120	2.80	3.36	3.69	3.92	4.10	4.24	4.36	4.47
∞	2.77	3.32	3.63	3.86	4.03	4.17	4.29	4.39

SOURCE: Table E is reprinted from *Biometrika,* 1952, *39,* 192.

Indexes

Index of Names

Index of Subjects

Abscissa, 64
Additive designs, 156
Adjustment, method of. *See* Method of adjustment
Agreement, method of. *See* Method of agreement
American Documentation Institute, 232
Amplification, 199–200, 202
Analysis of variance, 79, 89–102, 142
  assumptions underlying, 99
  comparisons after, 98–99
    table of Q-values, 241
  computations for, 94–97
  degrees of freedom and, 94, 97
  evaluation of, 99–102
  F-distribution, 93
    table of, 240
  F-test, 90, 100
  interaction and, 100
  one-way classification, 92–94
  variability, between groups, 90
    within groups, 90
  variance, between groups, 93, 97
    concept of additivity and, 91–92
    within groups, 93, 97
Annual Review of Psychology, 232
Approximation, successive, 30, 123

Artificial variation. *See* Method of artificial variation
Association, strength of. *See* Experimental effect
Asymptote, 37–38, 115
Averages, method of. *See* Method of averages

Baseline behavior, 9–11, 155–156
Bayesian statistical inference, 76
Behavior modification. *See* Operant conditioning
Best fitting curve, 102, 106, 109, 112–114, 143
  concepts of, 105–106
  definition of, 39, 110
  equations for, 110–111
Bias
  control of, 128
  sources of, 128–135
Biological Abstracts, 232

Calibration, 136, 163, 171, 198, 201
Catch trials, 177, 181
Causality
  concept of, 119–127

247

82 83 84 85 86 9 8 7 6 5 4 3 2 1